BOOKS BY OSBORN SEGERBERG JR.

Living To Be 100
New York: Scribners

Living With Death
New York: Dutton

The Immortality Factor
New York: Dutton

Where Have All The Flowers Fishes Birds Trees Water & Air Gone? What Ecology Is All About
New York: McKay

THE RIDDLES OF
JESUS
& ANSWERS OF
SCIENCE

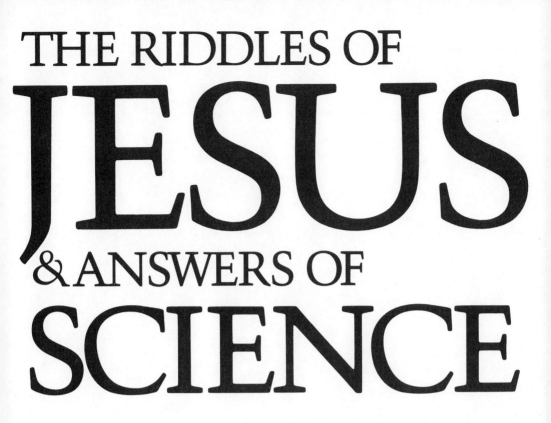

*Modern Verification of His Wisdom
& How It Can Help You*

OSBORN SEGERBERG JR.

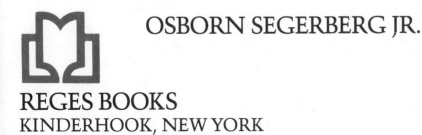

REGES BOOKS
KINDERHOOK, NEW YORK

Copyright © 1987 Osborn Segerberg Jr.

Library of Congress Cataloging-in-Publication Data

Segerberg, Osborn.
  The riddles of Jesus and answers of science.

  Bibliography: p.
  Includes Index.
  1. Jesus Christ — Teachings. 2. Religion and
science — 1946-   . I. Title.
    BS2415.S46 1987   232.9'54   87-12727

ISBN 0-9618626-0-2
ISBN 0-9618626-1-0 soft cover

First Printing

Printed in the United States of America

Book cover and design by Richard Kraham

ACKNOWLEDGMENTS

A book, especially, is the product, design and responsibility of its author. Yet, as in other human enterprises, the final result is shaped by the influences of many people. The process is particularly true for this book whose subject has touched so many minds. Some of the heritage of knowledge is indicated by sources give in REFERENCES & NOTES.

The author acknowledges gratefully contributions to the evolution of this book. First and foremost to Walter Donald Kring, S.T.B., LL.D., L.H.D., D.D. and Minister Emeritus of All Souls Unitarian Church in New York City. His sermons were a source of inspiration to me for many years. His Lenten lectures in 1977 called attention to the persistent mystery of the kingdom of God and to the difficulty in understanding Jesus' parables and ethical principles. Those revelations, rarely dealt with in church, supplied an important impetus for this inquiry. Over the years, Dr. Kring gave unwavering support and urged that the project be brought to completion.

To Martha Reutti, whose generous and timely financial assistance helped make this project possible.

And to the following persons for giving generously of their time to read the manuscript and comment: Rima Bostick, Chairman of the Columbia County Council on the Arts; Bernard T. Brennan and Kate Brennan; Jean Dubos; Cornelia Holbert and Roy Holbert, M.D.; Dr. Kring; R.W. Piwonka, Ph.D., Physiology, Pharmacology, for his surveillance in the light of the latest biochemistry; Edgar M. Reilly, Senior Scientist, Zoology, Emeritus, New York State Museum, for a rigorous reading in historic and religious as well as scientific aspects; Kate and Maggie Segerberg; Theodore Tracy, S.J., S.T.L. (Licentiate in Sacred Theology), Ph.D., for a thoughtful and detailed commentary.

And to Marcia Drennen who edited the manuscript into its final form and whose skill was a pleasure to behold.

Finally, but certainly not least, to my other editor, beloved wife and severest critic, Nancy.

Preface

There has been an incredible explosion of knowledge in the 20th century and especially during the last few decades — from quarks to the Big Bang, from space exploration to the discovery of DNA. We have found the Missing Links and given them such names as *Australopithicus afarensis* and *Homo erectus.*

We have gone in search of the Trojan War to yank it out of the mists of prehistory and confirm the songs of Homer. We have brought to light the glory of the boy-pharaoh Tutankhamen, who achieved his immortality by surviving the grave robbers. The Dead Sea Scrolls, long hidden, have informed us about the Essenes while the Nag Hammadi texts have illuminated Gnosticism.

Amidst these riches of discovery, there has been a glaring omission. And this may be understandable because it is not something tangible like the other finds. At least, we have no reason to believe that explanations for the teaching of Jesus exist in any tangible form. Yet the doctrine is visible for all to see, imbedded in paradoxes, parables and that tantalizing phrase, "the kingdom of God." Jesus' concept has endured the centuries like some redoubt impregnable to all attempts at comprehension.

In the wake of failure, something like a conspiracy of silence has developed. Jesus gave many similes, metaphors and parables to describe the kingdom of God, but not once declared outright what it was. Yet how many lay people are aware that the kingdom of God is a mystery and that no one is sure what Jesus meant by it even though the term appears nearly 100 times in the Gospels?

This book is another attempt to understand the doctrine of Jesus. But in addition to traditional knowledge about him, this inquiry makes use of an important body of knowledge not available to earlier investigators. The knowledge of life gained by biology, molecular biology, neurobiology, biochemistry, biomedicine, ecology and other life sciences is employed as a guide to Jesus' teaching. This new knowledge can be made useful in this way only because of what Jesus already had told us about life — told us, but until very recently we did not have the knowledge to understand him.

In 1974, my book *The Immortality Factor* mentioned some of the rational wisdom — what we today call science — that Jesus had brought to his people, whose state of knowledge could not appreciate it. At the time, the juxtaposition of religion and science, Jesus and biology, seemed strange. This strangeness, the result of the traditional ways we are taught to compartmentalize our concepts, disappeared with further research. Science and religion are two perspectives of reality, and in certain cases are far more congruent than we are accustomed to imagine. It was the Judeo-Christian view of reality, says molecular biologist Francois Jacob, that made modern science possible.

Two years after *The Immortality Factor* was published, during research for a book that essentially was addressed to the question "What is life?", the thought occurred that Jesus might have made many observations about life that would be useful to us today.

Coincidental to this, I came across a rare set of volumes containing interviews with hundreds of American centenarians, the first to be protected under the new Social Security provisions in the Depression 1930s. The interviews revealed that more than a few of these successful survivors for 100 or more years said that they lived by the Golden Rule and that they really did love their neighbors. A number said the key to living a long life is: Don't worry. This was the advice that Jesus gave in the passage about the lilies. Jesus may have been preaching about life in heaven, but his precepts brought added years in this world.

Could it be that Jesus used life, the way it really works, as a Rosetta Stone to decipher what God was about?

That question was the genesis of this book.

It begins with an examination of the prescient words of Jesus himself.

CONTENTS

4

PART ONE

THE SEARCH FOR THE KINGDOM OF GOD

ONE

The Greatest Story

"Repent: for the kingdom of God is at hand."

In the long, carefully-chronicled history of the Jews, a dialectic between this people and their God, these words, this phrase never appeared in the 39 books of the Old Testament. But now in the lst century A.D. the message was heard as a tocsin of hope. For many Jews, the reign of God was the only possible antidote to the reign of evil.

S P Q R — *Senatus Populusque Romanus* — Roman Senate and People, the brand of the Roman Empire, was stamped on Palestine. The Jewish people had been chafing under the domination and taxation of pagan Rome for more than 90 years. The Jews were stubborn, tenacious, fanatically religious, and the Romans let them retain administration of their religion. The Sanhedrin, a council of 71 priests, elders, Sadducees, Pharisees and scribes under the presidency of a high priest, claimed supreme authority over Jews everywhere and this power was acknowledged by all orthodox Jews. The Sanhedrin could punish violations of Jewish laws and even pass the death sentence on Jews in Judea for religious offenses, but could not carry out the penalty without consent of the civil authorities. Civil power was administered in Judea by a Roman procurator and in Galilee by Herod Antipas, a client ruler for the Romans.

The modicum of autonomy rested on a precarious balance in a fragile arrangement. The Sanhedrin and other Establishment members feared that at any sign of revolt the vaunted legions would be summoned to eradicate not only resisters but all Jewish authority. Most Jews hated not only the Romans, but their Jewish collaborators as well. This tension between hatred and fear was strained by Zealots who advocated armed rebellion. They and many other Jews believed it was immoral to pay Caesar the tribute that belonged to God. There was constant talk of and desperate hope for a Messiah, a new champion to restore freedom and sovereignty. Another Moses to lead the Jews to the Promised Land.

Their history had been marked by incredible vicissitudes and changes of fortune. After the Exodus from servitude in Egypt, after wandering in the Sinai wilderness for 40 years, the tribes of Abraham, Isaac and Jacob fought their way into Palestine under the leadership of their great general, Joshua. The tribes grew in power, and at the beginning of the 1st millennium B.C. formed a consolidated kingdom under their greatest symbol of strength, David, and his son Solomon, their pre-eminent exemplar of wisdom. After them, it was down hill. The United Monarchy split into a northern Israel and a southern Judah. At the time of the prophet Isaiah, Israel fell to the Assyrians in 721 B.C. The identity of these people, the "lost tribes of Israel," disappeared under the Assyrian policy of extirpation and dispersion. Judah lost its sovereignty in increments, first to Egypt and then to Babylon. In the ultimate conquest, provoked by continued Jewish resistance after an earlier defeat, Babylon's Nebuchadnezzar in the 6th century B.C. burned Jerusalem to the ground, inflicting the extreme calamity. He destroyed the Temple built by Solomon. Most of the Jews were carried off to Babylon in what became known as the Exile. But within half a century aging Babylon was swallowed by the behemoth Persian Empire.

Like the phoenix, Jerusalem was resurrected, but by the time Persia's king Cyrus allowed the Jews to go back and rebuild the Temple, the Jewish people had become intimate with the religion of Zoroaster, seductively like their own in the belief that there is only one God and in a counterpart to the Messiah. Iranians called him Savior. Some Jews absorbed other Zoroastrian beliefs in angels, devils, an end to history, resurrection of the dead and a judgment day to consign good people to heaven and evil ones to hell.

Alexander's conquests in Asia brought Palestine under the domination of the Greeks. This subjugation became increasingly virulent until the intolerable abomination of installing Hellenistic gods in the Second Temple. This execration incited a revolt in 165 B.C. led by the family of the Maccabees, and against all odds it succeeded. Israel came into a new golden age and grew almost to the size attained under David. Only to subside once again into internal squabbles. The Romans were invited to settle one of these disputes, and never left. Pompey enforced his decision by taking Jerusalem and making Palestine a part of the Roman province of Syria.

To the Jews, religion was the alter ego of their political reality. What God decided upon in heaven subsequently was manifested on earth. Through the series of hard-to-understand trials and unjustified oppressions, Jewish religious hopes persevered, but in some respects became unrealistic, even fantastic. Elements of the supernatural began to appear. Ezekiel, while still in the Babylonian Captivity, envisioned a New Jerusalem whose very natural environment would be miraculously transformed. The Book of Daniel, written shortly before the Maccabees' revolt, predicted that a Son of man would come down out of the clouds to found an everlasting kingdom of saints. Apocryphal and apocalyptic writings in the lst century B.C. saw the solution either in the direct intervention of God or the earthly coming of God's representative, the Messiah, who would usher in a time of joy and peace and plenty. There would be an end to poverty and evil. Justice would reign.

So added to the political unrest of the times, Palestine seethed with all kinds of imaginings and hopes. All things seemed possible. Magic and witchcraft, demons and angels, possession by and exorcism of spirits, miracles and prophetic divination all were accepted. The science of the time was astrology in which the heavens existed to foretell the affairs of human beings. Thaumaturgists, touring magicians, performed their wonders before the eyes of credulous villagers. The Magi were revered seers of the East. All things seemed possible.

But what was meant by the kingdom of God? Was it a resurgent political state of God's people? To the Sadducees, aristocrats and traditionalists who filled many priestly offices and scoffed at resurrection and afterlife, that was the only possible interpretation. Was the kingdom of God a domain of the spirit? That would have been the answer of the prophets. Was the kingdom of God a realm of eternal afterlife? That was a possibility for the Pharisees. The historian Josephus, himself a Pharisee, describes the sect as "a body of Jews who profess to be more religious than the rest." Like all Jews except for the Sadducees, Pharisees did believe in resurrection of the dead. Was the kingdom of God a society of morally righteous saints? The Essenes, having judged that the prevailing religious Establishment — the Sadducees, the Pharisees and the scribes who interpreted the law — was corrupt, practiced an ascetic and morally spotless life in an isolated desert encampment. The Essenes were awaiting just such a kingdom.

The man who first spoke of the kingdom of God being at hand resembled the Essenes in a number of respects. He led an ascetic existence, dressed only in a crude camel's hair frock with a leather girdle around his waist. He ate locusts and wild honey, for he, too, saw his mission in the desert and quoted Scriptures to show that he was fulfilling Isaiah's prophecy: "The voice of one crying in the wilderness. Prepare ye the way of the Lord, make his paths straight." This man's name was John and because he practiced baptism in the Jordan River, he was known as John the Baptist.

Like the Essenes, John the Baptist believed the Establishment practitioners of religion were corrupt. So when Pharisees and Sadducees joined the crowds streaming eastward from Jerusalem to hear this new star attraction, he castigated them. "O generation of vipers, who hath warned you to flee from the wrath to come?" John said that these Jews were not to assume they were safe just because they were descendants of Abraham and thus heirs to the religion. God can choose his elect. "God is able of these stones to raise up children unto Abraham."

When John's dismayed listeners asked what they should do, he answered, "He that hath two coats, let him impart to him that hath none; and he that hath meat, let him do likewise." Among those who wanted to be baptized by John were publicans. These were non-religious Jews who collected taxes for the Romans and often took something extra for themselves. When the publicans asked what they should do, John said, "Exact no more than that which is appointed you." He told soldiers to do no violence.

John so impressed the people that they put the burning question of the time to him: Are you the Messiah? No, he answered, "I indeed baptize you with water unto repentence, but he that comes after me is mightier than I, whose shoes I am not worthy to bear."

Among those who came to hear John was Jesus, all the way from Nazareth. He was about 30 years old. John baptized Jesus. As Jesus came up out of the water "he saw the heavens opened and the Spirit like a dove descending upon him: and there came a voice from heaven, saying, Thou art my beloved Son, in whom I am well pleased."

John's railing at the Establishment made him a troublemaker and bureaucrats uneasy. When John pointed the finger at Herod and accused him of violating Jewish law by taking his half-brother Philip's wife for his own, and cited other crimes, the prophet had overstepped his religious protection. Herod moved to silence this voice in the wilderness. John was thrown into prison and later decapitated.

The lesson was there for Jesus to see: if you crossed the authorities, the penalty could be your life.

In the wilderness on the way back to Galilee, Jesus was tempted by the Devil. This confrontation in the desert resembles the oral exams of a doctoral candidate. Satan said if Jesus were the Son of God, prove it: turn stones into bread, jump from a high place without hurting himself. Jesus refused to do both, citing Scriptures to live by the word of God and not to tempt God. Then the Devil offered a Faustian bargain — all the temporal power that Jesus desired, certainly enough to restore the sovereignty of Israel. In return, all Jesus had to do was to worship the Prince of Evil. "And Jesus answered and said unto him, Get thee behind me, Satan: for it is written, Thou shalt worship the Lord thy God and him only shalt thou serve."

Final exams were over. Jesus was ready to begin his mission impossible.

"Now after that John was put in prison, Jesus came into Galilee, preaching the gospel of the kingdom of God. And saying, The time is fulfilled, and the kingdom of God is at hand: Repent ye, and believe the gospel." Nobel laureate Albert Schweitzer, a great Biblical scholar, says the word repent in this case means "change your thoughts." It is a call for a new way of thinking. Gospel, of course, means good news. It would be like the town criers of colonial times — "Hear ye, hear ye" — or newsboys of yesteryear — "Wuxtry, wuxtry, read all about it." Today we get our news from the evening telecasts, but because the definition of what is news is man bites dog — something out of the ordinary — almost all the news is bad news. When a problem is on the way to being remedied, it disappears from the air waves. Jesus is announcing his discovery — something new, extraordinary, so even by today's definition it is news: "I have good news for you. Believe in it and change your thinking."

The quotation at the beginning of the previous paragraph is from the Gospel of Mark, but it's the same in the other two Synoptic Gospels. Matthew says: "From that time Jesus began to preach, and to say, Repent: for the kingdom of heaven is at hand." Matthew frequently substitutes kingdom of heaven for kingdom of God, but this Gospel does use the latter expression as well. Luke says people in Capernaum tried to keep Jesus from leaving, so taken were they with his message, but "he said unto them, I must preach the kingdom of God to other cities also: *for therefore am I sent.*" (Emphasis added) Jesus is saying unequivocally that the doctrine of the kingdom of God is central to, indeed the entire purpose of his mission.

Not only that, but it is something radically different from anything that had been taught before. "The law and the prophets were until John: since that time the kingdom of God is preached." A new regime is starting. Even if Jesus hadn't said so, we can infer it. John's message was that God's wrathful judgment was imminent and people should prepare for it by repenting their sins and showing that repentence with appropriate acts. Jesus says he is preaching the kingdom itself — telling people about it.

We also can judge the innovation from the corroborating reaction of the people who heard him. The three Gospels characterize those reactions nine times with the words *astonished* or *amazed.* "And they were astonished at his doctrine: for he taught them as one that had authority, and not as the scribes." "And they were astonished at his doctrine: for his word was with power." When he preached in the synagogue in his home town of Nazareth, "many hearing him were astonished, saying, From whence hath this man these things? and what wisdom is this which is given unto him, that even such mighty works are wrought by his hands? Is not this the carpenter, the son of Mary....?"

The mighty works wrought by his hands referred to Jesus' sensation-causing ability to heal people. His teaching about the kingdom of God often was accompanied by demonstrations of this healing. When the preaching and an incident of healing happened in conjunction at the synagogue in Capernaum, "they were all amazed, insomuch that they questioned among themselves, saying, What thing is this? What new doctrine is this? for with authority commandeth he even the unclean spirits, and they do obey him." At Nazareth, where people knew him as a carpenter and thus were unable to believe in his new role, Jesus couldn't perform miraculous recoveries. "A prophet is not without honor," he said, "but in his own country, and among his own kin, and in his own house."

Once, when Jesus wanted to preach by the Sea of Galilee, he asked some fishermen to use their boat. Anchored just off shore, it served as a pulpit for Jesus to talk to his audience on land. After he had finished, he told Peter, who owned the boat with his brother Andrew, to move out into the deep water and cast his net. Peter said they had been trying for a catch all night with no success. This time they caught so much fish that the boat was in danger of capsizing. Peter was awestruck. Jesus asked Peter and Andrew to come with him: "Follow me, and I will make you fishers of men." He recruited two more disciples, the fishermen brothers John and James, at the same time. The number of disciples would reach 12.

Mark and Luke say Jesus' fame spread throughout Galilee. Matthew says his fame went through Syria.

So far the Gospels have told us that there was a precursor for Jesus and the kingdom-of-God doctrine, that Jesus began his mission preaching the doctrine, that to teach the doctrine was the sole purpose of his mission, that Jesus said the doctrine was new and different from anything in the past, that people were astonished by it, and that he became famous throughout Galilee and Syria because of this doctrine and his impressive ability to heal people. After this introduction and preparation, we learn what the doctrine is about in the Sermon on the Mount, an incomparable masterpiece. It is the only sustained presentation of Jesus' teaching, and is likely a compendium of many sermons with various subjects grouped in appropriate sequences. Immediately we begin to see why his listeners were astonished.

The Sermon begins with the Beatitudes, the listing of nine states of being or character traits or activities that Jesus says are blessed. The Beatitudes single out the kinds of people and acts that had rarely if ever been extolled. Some of them, indeed, were despised. Then as now, praise and attention were devoted to kings, the success stories, the rich, those at the top of the heap. But Jesus said blessed are the meek and the poor in spirit, which is another way of saying humble. Glory usually was reserved for the great warriors. The Jews so admired David that it was almost inconceivable for them to believe the Messiah could be other than a descendant of David's line. Jesus said blessed are the peacemakers. He did hail a special kind of courage — those who are persecuted for righteousness' sake. Being persecuted is nobody's idea of a blessed state. But he valued righteousness so much that those who wanted it and strove for it are blessed. Grief is among the most excruciating human conditions, but he said those who mourn are blessed. Here was a champion of the underdog, the unfortunate, the common people — those who never had an ombudsman.

The next thing one notices is that there are differential rewards. The peacemakers shall be called the children of God. The pure in heart shall see God. Those who mourn shall be comforted, those who hunger and thirst for righteousness shall be filled, and the merciful shall obtain mercy. Now here's a curious distinction: the meek shall inherit the earth while the humble shall receive the kingdom of God.

And for those who are persecuted for Jesus' sake, "great is your reward in heaven" while those persecuted for the sake of righteousness receive the kingdom of God. For only two of the nine Beatitudes is the reward the kingdom of God: the poor in spirit and those persecuted for righteousness' sake.

Jesus then explains what he means by saying that the law and the prophets prevailed until John and now he is teaching something new. "Think not that I am come to destroy the law or the prophets: I am not come to destroy, but to fulfill." "For I say unto you, That except your righteousness shall exceed the righteousness of the scribes and Pharisees, ye shall in no case enter into the kingdom of heaven."

This is the beginning of a theme that runs like a thread through the Sermon: the distinction between outer and inner, the material and spiritual, pretense and deed, form and essence, ritual and being truly religious, sanctimony and virtue, hypocrisy and integrity. According to this thesis, the law is fine as far as it goes, but *it doesn't go far enough.*

Jesus starts with one of the Ten Commandments of Moses: Thou shalt not kill. Whoever kills "shall be in danger of the judgment: But I say unto you, That whosoever is angry with his brother without cause shall be in danger of the judgment." Therefore, Jesus says, before making your pious gift at the altar, first be reconciled with your brother, then make your gift. Agree with your adversaries quickly lest they bring you to court and you wind up in jail.

Then another of the Big Ten: Thou shalt not commit adultery. "But I say unto you, That whosoever looketh on a woman to lust after her hath committed adultery with her already in his heart."

Then a law so important that it was stated in three of the five books of the Pentateuch or Torah: Exodus, Leviticus and Deuteronomy. "Ye have heard that it hath been said, An eye for an eye, and a tooth for a tooth". This legal symmetry of exacting a like punishment for the offense goes back in the Middle East at least to the Code of Hammurabi, the greatest Babylonian king, in the 18th century B.C. It was an advance and restriction on the still more primitive custom of the individual taking his revenge indiscriminately on any member of the offender's tribe, clan or family. Now the state executed the penalty. If a patient died or lost an eye as a result of an operation, the physician's fingers were cut off; if a house collapsed and killed the buyer, the architect or builder must die; if the collapse killed the purchaser's son, the son of the architect or builder was executed; if a man killed a girl, it was his daughter who paid with her life. The penalties were moderated with the advance of civilization, many of them replaced with monetary fines. But it is apparent today that the spirit of this ancient law of revenge, with its unending chain of violence, still animates the Middle East. Jesus showed a way to break the chain.

"But I say unto you, That ye resist not evil: but whosoever shall smite thee on thy right cheek, turn to him the other also. And if any man will sue thee at law, and take thy coat, let him have thy cloak also. And whosoever shall compel thee to go a mile, go with him twain."

In still another illustration of this thesis, he referred back to a law stated in Leviticus 19:18: "Thou shalt not avenge, nor bear any grudge against the children of thy people, but thou shalt love thy neighbor as thyself." Jesus not only extended this obligation to relations with non-Jews, but expanded it to unheard-of limits. "Ye have heard that it hath been said, Thou shalt love thy neighbor and hate thine enemy. But I say unto you, love your enemies, bless them that curse you, do good to them that hate you, and pray for them which despitefully use you, and persecute you." "Be ye therefore perfect, even as your Father which is in heaven is perfect."

Is it any wonder that people were astonished or that shocked townspeople in Nazareth asked, what kind of wisdom is this?

So ends the fifth chapter of Matthew. Chapter six begins with instructions on how to practice the kind of religion he is preaching. There is this unstated question: do you want to be appreciated by men or by God? Because you can't have both. Why must they be mutually exclusive? Because God has no use for hypocrites. "When thou doest thine alms, do not sound a trumpet before thee, as the hypocrites do in the synagogues and in the streets, that they may have the glory of men. Verily I say unto you, They have their reward. But when thou doest alms, let not thy left hand know what thy right hand doeth: That thine alms may be secret: and thy Father which seeth in secret himself shall reward thee openly." Obviously his was not an easy religion to practice.

Jesus has the same instruction for prayer. Hypocrites, he says, love to pray where everyone can see how holy they are. You pray in secret "for your Father knoweth what things ye have need of, before ye ask him." Then he teaches the Lord's Prayer. Finally, some words on fasting, with the same point: don't put on a sad face so that everyone knows you're depriving yourself for a good cause. That's what hypocrites do and "they have their reward."

Then another wise, and famous, saying: "Lay not up for yourselves treasures upon earth, where moth and rust doth corrupt, and where thieves break through and steal: But lay up for yourselves treasures in heaven, where neither moth nor rust doth corrupt, and where thieves do not break through nor steal: for where your treasure is, there will your heart be also." The same thought is expressed differently in a succeeding passage: "No man can serve two masters: for either he will hate the one, and love the other: or else he will hold to the one and despise the other. Ye cannot serve God and mammon." If your goal is to attain material wealth, that's one thing; if your goal is to serve God, that's another. The twain can't meet. An interesting application of this was given by the newspaper editor Horace Greeley to Henry Thoreau who had come to New York City seeking a newspaper job. When Thoreau described what he wanted to write, Greeley advised that he couldn't do what he wanted if he became a newspaperman. Even in writing, Greeley said, you cannot serve God and mammon. So Thoreau went back to Massachusetts, led a pauper's existence, wrote *Walden* and became enshrined in history. In that book, Thoreau wrote he learned that "trade curses everything it handles; and though you trade in messages from Heaven, the whole curse of trade attaches to the business."

These sayings about where your heart is and how you're going to direct your life lead up to and culminate in a passage sublime in beauty and profound in wisdom. "Take no thought for your life, what ye shall eat, or what ye shall drink; nor yet for your body, what ye shall put on....behold the fowls of the air: for they sow not, neither do they reap, nor gather in barns; yet your heavenly Father feedeth them....Consider the lilies of the field, how they grow; they toil not, neither do they spin: And I say unto you, That even Solomon in all his glory was not arrayed like one of these....Therefore take no thought, saying, What shall we eat? or, What shall we drink? or, Wherewithal shall we be clothed?....for your heavenly Father knoweth that ye have need of all these things. But seek ye first the kingdom of God, and his righteousness; and all these things shall be added unto you."

The end of chapter six. The first 11 verses of chapter seven are prelude to the Golden Rule. "Judge not that ye be not judged. For with what judgment ye judge, ye shall be judged." Don't point to what's wrong with your brother — look to your own faults, hypocrite. Then this inspiring passage of hope and promise: "Ask, and it shall be given you; seek, and ye shall find; knock, and it shall be opened unto you. Or what man is there of you, whom if his son ask bread, will he give him a stone? Or if he ask a fish, will he give him a serpent? If ye then, being evil, know how to give good gifts unto your children, how much more shall your Father which is in heaven give good things to them that ask him?"

Then Matthew 7:12, the Golden Rule: "Therefore all things whatsoever ye would that men should do to you, do ye even so to them: for this is the law and the prophets." Jesus expressed this same thought but expanded it into a declaration of divine justice in a note of explanation after the Lord's Prayer in chapter six. If you forgive other people their trespasses, God will forgive you; if you won't, God won't.

Next there are inserted two verses, standing by themselves, that have been called the Two Ways. "Enter ye in at the strait gate: for wide is the gate, and broad is the way, that leadeth to destruction, and many there be which go in thereat: Because strait is the gate, and narrow is the way, which leadeth unto life, and few there be that find it." The word strait as it is used here is archaic, meaning restricted, constricted, tight.

We're nearing the end of the Sermon now with the lesson on how to distinguish false from true prophets. "Beware of false prophets, which come to you in sheep's clothing, but inwardly they are ravening wolves." In our day, they could be advertisers, salesmen, politicians, demagogues, suitors, even prophets. The Reverend Jim Jones, a charismatic and tyrannical evangelist who formed his own church with lost and forsaken followers, led his flock from California to Guyana where he presided over a hideous mass suicide/murder of 912 people in November 1978. "Ye shall know them by their fruits. Do men gather grapes of thorns, or figs of thistles? Even so every good tree bingeth forth good fruit; but a corrupt tree bringeth forth evil fruit."

You can tell what they are by what they do. "Not every one that saith unto me, Lord, Lord, shall enter into the kingdom of heaven, but he that doeth the will of my Father which is in heaven."

The Gospel of Luke has a Sermon on the Plain that somewhat parallels the Sermon on the Mount but does not possess its felicity of language. Luke's Sermon is not as sustained and cannot generate the same cumulative power. And there are some major differences in interpretation: instead of blessed are the poor in spirit, Luke makes it blessed are the poor; for blessed are they who hunger and thirst after righteousness, the Plain Sermon has it blessed are you who hunger.

Luke has Jesus say explicitly that he has come to minister to the downtrodden, outcasts and casualties of life. In his first return to Nazareth, he goes to the synagogue and reads from the prophet Isaiah: "The Spirit of the Lord is upon me, because he hath anointed me to preach the gospel to the poor; he hath sent me to heal the brokenhearted, to preach deliverance to the captives, and recovering of sight to the blind, to set at liberty them that are bruised."

Then Jesus preached the gospel of the kingdom. When people questioned his doctrine, as Mark reported, Luke says that Jesus not only told them that a prophet is without honor at home, but upbraided them with Biblical references to how the prophets Elijah and Elisha punished the Jews. His listeners became so incensed they formed a lynch party. They "were filled with wrath, and rose up, and thrust him out of the city, and led him unto the brow of the hill whereon their city was built, that they might cast him headlong." Jesus managed to escape with his life, but he learned another lesson from his early ministry experience at Nazareth. His powers of healing depended upon the other person's perception of him. The other person's faith in him was crucial for success.

The episode in Nazareth was an exception. Jesus was a miracle worker who became a peripatetic magnet attracting ever bigger crowds. People came to see for themselves, some to be cured, and all were told of the kingdom of God. He said his healing was a demonstration of or means of access to the kingdom.

Jesus performed three kinds of miraculous cures: of people who were physically ill with disease, mentally ill — possessed by devils or unclean spirits — and sometimes raising from the "dead" people whom Jesus said were only sleeping or in what we would call a coma. The common denominator in all of these acts of healing was the faith of someone involved.

When two blind men beseeched Jesus to have mercy on them, he said, "Believe ye that I am able to do this? They said unto him, Yea, Lord. Then touched he their eyes, saying, According to your faith be it unto you. And their eyes were opened." Once, the head of a synagogue named Jairus begged Jesus to come with him and save his dying daughter. Pushing through crowds, Jesus felt someone touch his clothes. He demanded to know who did it. It was a woman who had been bleeding for a dozen years. She "had suffered many things of physicians, and had spent all that she had, and was nothing bettered, but rather grew worse." After she touched Jesus' garment, she felt cured. The woman threw herself at his feet and confessed. He said to her, "Daughter, thy faith hath made thee whole". Continuing to Jairus' house, they were met by a servant who said the daughter had died. Jesus told the father: "Be not afraid, only believe." They went to the house, Jesus took the girl's hand, told her to arise and she awoke.

A man came to Jesus and said his son was mentally ill and often injured himself. The man said the disciples tried but were unable to cure him. The boy was brought to Jesus who after a struggle healed the lad. The disciples wanted to know why they had failed. Jesus told them, "Because of your unbelief: for verily I say unto you, If you have faith as a grain of mustard seed, ye shall say unto this mountain, Remove hence to yonder place; and it shall remove; and nothing shall be impossible to you."

A Roman centurian wanted Jesus to cure his servant who was gravely ill. The centurian said he had such faith in Jesus that he didn't have to go to the house. Jesus said he had not seen such faith in all Israel. If that implied a slap at the Jews, Jesus made explicit his dissatisfaction with the reception his doctrine had been receiving. He said that outsiders, gentiles, would enter the kingdom of God while Jews, the natural inheritors, would not. "Many shall come from the east and west, and shall sit down with Abraham, and Isaac, and Jacob, in the kingdom of heaven. But the children of the kingdom shall be cast out into outer darkness: there shall be weeping and gnashing of teeth." This early reproach is expressed soon after the Sermon on the Mount.

Jesus' acts of healing aggravated friction with the Pharisees and scribes. Both groups were punctilious in observations of the many Jewish laws and were intolerant of infractions. The Pharisees numbered about 6,000, kept themselves apart from the common people, were respected by many Jews for their interpretations of the law and were powerful in enforcing Jewish doctrine. Their piety was especially zealous in matters pertaining to dietary laws, ritual purity and tithing.

It was forbidden to work on the sabbath and Jesus' acts of healing were taken as violations of the prohibition. Jesus used his wits to deflect indictments. He asked his accusers if they didn't tend their cattle on the sabbath. Was a human being any less worthy than an ox? Another time, he asked if one were supposed to do good or evil on the sabbath. On neither occasion were his adversaries able to answer. When Pharisees caught Jesus and his disciples picking corn on the sabbath, Jesus retorted that David had broken the law in order to relieve his hunger and added: "The sabbath was made for man, and not man for the sabbath."

Another time, when Jesus said to a young man sick with palsy, "Son, thy sins be forgiven thee," some scribes said Jesus was blaspheming because only God can forgive sins. Blasphemy was a capital offense. Jesus asked what difference it made whether he said sins were forgiven or arise. But just to show that he could forgive sins, Jesus said to the palsied man, "Arise, and take up thy bed, and go thy way into thine house. And immediately he arose, took up the bed, and went forth before them all; insomuch that they were all amazed, and glorified God, saying, We never saw it on this fashion."

The Establishment resented the growing popularity of Jesus and sought to discredit him. The Pharisees devised what seemed to be an incontrovertible argument. They charged that the reason Jesus was able to cast out devils was because he had the help of the Prince of Devils. In other words, Jesus was a sorcerer. Sorcery was another crime punishable by death.

Jesus responded with a brilliant refutation. "Every kingdom divided against itself is brought to desolation; every city or house divided against itself shall not stand: and if Satan cast out Satan, he is divided against himself; how shall then his kingdom stand?....But if I cast out devils by the Spirit of God, then the kingdom of God is come to you." In Luke it was: "But if I with the finger of God cast out devils, no doubt the kingdom is come upon you."

All the while the disciples were learning, being prepared for their mission. An important part of their training was to show them how to preach the kingdom of God. A major instrument in this teaching was the parable, a form that Jesus apparently turned to sometime after he began his ministry. The parable is a simple story that could be readily grasped, at least on the surface level, by his most untutored listener. But while Jesus' parables told an obvious story, on a deeper level they taught a truth, had a moral, and almost always contained a secret about the kingdom of God.

When Jesus started to use this seeming transparent but often opaque vehicle, the disciples were curious about it. This is detailed in the parable of The Sower, the first extended parable in each of the three Synoptic Gospels. Some of the sower's seeds fall by the wayside where birds eat them. Some seeds fall on stony places where few seeds take root. Those that do sink roots get little nourishment from the earth and wither. Some seeds fall among fast-growing thorns which choke them. But some seeds "fell into good ground, and brought forth fruit, some an hundredfold, some sixtyfold, some thirtyfold."

After the public sermon, the disciples asked Jesus in private why he spoke in parables. "Because," he replied, "it is given unto you to know the mysteries of the kingdom of heaven, but to them it is not given. For whosoever hath, to him shall be given, and he shall have more abundance: but whosoever hath not, from him shall be taken away even that he hath. Therefore I speak to them in parables: because they seeing see not: and hearing they hear not, neither do they understand. And in them is fulfilled the prophecy of Isaiah, which saith, By hearing ye shall hear, and shall not understand; and seeing ye shall see, and not perceive: For this people's heart is waxed gross." They have lost the ability to understand and be converted by his doctrine.

Then Jesus explains the parable to his disciples. In Mark, Jesus says the sower sows the word; in Luke, Jesus says it is the word of God. In Matthew, "When one heareth the word of the kingdom, and understandeth it not, then cometh the wicked one, and catcheth away that which was sown in his heart. This is he which received seed by the way side. But he that received the seed in stony places, the same is he that heareth the word, and anon with joy receiveth it; Yet hath he not root in himself, but dureth for a while: for when tribulation or persecution ariseth because of the word, by and by he is offended. He also that received seed among the thorns is he that heareth the word: and the care of this world, and the deceitfulness of riches, choke the word, and he becometh unfruitful. But he that received seed into the good ground is he that heareth the word, and understandeth it; which also beareth fruit, and bringeth forth, some an hundredfold, some sixty, some thirty."

"The kingdom of heaven is like to a grain of mustard seed, which a man took, and sowed in his field: Which is the least of all seeds: but when it is grown, it is the greatest among herbs, and becometh a tree, so that the birds of the air come and lodge in the branches thereof."

"The kingdom of heaven is like unto leaven, which a woman took, and hid in three measures of meal, till the whole was leavened."

"The kingdom of heaven is like unto treasure hid in a field; the which when a man hath found, he hideth, and for joy thereof goeth and selleth all that he hath, and buyeth that field.

"Again, the kingdom of heaven is like unto a merchant man, seeking goodly pearls: Who, when he had found one pearl of great price, went and sold all that he hath, and bought it."

Another obscure saying, one that probably is more a paradox than a parable, also came with an explanation. It was an illustration of his great theme of the difference between form and essence and, in this case, a downgrading of the spiritual value of Jewish dietary laws. "Not that which goeth into the mouth defileth a man; but that which cometh out of the mouth, this defileth a man." Afterwards, the disciples told Jesus that the Pharisees were offended. "Let them alone," Jesus said, "they be blind leaders of the blind. And if the blind lead the blind, both shall fall into the ditch."

Then Peter asked what the saying meant, and Jesus answered: "Are ye also yet without understanding? Do not ye yet understand, that whatsoever entereth in at the mouth goeth into the belly, and is cast out into the draught? But those things which proceed out of the mouth come forth from the heart; and they defile the man. For out of the heart proceed evil thoughts, murders, adulteries, fornications, thefts, false witness, blasphemies: These are the things which defile a man: but to eat with unwashen hands defileth not a man."

When Jesus sends his disciples-about-to-become-apostles on their first mission, he counsels them like a solicitious father. From his cautionary instructions, one can appreciate the threatening and potentially hostile world into which these lowly, uneducated, naive do-gooders were venturing. Their mission was to preach the kingdom of God to the lost sheep of Israel and heal the sick. They were to take no money nor food with them. They were to find a friendly house and use only that as a base for the time they remained in one location. "And whosoever shall not receive you, nor hear your words, when ye depart out of that house or city, shake off the dust of your feet." Be done with them. "I send you forth as sheep in the midst of wolves: be ye therefore wise as serpents, and harmless as doves. But beware of men: for they will deliver you up to the councils, and they will scourge you in their synagogues". If the missionaries are seized, they're not to worry about what to say — that will come to them at the time. Fear not. But don't expect it to be easy.

And off they went in pairs.

The life of an itinerant preacher was unenviable despite the punctuated exhilarations of spellbound audiences. It was a constant, wearing, wearying always-on-the-go. From A to B to C to D and back to B — a series of one-day stands with catch-as-catch-can meals, not sure of the night's lodging, no place for rest or privacy. Jesus would go into the desert or mountains in order to be alone and pray. Once, when he saw a crowd approaching, he tried to escape. A scribe caught up with him and said he would follow wherever Jesus went. Jesus gave this poignant reply: "The foxes have their holes, and the birds of the air have their nests; but the Son of man hath nowhere to lay his head."

Not only was the life of a preacher and social critic arduous, it was dangerous. Jesus learned at this time of the execution of John the Baptist. We know that this event had significant import for Jesus. Did it influence his plans?

Immediately after the apostles returned, Jesus took them to a desert for a private meeting. They reported on their endeavors. There is no mention of any great successes, no talk of large-scale conversions. Jesus must have expected, indeed been confident of early success to his mission. He had told the apostles before their departure: "Ye shall not have gone over the cities of Israel, till the Son of man be come." But Luke dismisses the homecoming with one brief sentence: "And the apostles, when they were returned, told him all that they had done." The single sentence in Mark isn't much longer. In Matthew, where the instructions for the apostles' mission was given in great detail, the return isn't even mentioned.

This was a bold experiment, an unprecedented effort to broadcast a doctrine evangelically. Did it fail? Was the private meeting some kind of strategy session to see what went wrong? To see what should be altered? To adopt a new program? The apostles went back to being what they had been, disciples. Their intended function as traveling representatives of their teacher foreclosed, they remained as foils for elucidating Jesus' ideas and also performed the role of a Greek chorus as intimate witnesses to the drama that was about to unfold.

Jesus already had expressed his dissatisfaction at the reception the kingdom-of-God doctrine was getting. The people weren't understanding it, weren't believing it, even as they mobbed him to see the miraculous cures. Jesus sought to recruit one man. "But he said, Lord, suffer me first to go and bury my father. Jesus said unto him, Let the dead bury their dead: But go thou and preach the kingdom of God. Another also said, Lord, I will follow thee: but let me first bid them farewell, which are at my house. And Jesus said unto him, No man, having put his hand to the plough, and looking back, is fit for the kingdom of God."

Jesus' disappointment with the lack of understanding of his doctrine extended, as we have seen, to the disciples who by this time should have comprehended what he was talking about. Aside from the disciples, however, there didn't seem to be many converts. Early, we were told that people were astonished by the doctrine. Later, there is no characterization of the general reaction.

After the return of the apostles and the meeting in the desert, a dramatic change takes place in the story. First, there is the miracle of the loaves and fishes. Starting with five loaves of bread and two fishes, Jesus feeds five thousand men plus, Matthew adds, women and children. Next, Jesus is seen, by his disciples, walking on the Sea of Galilee. Then another mass feeding, this time of four thousand.

Even after these feats, however, there seemed to be a problem with his credentials: proof that he was indeed a true prophet. Nor did his good works in healing appear to be enough. The Pharisees demanded that he produce a sign, a sign from heaven, to verify his authenticity. He "sighed deeply in his spirit, and saith, Why doth this generation seek after a sign? verily, I say unto you, There shall be no sign given to this generation." That was a pretty weak answer. There was a crisis of belief.

Jesus asks his disciples who people say he is. They reply that some say he is John the Baptist, some say Elijah, others say Jeremiah or some other prophet. "But whom say ye that I am?" Peter says he is the Messiah. Jesus, in Mark and Luke, tells his disciples not to say anything about this. But in Matthew he calls Peter blessed "and upon this rock I will build my church; and the gates of hell shall not prevail against it. And I will give unto thee the keys of the kingdom of heaven: and whatsoever thou shalt bind on earth shall be bound in heaven: and whatsoever thou shalt loose on earth shall be loosed in heaven." Then, as in the other Gospels, he instructs his disciples not to reveal to anyone that he is the Messiah.

Jesus now tells the disciples that he must go to Jerusalem, suffer many things, be killed and raised again on the third day. When Peter objects to such a fate, Jesus rebukes him for not appreciating God's will, but valuing the things of men. The disciples still weren't fully persuaded. They still didn't have implicit faith. Irrefutable proof was needed.

About a week after the Recognition, Jesus invites Peter, John and James up into a mountain with him to pray. Jesus "was transfigured before them: and his face did shine as the sun, and his raiment was white as the light. And behold, there appeared unto them Moses and Elijah talking with him." A cloud came, covering them, and out of the cloud a voice said: "This is my beloved Son, in whom I am well pleased; hear ye him." The disciples were frightened and fell on their faces. Jesus touched them, told them to arise and not to be afraid. "And when they had lifted up their eyes, they saw no man save Jesus only. And as they came down from the mountain, Jesus charged them, saying, Tell the vision to no man until the Son of man be risen again from the dead."

The disciples ask why the scribes insist that Elijah must precede the Messiah — this was a prophecy of Malachi. Jesus answers that Elijah must appear first to set things straight. "But I say unto you that Elijah is come already, and they knew him not, but have done whatsoever they listed. Likewise shall also the Son of man suffer of them. Then the disciples understood that he spake unto them of John the Baptist."

This is the watershed of the Gospels. Now the story is headed in a new direction toward a different horizon. There is a shift from a major to a minor key. Before was the bright morning of promise and hope, of the optimistic introduction of a new doctrine that will give people a new life, a new wine in new bottles, preaching of love and mercy and goodness and divine justice. Increasingly, in the long afternoon's journey toward night the shadows lengthen although there still are some shafts of the setting sunlight. The ambience is foreboding. One can almost hear the ominous rumble of distant thunder. Always the allusions to some awful rendezvous; always, like a Greek tragedy, the inexorable progress toward an inescapable fate. Where the story had been life-oriented, now it becomes death-oriented.

Now in addition to exhortations to practice love and righteousness, there are fulminations against enemies, predictions of dire things to come — woes to the cities that have not heeded his words and deeds. As though to compensate for the flaw or weakness in the earlier mission, there is almost an obsessed insistence on belief in him as the requisite for salvation, an element that is absent in his earlier preaching. There was an early indication of this attitude in his instructions to the apostles, as though there were a premonition that their mission would not succeed. "But whosoever shall deny me before men, him will I also deny before my Father which is in heaven.

Think not that I am come to send peace on earth: I came not to send peace, but a sword."

There is more talk of resurrection after three days — the sign of his credentials is changed to that of Jonah who spent three days in the belly of a whale. There are increasing references to his messianic importance and other-worldly concerns, an increasing shift toward the supernatural. "This gospel of the kingdom shall be preached in all the world for a witness unto all nations; and then shall the end come." "And then shall they see the Son of man coming in a cloud with power and great glory. And when these things begin to come to pass, then lift up your heads; for your redemption draweth nigh....when ye see these things come to pass, know ye that the kingdom of God is nigh at hand. Verily I say unto you, This generation shall not pass away, till all be fulfilled." "In the regeneration when the Son of man shall sit in the throne of his glory, ye also shall sit on twelve thrones, judging the twelve tribes of Israel."

How can we account for this abrupt and radical shift in the tenor of his ministry? Albert Schweitzer believed that when Jesus saw his campaign wasn't working, he switched to a new strategy modeled on the Suffering Servant. The Suffering Servant as described in the Book of Isaiah is a paragon, a savior of the Jewish people who leads them to righteousness through the sacrifice of his life.

Isaiah preached in the second half of the 8th century B.C. before and after the fall of Israel to the Assyrians. Isaiah criticized the moral and social conditions in both kingdoms of Israel and Judah, and he viewed the Assyrian onslaught as the intervention of the Jewish God Yahweh in history. Assyria was an instrument of divine vengeance.

This theme was echoed by Jeremiah during the decline and fall of Judah, and by Ezekiel in the Babylonian Exile. But in the last years of the Exile there appears a prophet with a message in strong contrast to this tradition. This prophet interprets contemporary history with hope and optimism. He sees God's instrument this time as the Persian King Cyrus who will destroy Babylon and liberate the Jews, which is just what happened.

The work of this unknown prophet and his creation, the Suffering Servant, were inserted into the Book of Isaiah, chapters 40 through 55. For that reason this later prophet has come to be known as the Second Isaiah or Deutero-Isaiah. For him, there no longer are superior and inferior gods. There is only one God, for all. And God's purpose is universal justice. It is the role of the Suffering Servant to reveal God's truth to the people so that they can have a new relationship with God.

The Suffering Servant accomplishes his mission by bearing the sins and suffering of many and laying down his life for them without complaint in order to bring them to righteousness. See how this passage from the Second Isaiah can serve as a template for the remainder of Jesus' life: "All we like sheep have gone astray....and the Lord hath laid on him the iniquity of us all. He was oppressed and he was afflicted, yet he opened not his mouth: he is brought to the slaughter....He was taken from prison and from judgment....for the transgression of my people was he stricken....because he had done no violence, neither was any deceit in his mouth....Yet it pleased the Lord to bruise him....by his knowledge shall my righteous servant justify many: for he shall bear their iniquities. Therefore will I divide him a portion with the great, and he shall divide the spoil with the strong; because he hath poured out his soul unto death: and he was numbered with the transgressors; and he bare the sins of many, and made intercession for the transgressors."

People regarded the servant as a criminal, persecuting and condemning him. They rationalized his suffering as the punishment of God. But after his death, in retrospect, people see that they were wrong. They revise their estimate of him. They deserved the punishment for their iniquity. But God willed it to happen this way for their benefit. *They* have been made better people because of his sacrifice.   The Suffering Servant wasn't an actual historical person, but rather an ideal. The job was open to any Jew who wanted to apply.

We already have seen the influence of Deutero-Isaiah on Jesus' doctrine in his emphasis on divine justice and his mission to reveal God's truth so that people could live better lives. Now we see evidence that Jesus even was willing to sacrifice his life in order to accomplish his mission if that were required. And still another theme is now introduced: the necessity of being a servant to all.

Soon after the Transfiguration, Jesus started for Jerusalem. The significance of his decision to go to Jerusalem is that by entering Judea he came under the temporal authority of the Sanhedrin. He no longer would enjoy the political immunity he had in Galilee when he challenged orthodox doctrine and leaders. Any confrontation could be dangerous. He deliberately chose to test and rest his destiny in the ultimate crucible.

Along the way, he heard the disciples arguing about who should be first among them. After they reached Capernaum, he asked them what the dispute was about. They wouldn't tell him, but he knew anyway and said to them: "If any man desire to be first, the same shall be last of all, and servant of all." The Zebedee brothers, John and James, asked Jesus if they could sit beside him, at his right hand and left hand, when he came into his kingdom. Jesus said it was not within his power to grant this. As one might imagine, when the other disciples heard about this special pleading, they were angry. Jesus gathered them all together and said that "whosoever will be great among you, shall be your minister: and whosoever of you will be chiefest, shall be servant of all. For even the Son of man came not to be ministered unto, but to minister, and give his life a ransom for many."

When the disciples asked Jesus who then is the greatest in the kingdom of God, "Jesus called a little child unto him, and set him in the midst of them. And said, Verily I say unto you, Except ye be converted, and become as little children, ye shall not enter into the kingdom of heaven."

Some Pharisees, again baiting him, asked when the kingdom of God would come. Jesus answered: "The kingdom of God cometh not with observation: Neither shall they say, Lo here! or, lo there! for, behold, the kingdom of God is within you."

This contrapuntal theme of challenge to Jesus was introduced early, with the first declaration of menace coming after one of these encounters in Mark 3:6: "The Pharisees went forth, and straightway took counsel with the Herodians against him, how they might destroy him." This counterpoint is skillfully orchestrated into the narrative, reappearing intermittantly after sections of reassuring hiatus.

After Jesus entered Jerusalem, the testing intensified, the plot to kill him thickened. But he was as much challenger as challenged, driving the money changers from the Temple, preaching his own doctrine in this holiest of holies, debating with Pharisees, Sadducees, priests, lawyers, scribes and giving better than he got. Such provocation couldn't be allowed to go on. Some people were wondering: is this truly the Messiah? Such speculation out in the boondocks is one thing, but it was far more dangerous, and intolerable, in the religious and political heart of Palestine. It was being bruited that Jesus had claimed he was King of the Jews, an unallowable affront to the authority of Rome. Any spark might ignite the people's yearnings. And it was a volatile moment with Jerusalem crowded for Passover. The high priest Caiaphas already had said of Jesus that it was better for one man to die than for the whole nation to be destroyed.

Still, Jesus was known now. It had to be handled carefully. What better time to mount a martial strike than during a holiday night?

The Last Supper. Anguish at Gethsemane: "0 my Father, if it is possible, let this cup pass from me: nevertheless not as I will, but as thou wilt." The betrayal by Judas. Arrest. Jesus before Caiaphas. Jesus before Pilate. Jesus before Herod. Pilate sentences Jesus. The Roman soldiers "clothed him with purple, and platted a crown of thorns, and put it about his head. And began to salute him, Hail King of the Jews! And they smote him on the head with a reed, and did spit upon him, and bowing their knees worshipped him. And when they had mocked him, they took off the purple from him, and put his own clothes on him, and led him out to crucify him." Crucifixion was the form of execution the Romans used for subversion or treason to the state. A sign, KING OF THE JEWS, was put on the cross.

He was crucified between two thieves. "And the scripture — [Second Isaiah] — was fulfilled, which saith, And he was numbered with the transgressors". As he hung in agony on the cross, a man, still testing, gave him a spongeful of vinegar to slake his thirst. People reviled him: Son of God, King of Israel, you have saved others, now save yourself. Come down from the cross and we will believe. His flock was scattered, his staunchest disciple had denied Jesus to save his own skin. This was utter defeat, utter ignominy. And, too, that most galling of events: the unjust execution of an innocent man, a man who had done no violence, from whose mouth had come no deceit. There was his undoing, for on too many things he had spoken with uninhibited candor.

"My God, my God, why has thou forsaken me?" said Jesus, the man. "Father, into thy hands I commend my spirit," said the Son of man. "Father, forgive them; for they know not what they do," said the Suffering Servant. And to one of the thieves being crucified with him, "To day shalt thou be with me in paradise," said Jesus, the Christ.

In the long Jewish history with its incredible vicissitudes, this is the most incredible story of all. Certainly the most improbable. Three days after the death of this man would begin a revolution that would conquer the Roman Empire, capture western humanity and profoundly influence the development of civilization. He would become comforter, solace, companion, confidant, hope, inspiration, redeemer for more people than any person in history. The religion that would ensue would reject and be rejected by Judaism, but would give to the gentiles the Jewish Bible so that, just as Jesus had said, these outsiders sat down with Abraham and Isaac and Jacob. And just as the Suffering Servant had predicted, people did come to believe that Jesus sacrificed his life to expiate their sins.

Three days after the crucifixion, the stone was found rolled away from the entrance to the sepulcher. The body of Jesus was not inside. Instead, Mary Magdalene saw two angels sitting where the corpse had been. Then she saw Jesus alive. She addressed him and he talked to her. He was seen by the disciples in post-resurrection appearances. One report told of witnesses to his ascension into the clouds.

It is beyond our power to make a judgment of these accounts. Beyond question, however, *something happened.* In its effects, it was a supernova in human history. His followers believed! So much so that they were absolutely certain that he soon would reappear in the Second Coming. This conviction so overwhelmed their thinking that the things of this world hardly mattered. They impatiently awaited the return of Christ — for the Resurrection confirmed and manifested his authenticity — to supervise in the resurrection of all and to usher all of the faithful into his heavenly kingdom of God.

In this white-hot fervor, the indefatigable apostle Paul — who never met Jesus but was converted by a mystical experience and vision on the road to Damascus — was busy forging a religion and a theology. They were not so much of Jesus as about Jesus, not so much that Jesus had lived for us as that he had died for us.

Paul introduced the concept that as the first man, Adam, had brought Original Sin and death to humankind through his disobedience to God, so Jesus Christ was sent to provide salvation from the transgression. "Now is Christ risen from the dead, and become the first fruits of them that slept, For since by man came death, by man came also the resurrection of the dead. For as in Adam all die, even so in Christ shall all be made alive." Paul built the religion on one foundation. "If there be no resurrection of the dead, then is Christ not arisen: And if Christ be not risen, then is our preaching in vain, and your faith is in vain."

By the time the fourth and last canonized Gospel, the Gospel of John, was written, the term kingdom of God appears only twice.

Instead and substituting for it are such terms as life eternal, everlasting life or, simply, life. The idea of an always-existing soul detached from the body was familiar and agreeable to the Greek mind. Plato had talked about these soul entities that pre-existed as well as post-existed their habitation in the fleshly container.

Jewish thinkers never had split apart body and soul. To them, resurrection meant revival of the whole being. This was an alien and unacceptable concept to Hellenistic culture where people were interested only in immortality of the soul. Paul's solution, since the new religion was finding fertile ground in the Greco-Roman world, was to merge the two concepts, a marriage that never has been entirely compatible. The Logos, the Word, that appears at the beginning of the Gospel of John is a Greek concept that went back at least six centuries to Heraclitus. The term Son of man had no additional meaning in Greek and became Son of God. The Jewish Messiah became the Greek Christos.

The Hellenistic world beyond Palestine already had put faith in savior gods — Dionysus, Attis and Cybele, Isis, Mithra among others — who had conquered death and who could reward worshipers with salvation. Jesus Christ conquered them just as he did the Roman Empire.

Almost certainly the doctrine of Jesus would have disappeared without the Resurrection. When the Second Coming didn't occur right away, an effort was made to collect the sayings of Jesus and the story of his life in more permanent form. This was 30 or more years after his death, and so it is understandable if there are gaps and if fragments are not always the same or sometimes are placed in different order in the Synoptic Gospels. The oral traditions were written. There was no need to hide or suppress anything because he had proved himself beyond anyone's doubt. If some meanings were obscure or there were some discrepancies, they were included for the record since they were believed to have occurred. Jesus had said these things and to greater or lesser degrees they were background material and prelude to the event that revealed and confirmed the significance of his mission. It was what he had done, not what he had said, that really mattered. His actions had told them that the kingdom of God was life everlasting after death. In the blinding light of this revelation, it didn't seem to matter that *Jesus never had said publicly what the kingdom of God was, never said overtly or unambiguously what he meant by the kingdom of God.*

When Mary Magdalene recognized Jesus in the sepulcher, she

addressed him as *Rabboni*. Teacher. Not the least incredible part of the story is that during nearly two millennia Christianity has grown to be the world's largest religion without Christians knowing what is meant by the central tenet of Jesus' teaching.

TWO

The Mystery of History

The Resurrection fused Jesus Christ, but over the centuries the Jesus of life faded into the Christ of faith.

The symbolic Christ began to be challenged by the Enlightenment, the intellectual quickening of the 18th century that believed in the efficacy of reason and knowledge to produce the betterment of humankind. Thinkers stimulated by the premise and promise of the Enlightenment believed they could, and should, disinter the Jesus who once had lived from the dead icons of Christ.

To Thomas Jefferson, Jesus was "a man, of illegitimate birth, of a benevolent heart, enthusiastic mind, who set out without pretensions of divinity, ended in believing them, and was punished capitally for sedition by being gibbeted according to Roman law." In private correspondence, Jefferson wrote that he had begun abstacting from the Gospels "what is really his from the rubbish in which it is buried, easily distinguished by its lustre from the dross of his biographers, and as separable from that as the diamond from the dung hill."

The picture of Christ had been layered image over image over image over the original portrait of Jesus. At first, Jesus was called teacher or sometimes prophet, then Messiah or Lord. With the apocalyptic expectation of the end of the world and the Son of man to arrive in the clouds of glory to introduce the reign of God, Christ came to be seen as the turning point in history for all nations. As he became more important in the Greco-Roman world, Christians found gentile forerunners. The Roman poet Virgil at about 40 B.C. had predicted the birth of a child who would begin a new golden age, eliminating wickedness and fear. Socrates was said to have been a Christian before Christ and was put to death by enemies of the Logos. In Plato's *Republic,* written three and a half centuries B.C., before Christ, Glaucon supposed that unlike all other mortals there was one completely righteousness man, a man "who desires....to be a good man and not merely to give the impression of being a good man." He is accused of being unrighteous even though he is righteous, and does not yield. What will become of this man? Glaucon answers his own question: "He shall be scourged, tortured, bound, his eyes burnt out, and at last, after suffering every evil, shall be impaled or crucified."

Jesus had told Pontius Pilate, "My kingdom is not of this world." But in 312 the Emperor Constantine won a battle under the insignia of Christ. This alliance would be consumated by Christianity becoming the state religion of Rome. Caesar genuflected before Christ. The man who had been crucified under the sarcastic sign, THE KING OF THE JEWS, had a new title: King of Kings.

Just 13 years after Constantine's victory at Milvian Bridge and immediately after he had consolidated his power as sole ruler of the Empire, the Council of Nicea consecrated the elevation of Christ to Godhood. The Son of God was co-equal with the Father and the Holy Ghost in the Trinity. The Nicene Creed makes Christ the pre-existent Logos, "the only-begotten Son of God, begotten not made, of one substance with the Father, through whom all things were made, who for us men and our salvatation came down from the heavens, and was made flesh of the Holy Spirit...." The next important council, at Chalcedon in 451, confirmed that the two natures — the divine and the human — coexisted in Jesus Christ at the same time. This doctrine no longer was promulgated as a creed of belief, but was stated as fact.

Christ also became known in later centuries as the Bridegroom of the Soul, the Mirror of Eternity, and The Prince of Peace. This third title came from a passage in Isaiah: "For unto us a child is born, unto us a son is given....and his name shall be called....The Prince of Peace." The title was advanced after eight Crusades had been launched at the urging of the Papacy from Christian Europe to regain Jerusalem and the Holy Sepulcher from the Moslems. The most permanent achievement of the centuries-long effort was the sack of Christian Constantinople by Crusaders causing the irreparable loss of a good part of the heritage of western civilization and the decline of Eastern Christianity. Not too long after the title was nominated came the Thirty Years War between Catholics and Protestants, devastating central Europe and reducing the population of Germany by more than a third. Christian theologians — including Augustine, Thomas Aquinas and Martin Luther — had managed to justify wars and individuals fighting in spite of Jesus' preaching nonviolence.

The first public round against the miraculous, cosmic, protean Christ was fired in 1773 and it sparked a remarkable struggle that carried into the 20th century. The battleground again was Germany, but unlike the Thirty Years War, this one was fought with books. Another curious fact is that most of the books had the same title: Life of Jesus, or some variation of it.

Hermann Samuel Reimarus was a scholar, philosopher, professor of Hebrew and cultural leader in Hamburg who wrote on many subjects. Among the things Reimarus wrote, in secret, was an exhaustive attack upon Christianity. Reimarus used all the force of his scholarship and logic to deny revelation and miracles, to label Jesus an irresponsible seeker after political power, and to argue that the Resurrection was a deliberate hoax. It took Reimarus *4,000* pages to make his points, but he never published this material for fear of the impact upon himself and his family. After his death, however, his daughter showed the papers to a leading German critic and writer, Gotthold Lessing, who went ahead and published them in fragments without at first disclosing who was the author. Church leaders, naturally, were outraged. And when friends and colleagues learned that the author was Reimarus, they were shocked.

Reimarus' attack had the effect of producing an attitude that could be summarized as: all right, let's get to the bottom of this, let's find out who the real Jesus was. This attitude reflected the confidence born of the Enlightenment in the new powers of historical research. Historians, scholars, theologians leaped into the fray, dispatching fusilades of words and volleys of arguments. But for the most part these were ponderous tomes often filled with "and yet, on the other hand, notwithstanding," as Albert Schweitzer put it.

Schweitzer performed the heroic service of reading all these volumes. Soon after the turn of the 20th century, Schweitzer published his review of more than 250 authors in *From Reimarus to Wrede: A History of Research on the Life of Jesus.* In English translation the book became *The Quest of the Historical Jesus.* Schweitzer was still a young man when the book was published and it made him a world-wide celebrity.

Schweitzer appears to be a disinterested editor, using his erudition and vantage point of retrospection to judge the parade of arguments, but in fact he has come to his own conclusion. He is doing no less than Aristotle did in *Metaphysics:* reviewing the positions of those who went before in order to make his own case.

After discussing Reimarus, Schweitzer presents examples of the rationalist school with escalating attacks that lead to Karl Hase in 1829. Hase, Schweitzer writes, "surrenders the birth-story and the 'legends of the Childhood' — the expression is his own— almost without striking a blow. The same fate befalls all the incidents in which angels figure, and the miracles at the time of the death of Jesus. He describes these as 'mythical touches.' The ascension is merely 'a mythical verson of His departure to the Father.'" Schweitzer says Hase developed the two-period view of Jesus' life. "In the first He accepted almost without reservation the popular ideas regarding the Messianic age. In consequence, however, of His experience of the practical results of these ideas, He was led to abandon this error, and in the second period He developed his own distinctive views." Schweitzer says this idea of the two periods was new and prevailed until the end of the century.

A culmination of these arguments and attacks came in 1835 with publication of *Life of Jesus* by David Friedrich Strauss. As an indication of how this genre of writing had been tightened, Strauss' work was a mere 1,480 pages. Nevertheless, it caused a sensation. Strauss rejected the idea of a personal immortality. He said that even if only a single generation had elapsed between the death of Jesus and the writing of the Gospels, we must assume that it was sufficient time for the historical material to become mixed with myth. We also must assume that the historical Jesus will be clothed in the messianic ideas of the Old Testament and the expectations of primitive Christians. In addition to trying to prove that the Gospels had a mythical origin and growth, Strauss denied the historicity of all supernatural elements. According to Schweitzer, Strauss made study of the life of Jesus an either-or proposition: "*either* purely historical *or* purely supernatural." By the middle of the century, sceptic Bruno Bauer would go so far as to deny that any historical Jesus ever existed.

These investigations had started with the assumption that the four Gospels were co-equal and produced in the order in which they appeared in the Bible: Matthew, Mark, Luke and John. Also that the authors were who they said they were: Matthew, the publican disciple; Mark, an early Christian in Jerusalem; Luke, the physician-follower of Paul; and John who liked to think of himself as the favorite disciple. But research showed that the Gospel of John probably was written too late to have been composed by the disciple. (Scholars today believe the four Gospels were written between 60 A.D. and 110 A.D. Authorities generally agree today that both Luke and Acts were written by the same author, but no one is completely sure who were the actual authors of the Gospels.)

During the course of the German inquiry, doubts began to arise about the priority in time of Matthew. The weight of evidence seemed to point to Mark as the original book. It seemed to be more primitive. It told the essential story in nuts-and-bolts fashion with no frills where Matthew and Luke were embroidered with far more details and eloquence. Scholars discovered that in addition to the story covered by Mark, Matthew and Luke made use of an unknown source of Jesus' sayings. This led to a conviction that Matthew and Luke were based on Mark and the sayings source.

As for the Gospel of John, the scrutiny of investigators showed that it varied wildly from the other three. The historians decided that John wasn't trying to document Jesus' life so much as he was trying to promote Jesus Christ. This led to what Schweitzer called the second mutually-exclusive alternatives: "*either* Synoptic *or* Johanine." John was dropped as an historical source. Today, Mark generally is considered the earliest Gospel, but there is a rival theory that Matthew is the original Gospel with Mark in third place, a distillation of Matthew and Luke. And there is a growing inclination to restore the status of John as an effort to fill in the gaps left by the first three Gospels.

A third theme developed toward and into the final quarter of the 19th century, what Schweitzer called the eschatological (end of the world) question. Eschatology is future oriented: it encompasses belief in resurrection after death, immortality, a day of judgment, a new age and drastically-changed future state. Apocalyptic eschatology — hope and belief in the coming of a Messiah and a dramatic transformation of fortunes — was an important element in Jewish thinking of the lst century B.C. But the belief was not held by every Jew, and it varied from a realistic new Maccabean revolt to the most fantastic and supernatural change of the world. The first Christians awaited such a transfiguration with the Second Coming of Christ and there were elements of the expectation in the latter parts of the Gospels. But how big a role did it have in Jesus' thought?

Timothee Colani, a Strassburg pastor, started the debate by saying that the spiritual conception of the kingdom of God cannot be combined with the thought of a glorious Second Coming because they are incompatible. If Jesus believed in the Second Coming, then he had to consider the present life as a kind of prologue to the second existence. Therefore, Colani believed, the eschatological statements in the Gospels did not belong to Jesus' teaching and should be discounted.

This led to Schweitzer's third arbitrary either-or: "*either* eschatological *or* non-eschatological."

Eschatology in Judaism began with Deutero-Isaiah, the unknown prophet in the Babylonian Exile whose Suffering Servant appeared to serve as a role model for Jesus. Deutero-Isaiah successfully prophesied that Cyrus and Persia would destroy Babylon and effect the liberation of the Jews so that they could repatriate their homeland. It was he who said "make straight in the desert a highway for our God." This was for the people's return to Jerusalem. The Second Isaiah promised more. God was finished punishing the Jewish people. They had earned their redemption and now a new age marked by God's love and kindness was dawning, the return of all the Hebrew people to Zion, the transformation of the land by rebuilding it virtually into a new Eden, the end of sorrow and beginning of everlasting joy, and the conversion of all nations with the triumph of God, the new universal God. The eschatologies that followed all contained some of these elements along with the messianic expectation and a growing supernatural quality. The Christian eschatology from this derivation was built around the Second Coming.

Johannes Weiss, a prominent theologian at the end of the 19th century, championed eschatology. Schweitzer writes: "The general conception of the Kingdom was first rightly grasped by Johannes Weiss. All modern ideas, he insists, even in their subtlest forms, must be eliminated from it; when this is done, he arrived at a Kingdom of God which is wholly future; as is indeed implied by the petition in the Lord's prayer, 'Thy Kingdom come.'" Where Jesus seems to be saying the kingdom is present, Schweitzer writes, "He only proclaims its coming. He....waits, like others, for God to bring about the coming of the Kingdom by supernatural means."

Wilhelm Bousset led the counter-attack. He said that Weiss, by putting so much emphasis on eschatology, let the "essential originality and power of the personality of Jesus slip through his fingers." For Bousset, the trait most characteristic of Jesus was his joy in life. Now, Bousset concedes, this joy could be associated with the eschatological mood, as an expression of indifference to this world. Even though early Christians held this eschatological attitude, Bousset thinks it "does not give the right clue for the interpretation of the character of Jesus as a whole....The present as contrasted with the beyond is for Him no mere shadow, but truth and reality; life is not for Him a mere illusion....And as, moreover, the righteousness which he preaches is one of the goods of the Kingdom of God, He cannot have thought of the Kingdom as wholly transcendental."

Schweitzer sums up Bousset's efforts: "This is the last possible sincere attempt to limit the exclusive importance of eschatology in the preaching of Jesus, an attempt so gallant, so brilliant, that its failure is almost tragic". *Exclusive* importance!

Schweitzer declares categorically that "the teaching of the historical Jesus was purely and exclusively world-renouncing." The question of whether Jesus' preaching was wholly or only partly eschatological, Schweitzer says, turns on his ethical teaching, which everyone knows was not designed for this world but was preparation for the next. Schweitzer saw his thoroughgoing eschatology as the triumphant thesis in still a fourth set of arbitrary opposites, scotching the antithesis, thoroughgoing scepticism.

Schweitzer terminated the 130-year quest abruptly, decisively and in surprising fashion with the judgment that the search to find the historical Jesus had failed. Furthermore, he said, the effort had shown that such a quest could never succeed! What the sceptics had destroyed was their own modern conception of Jesus. "The Jesus of Nazareth who came forward publicly as the Messiah, who preached the ethic of the Kingdom of God, who founded the Kingdom of Heaven upon earth, and died to give his work its final consecration, never had any existence. He is a figure designed by rationalism, endowed with life by liberalism, and clothed by modern theology in historical garb....What surprised and dismayed the theology of the last forty years was that, despite all forced and arbitrary interpretations, it could not keep Him in our time, but had to let Him go. He returned to His own time."

The only way that Jesus could be known today, Schweitzer said, is by people who experienced him mystically. The historical Jesus will always be for us "a stranger and an enigma."

Schweitzer won the field for an eschatological Jesus. Schweitzer saved the historical Jesus by putting him beyond the range of modern criticism, silencing the anti-Jesus batteries. This was no mean achievement. At the time, Arthur Drews in Germany was culminating Bruno Bauer's Jesus-is-only-a-myth thesis. The denial of the historical reality of Jesus also was finding exponents in England and Holland. In France, a Roman Catholic theologican directed such a severe textual analysis at the New Testament that he was excommunicated.

There was a price, however, for the Schweitzer maneuver. It exiled the historical Jesus to the shadows of understanding.

It wasn't just a tactical finesse. Schweitzer felt that eschatology had fallen out of fashion because the Second Coming never happened but that, nevertheless, this expectation of the Second Coming was the real inner history of Christianity. By reviving eschatology, he was restoring the belief that gave birth to Christianity. But is it possible, to use Jefferson's metaphor, that Albert Schweitzer chose the dross and left the diamonds?

Eschatology had been a part of many beliefs and an important element in the Zoroastrian religion that was absorbed into Judaism. Expectation of a glorious, perfect future was gouged from Jewish mentality by Roman arms. In 66 A.D., the uprising that had been feared at the time of Jesus did erupt in Jerusalem. The apocalypse came, and it annihilated the eschatological fantasy. The Romans required four years to do it, but they razed the Jewish civilization. The Temple disappeared. The Sanhedrin disappeared. The priests disappeared. The Sadducees disappeared. The Essenes disappeared. The Zealots disappeared. Most of the rest of the Jewish population had fled or was dispersed. The Diaspora began, along with the beginning of realism.

Can Jesus' teaching be expained as *solely* other-worldly? Can it be understood *solely* as eschatological? Is mystical experience our only link to him? Could it be that the epical debate was addressed to the wrong question? It is not the life of Jesus so much as his *doctrine* that is important to us. There still are those jewels of his sayings. For 20 centuries people have stared at them in awe and wonder, trying to read their meaning.

Two reasons it is difficult to perceive what Jesus meant are his background and his foreground. Jesus existed at a geographical, temporal and ideological crossroads of intellectual-religious influences. Afterwards, his disguised teachings became a subject for multiple interpreters.

Some causes for the confusion already have been presented. Jesus was imbued with the heritage of the Jews, a culture and religion anchored in this world. Yet some Judaism was colored by Zoroastrianism. There was the eschatology of Second Isaiah. There were the apocalyptic expectations of Daniel. And we know that Jesus' teaching was not strictly orthodox. Those various strains of belief are understandable because Jews of Palestine were in some ways a diverse people.

Jews of Judea, the land of the orthodox and cultured, scorned Galileans as peasant backsliders. Galileans regarded Judeans as legalistic snobs. Both regions were on poor terms with Jews of Samaria, which lay between Galilee and Judea. Judea and Samaria had a running feud over Samaritans' claims that Yahweh had chosen their Mount Gerizim, not Zion, for his home. Samaritans rejected all

Old Testament books except the Pentateuch, and their religious views were suspect among other Jews. That parable of the Good Samaritan emphasized Jesus' ecumenism precisely because he offered the startling notion that a Samaritan could be one's neighbor and treat one with mercy. Pharisees and Sadducees argued over the law (Sadducees accepted only the written law of the Pentateuch, Pharisees observed oral law as well). Non-sectarian Jews and Essenes had little use for the two dominant sects, and there is ample evidence of the hostility between Jesus and Pharisees, Sadducees, scribes and lawyers. We get some idea of how rampant Jesus considered deceit to be among his people from his remark when he saw Nathanael, a Galilean who had come to be a disciple: "Behold an Israelite, indeed, in whom is no guile."

But Palestine was not simply homeland for the Jews. There were more gentiles than Jews in most coastal cities and in the Decapolis or ten cities of the Jordan. Except for the interior villages, which were solidly Jewish, Greek culture was by now pervasive in Palestine. Aramaic was the principal language of the people and the one used by Jews. Priests and scholars understood Hebrew. Officials and most authors used Greek. Herod the Great, who ruled at the time of Jesus' birth, was neither a Jew by origin nor conviction. While he strived to maintain public peace and order, he pushed Hellenistic values and customs. Jews feared and hated Herod, Rome, and competing religions that Jews felt threatened to swallow their identity.

The intellectual revolution begun by Alexander's vast conquests in Asia abetted a process already unleashed under the Persian Empire. The forced relocation of populations, the detaching of parochial beliefs from their places of origin, the collisions of cultures, the exposure of people to foreign ideas was in effect a gigantic intellectual experiment. The mixing of gods, the borrowing, assimilation and remolding of beliefs blossomed into a creative intellectual adventure. At first the Hellenic world was dominated by secular Greek culture. Oriental ideas had been conveyed in images and symbols, myths and rites. The Greeks invented the *logos,* the abstract concept, the reasoned system, the method of theoretical expression. Mystery cults became infused with logic. Religions became capable of formulating theologies: intellectual systems that approached rational doctrines. Whatever was radically different in Eastern beliefs and could not be accepted by Greek culture went underground and became secret teaching.

The ferment reached an incandescent threshold in the eastern

Mediterranean world. The percolation of ideas produced an intellectual-spiritual crisis, one that could be grasped and articulated only in religious terms. Everywhere, not just among Jews, religion had become the mode for the advancement of thought. The initiating Greek philosophical methods had both liberated and fueled Eastern religious beliefs, resulting in a vitality that gained the ascendancy and presented a dizzying array of possibilities.

There was a radical dualism from the Iranian tradition: God and the world, spirit and matter, soul and body, light and darkness, good and evil, life and death. Diverse Eastern mystery cults developed into full-fledged spiritual mystery religions. A liberated Iranian eschatology offered the possibility of anything taking place. The concept of a transcendent, other-worldly God excited imaginations and readily merged into the concept of the gods of salvation. There was the most exhilarating possibility of all: the almost inconceivable phenomenon of resurrection and the reward of eternal life.

Ceremonies of the salvation religions often ritualized a symbolic resurrection. In the Mysteries of Cybele, the neophyte was regarded as in the process of dying, with the mystical death followed by a new, spiritual birth. Initiates were fed milk as if they had been reborn. The Mysteries of Mithra talked of being born again. Inductees were served bread and wine for strength and wisdom in this life and for glorious immortality in the afterlife.

At the same time, these salvation cults also were mystery religions. The mystery cult in Greece goes back to the 16th century B.C. with the Eleusinian Myteries. So well were these mysteries kept that scholars still know little about them. Nor was security breached much in the other mystery religions. Secrecy was regarded as heightening religious value and importance. The postulant was initiated into the cult with secret rites. Then the mysteries of the myth on which the religion was founded were revealed through esoteric teaching.

The desire for a spiritual renewal in the environment of the times promoted the spread of Hellenistic Judaism and mystery cults, the almost chain-reaction mushrooming of Christianity, and the appearance of a belief that fed on the other religions, magnified and compounded, exaggerated and distorted every new element, and above all raised esoteric teaching and learning to the core of the religion. This was Gnosticism, from the Greek word *gnosis,* knowledge. Gnostics referred to themselves as "the knowing ones." The origins of Gnosticism are unclear, but the Hellenic influences of Plato and Greek philosophy are unmistakable. There are Jewish, especially apocalyptic, elements, and great emphasis on Christianity. The Iranian traditions of dualism and eschatology are in evidence along with a new preoccupation with the Babylonian interest in the heavens.

The goal of gnosis is knowledge of God. Since a transcendent God is naturally unknowable, this kind of knowledge is radically different from what we would call rational or scientific knowledge. Knowledge of God is attained through experiencing supranatural revelation, receiving truth through secret lore or inner illumination: it is realized self-knowledge. This enlightenment brings salvation because the knower is able to take part in divine existence. Gnosis is both the instrument and goal of salvation: achieving perfection.

The Gnostic God, unlike the God of Judaism and Christianity, did not create the world and the universe, but is alien to them, is their antithesis. The creation of the cosmos is the work of demons known as Archons. The Archons reside in seven concentric spheres (taken from Babylonian cosmology) that imprison the innermost dungeon, the Earth. The Archons and their shells are what separate humans from their God and prevent souls from ascending after death to return to God. Through the human body and soul, each person is tied to the world and subject to the rule of Fate — the physical laws of nature and psychological enslavement through religious edicts such as the laws laid down by Moses, the Mosaic Code. But within each soul there is the spirit or divine spark. After this divine substance fell to Earth, the Archons deliberately created human beings in order to imprison the spirit. The divine essence is unconscious of itself — ignorant — until awakened and freed by Gnostic knowledge. The process of self-discovery begins as a person experiences the anguish and terror of the human condition. Evil is not conceived so much in moral terms as psychological — emotional harm, particularly fear, confusion and grief. Suffering derives not from sin, but from ignorance.

In order to release the "inner man" from the prison of his body, the individual must know about both the existence of the other-worldly God and about himself — his divine origin and his present predicament. This knowledge is brought and imparted by a savior-messenger obviously modeled on Jesus Christ. The transcendent son of God outwits the Archons to reach Earth. He becomes incarnate in human flesh in order to communicate the gnosis to chosen people and awaken their spirits from earthly slumber. He suffers all kinds of humiliation before returning to the realm of light beyond the cosmos.

It is a strange blend of the familiar turned inside out. Things of the spirit are opposed to things of this world, but this world is inherently evil along with its creators. Gnosis causes the person to hate this world and worldly things. The Gnostic was totally divorced from nature, which was evil. He was alone in an alien and hostile universe. Never before had there been such a bleak and terrifying view of reality.

It is not known exactly where Gnosticism first began to exert an influence, but its origins are believed to have been pre-Christian. Jesus uses a Gnostic image as a form of ultimate punishment. In Matthew 8:12, the castigation is for Jews who should have responded to his teaching, but have not: "the children of the kingdom shall be cast into outer darkness: there shall be weeping and gnashing of teeth." In Gnosticism, the outer darkness was a huge earth-encircling dragon with its tail in its mouth, the original chaos or evil principle of this world.

The uncharacteristic phrase, repeated twice more in Matthew, may have been interpolated when the oral traditions were being written. For Gnostic thought was flourishing by 80 A.D., when the Gospels still were in formative states. By the end of the 2nd century, Gnosticism was challenging orthodox Church leaders for control of Christianity. It was Marcion in about 140 A.D. who started the notion of two Gods (the second being the God of the Archons). Marcion noticed that the kindly God of Jesus was quite different from the ancient Jewish God Yahweh who was vindictive, wrathful and forever punishing his errant followers. Another heresy was the speculation that if Christ were the Son of God, divine and transcendent from his inception, he could not have suffered on the cross. Some Gnostics were saying that the Resurrection was only symbolic, that a person became resurrected in this life when he was born again with Gnostic knowledge.

Such interpretations not only were theoretical alternatives, but, as Elaine Pagels wrote in *The Gnostic Gospels*, they had political significance and real consequences for the development of the Church. Martyrs were Christian shock troops whose willingness to defy the imperium of Rome cemented the bonds of the churches and spurred the recruiting of members. If the Resurrection were only symbolic and Christ had not suffered the real pain of a human being to become the paragon and inspiration of martyrs, the Church's ability to attract candidates willing to sacrifice their lives would have been nullified.

Furthermore, the cerebral and individualistic nature of Gnosticism splintered Christian unity by becoming a do-it-yourself religion with each person working out his own brand of salvation and with church groups that were theologically estranged. Gnosticism was turning a religion that could be understood by all and thus open to all into an abstruse, idiosyncratic and elitist obsession for the initiated. The success of Gnosticism almost certainly would have led to the disintegration of Church organization and ultimately the failure of Christianity.

For all these reasons, Church doctrine had to be spelled out, chapter and verse, in the approved canon. And the wording of the creed becomes entirely understandable, simple and explicit. There is one God, Jesus was a man who was crucified by a Roman official, Jesus suffered, he was resurrected bodily. He was human as well as divine.

At their deepest bases, if all the similarities and entanglements are cleared away, the two religions were incompatible. One is life-affirming. The other life-denying.

Gnostics were able to infiltrate their confusing and contradictory doctrine because there was a tradition that Jesus' secret wisdom had been passed down orally from the apostles to certain qualified members of succeeding generations. A raft of Gnostic gospels purported to reveal the esoteric teaching of Jesus. This Gnostic claim to reveal the secret tradition of the apostles challenged the authority of the bishops who were the legitimate successors to the apostles. In order to counter this threat, in addition to codifying accepted doctrine, the orthodox leaders began to fight esotericism (from *esoterici,* the cult students entitled to learn the clandestine knowledge of Pythagoras) within the Church. They denied that there ever were any secret teachings of Jesus.

But such denials must be put into historical perspective. "Esotericism," writes the eminent historian of religion Mircea Eliade, "is documented in all the great religions in both the Hellenistic period and near the beginning of the Christian era." Clement of Alexandria, a Church leader early in the 3rd century, wrote that his teachers preserved "the true tradition of the blessed teachings, come directly from the holy Apostles Peter, James, John and Paul, transmitted from father to son". Origen a little later wrote: "Jesus explained all things to his own disciples privately, and for this reason the writers of the Gospels concealed the clear exposition of the parables."

The oral tradition of Jesus' secret teaching must have been erased. But we know from the Gospels themselves that only the *esoterici* around Jesus were entitled to know the mysteries of the kingdom of God. Only disciples were given explanations of the parables. And Jesus in his public sermon advised not to cast your pearls before swine, lest they trample them and attack you.

The most obvious reason that we don't know what Jesus meant by the kingdom of God is that he chose to conceal it in riddles.

THREE

Riddles

Jesus taught with proverbs, paradoxes and parables, and with three levels of clarity: transparent, translucent and opaque. Most of the proverbs seem perfectly clear, at least at first. As in gazing into the crystal waters of a still lake, the limpid medium magnifies and illuminates, but in providing access to great depths leads to uncertainty. Is all the transparent meaning really at or near the surface?

Man shall not live by bread alone. Ye are the salt of the earth: but if the salt have lost his savor, wherewith shall it be salted? Ye are the light of the world. A city that is set on a summit cannot be hid. Don't let your left hand know what your right hand is doing. Where your treasure is, there will your heart be also. No man can serve two masters. Consider the lilies of the field, how they grow; they toil not, neither do they spin. Take therefore no thought for the morrow; for the morrow shall take thought of the things of itself. Sufficient unto the day is the evil thereof. Judge not, that ye be not judged. Ask, and it shall be given unto you; seek, and ye shall find; knock, and it shall be opened unto you. Therefore all things whatsoever ye would that men should do to you, do ye even so to them. Wide is the gate and broad is the way that lead to destruction; strait is the gate and narrow is the way that lead to life. By their fruits ye shall know them. Fear not them which kill the body, but are unable to kill the soul: but rather fear him which is able to destroy both soul and body. The very hairs of your head are all numbered. What is a man profited, if he gain the whole world, and lose his own soul? What God has joined together, let not man put asunder. Render unto Caesar the things which are Caesar's. If a house be divided against itself, that house cannot stand. Which of you with taking thought can add to his stature one cubit? To whom much is given, of him shall be much required. He that is without sin among you, let him cast the first stone at her. The truth shall make you free. A new commandment I give unto you. That ye love one another. In my Father's house are many mansions. Greater love has no man than this, that a man lay down his life for his friends.

We recognize these sayings as facets of deep truths. "In every work of genius," Emerson said, "we recognize our own rejected thoughts;

they come back to us with a certain alienated majesty." Whatever the transparent or deepest meanings of these proverbs, they inform us that they are products of a superb intelligence.

Jesus loved to use paradoxes. A paradox is a statement or situation that seems to have a built-in contradiction, a statement that flies in the face of accepted wisdom or an invention that at first seems impossible. And yet the possibility that it might be true cannot be ruled out.

The blind are leading the blind. Let the dead bury their dead. Not that which goes into the mouth defiles a man, but what comes out. They seeing see not and hearing hear not. He who has ears, let him hear. The person who finds his life will lose it, and the person who loses his life will save it. Many are called, but few are chosen. The last will be first, and the first last. "Among them that are born of women there hath not risen a greater than John the Baptist: notwithstanding he that is least in the kingdom of heaven is greater than he." Whoever exalts oneself shall be humbled, and whoever humbles oneself shall be exalted. Whosoever shall humble himself as this little child, the same is the greatest in the kingdom of heaven. Blessed are the humble. Blessed are the meek. Blessed are the poor. Blessed are those who weep. Blessed are those who hunger. To him who has shall be given and he shall have more abundance, but from him who has not shall be taken away, even what he has.

Jesus himself supplied explanations for some of the paradoxes. The saying about the blind comes after the disciples report to Jesus that the Pharisees were offended by his criticism of dietary laws. Jesus says, "Let them alone: they be blind leaders of the blind." The Pharisees posed as religious leaders, but actually they were incorrect in their beliefs. The misguided are leading the ignorant.

Similarly, the saying "let the dead bury their dead" is another use of double entendre. Jesus had just asked a man to follow him, but the man made an excuse, saying he had to bury his father. That seems valid enough, but it creates a doubt about his sincerity. Jesus has offered the man a new life, a chance to emerge from his somnam-bulance, to become awake to the world of the spirit. In this case, the saying means: let those who are sleepwalking through life bury the dead. A widely-used and venerable religious metaphor analogized sleep to both ignorance and death.

What defiles a man, Jesus explained, are the ugly, mean thoughts he utters. They are manifestations of the filth inside.

Jesus also explained "they seeing see not: and hearing they hear not, neither do they understand." He told his disciples he was fulfilling a similar saying by the prophet Isaiah. That saying, too, employs double entendre: "By hearing ye shall hear, and not understand; and seeing ye shall see, and not perceive". Mental apprehension is substituted for physical perception. People no longer can understand because the values they have developed interfere with their ability to grasp and appreciate his doctrine. When Jesus says "He who has ears, let him hear," he is alerting his audience to something important. Pay attention, really listen, see if you can get it.

I could not understand the meaning of "The person who finds one's life will lose it, and the person who loses one's life will find it" until I read as a young man in a publication long since forgotten this offered explanation: it is only when we human beings can lose ourselves in a project, immerse our lives in working toward some goal that we can find ourselves, learn who and what we are. With purpose in our life, we terminate the drift. The late actor Jimmy Cagney grasped the importance of this point when he said, "Absorption in things other than self is the secret of a happy life."

The expression "Many are called, but few are chosen" does not appear to be abstruse. We can readily imagine a government or manufacturer announcing that X number of jobs are available. The would-be employers hope to attract more job-seekers than are needed. In that way, through a process of selection the employers will be able to hire the best possible workers. The same weeding-out would apply to proselytizing followers.

In one place where the paradox appears, it shares its position with an entirely different moral. The juxtaposition in this instance appears in the King James Bible, but not other versions. And the parable it follows is difficult to understand. A householder goes out early in the morning to hire laborers for his vineyard. They agree to be paid one penny for the day's work and he sends them into his vineyard. A few hours later the man rounds up more laborers. Three more times during the day, the owner hires men for his vineyard. In the evening, the owner tells his steward to pay the laborers, starting with those who were hired last. The steward gives each of them a penny. Those who were hired first expect to be paid more. When they each are given the same one penny, they complain: "These last have wrought but one hour, and thou has made them equal unto us, which have borne the burden and heat of the day." But the householder says, didn't you agree to that wage? "Is it not lawful for me to do what I will with mine own?" And then the double paradox moral: "So that last shall be first, and the first last: for many be called, but few chosen."

The colon makes the two paradoxes equivalent. The meaning of the parable itself is obscure. Certainly the action of the owner seems unfair even if he is technically or legally within his rights since the early laborers did agree to the deal. But why in effect reward the Johnny-comes-latelies?

Perhaps the equivalency may become more understandable by turning to a place where the first paradox is used without the second. This is in Luke where some passages in the Sermon on the Mount are presented in a somewhat different context. Jesus is asked, "Are there few that be saved?" And Jesus answers: "Strive to enter in at the strait gate: for many, I say unto you, will seek to enter in, and shall not be able." He goes on to say that once the master of the house is up and has shut the door, you can knock, but he will say, "I know you not." It's too late. You should have followed his doctrine earlier. "There will be weeping and gnashing of teeth, when ye shall see Abraham, and Isaac, and Jacob, and all the prophets in the kingdom of God, and you yourselves thrust out. And they shall come from the east, and from the west, and from the north, and from the south, and shall sit down in the kingdom of God. And behold, there are last which shall be first, and there are first which shall be last."

The Jews were first offered the opportunity to enter the kingdom of God and disdained to do so. Then the gentiles are called, and they are the first to enter. The few-are-chosen theme is expressed from the outset and the first-last/last-first paradox from the master-of-the-house portion.

Jesus explained to his disciples the paradox of the one who wants to be first must be last in terms of the Suffering Servant.

The paradox about John the Baptist is a stumper. And why is a little child the greatest in the kingdom of heaven? How are the humble blessed? Why are the poor blessed? In what way are they blessed? The same for the meek. Why are those that weep blessed and why shall they laugh? And to him who has shall be given, from him who has not shall be taken away, even what he has, seems eminently unfair and antithetical to the ethic of Christian charity.

The economic and social conditions of Palestine provided the fabric for Jesus' teaching parables. Palestine at the time was prosperous. The country was largely agrarian; peasants tilled the soil, tended the orchards, vineyards and flocks. Palestine was an exporter of wheat as well as prized dates, figs, grapes, wine, olives, and oil. Small trade flourished. And there was the fishing industry at Lake Galilee.

There are nearly five dozen parables in the three Synoptic Gospels, none in John. Seven of the parables appear in all three Gospels and four parables are told in both Matthew and Luke. There are about 40 different parables.

Mark 4:33-34 says: "And with many such parables spake he the word unto them, as they were able to hear it. But without a parable spake he not unto them: and when they were alone, he expounded all things to his disciples."

"Because of their form distinct from the allegorizing proclivity of the primitive church," writes James M. Robinson, one of today's foremost theologians, "the parables have become the segment of the teachings of Jesus most widely accepted as authentic by scholars today." Because, also, the parables are obscure, they lend themselves to interpretation consistent with thinking that happens to be in vogue. Robinson says that rationalists viewed the parables as expressing rational principles. In the Victorian period, when Jesus was regarded primarily as a moralist, interpreters looked for a moral point, as distinct from the point of a moral.

With the eschatological interpretation, the parables were seen as signposts to the future. They were said to describe how the kingdom of God was developing, unfolding and would arrive. An example of this was one of the two parables original in Mark: "So is the kingdom of God, as if a man should cast seed into the ground: And should sleep, and rise night and day, and the seed should spring and grow up, he knoweth not how. For the earth bringeth forth fruit of herself; first the blade, then the ear, after that the full corn in the ear."

Because some of the parables indicated a time frame in the present, theologican C.H. Dodd maintained that the kingdom was here. But since he couldn't throw out the eschatological element entirely, he coined the term "realized eschatology": Israel's hope for the future had been realized in the ministry of Jesus. Dodd's antithesis to Schweitzer's thesis led to a synthesis of sorts. Through Jesus' mission God's kingdom has been dawning and is breaking in.

German theologian Rudolph Bultmann tried to finesse the time question. He said Jesus is timeless. His parables should be interpreted existentially — make sense out of them in terms of contemporary life rather than regarding them as chronological formulations. This led to an opinion that in the parables Jesus wasn't talking about our relation to God, but he was talking about his relationship with us.

A Parables Seminar of the Society of Biblical Literature decided that the parable is not coded theology, but, in Robinson's words, "irreplaceable loaded language, itself triggering the reality of what it is talking about; Jesus' metaphor shatters the familiar world of us all....thus freeing the attentive listener....for God's reign, the strange world that....is our shattered familiar world returned to us anew."

Twenty one parables, 15 different ones, make explicit reference to the kingdom of God. Presumably, a number of or all the others — since Jesus said he was preaching the kingdom of God — relate to the kingdom.

Two of the explicit parables — The Sower and The Mustard Seed — appear in each of the three Gospels. The Mustard Seed is hardly more than a simile. The kingdom of God is like a mustard seed, the smallest of the seeds which grows to be the tallest of herbs. The parable of The Leaven, which is in Matthew and Luke, is similar in form. "It is like leaven, which a woman took and hid in three measures of meal, till the whole was leavened." The other two condensed similes — is like a treasure hidden in a field, is like a pearl of great price — appear only in Matthew.

There are several other brief parables that appear in the form of metaphors. You don't sew a new cloth onto an old garment because in so doing you risk tearing the worn material and making matters worse. Similarly, you don't put new wine in old bottles for fear of breaking the bottles and thus ruining both the wine and the containers: "new wine must be put into new bottles." We can infer that Jesus is talking about the gospel of the kingdom. It is something new. But while we can decipher these two parables they do not tell us what the kingdom is.

Another aphoristic metaphor is that people don't light a candle and then put it under a bushel, but on a candlestick for all to see and to light the way. In Mark and Luke this parable follows immediately after the explanation of the parable of The Sower. The candle parable goes on to say that nothing will remain hidden or secret, but be made manifest. "Take heed therefore how ye hear: for whosoever hath shall be given; and whosoever hath not, from him shall be taken even that which he seemeth to have." That is associated with the parable of The Sower in Matthew. Since the Lamp-Under-a-Bushel parables in Mark and Luke immediately follow The Sower and have the same moral, they would seem to be making the same point.

The parable appears again a few chapters later in Luke, and makes an entirely different point. After restating the candle metaphor, the parable goes on: "The light of the body is in the eye: therefore when thine eye is single, the whole body also is full of light; but when thine eye is evil, thy body also is full of darkness."

Three other parables in addition to those given earlier come with explanations and all make the same point. One is the parable of The Wheat and the Weeds. "The kingdom of heaven is likened unto a man which sowed good seed in his field: But while men slept, his enemy came and sowed tares among the wheat". Tares are worthless weeds. When the plants grew, the field hands told the owner what had happened and asked if they should pull out the weeds. No, said the landowner, because of the danger of uprooting the wheat as well. At harvest, the reapers will be told to gather the weeds and burn them. Then the wheat will be reaped and stored.

Later, in private, Jesus explains the parable to his disciples. "He that soweth the good seed is the Son of man; the field is the world; the good seed are the children of the kingdom; but the tares are the children of the wicked one. The enemy that sowed them is the devil; the harvest is the end of the world; and the reapers are angels. As therefore the tares are gathered and burned in fires; so shall it be at the end of the world. The Son of man shall send forth his angels, and they shall gather out of his kingdom all things that offend, and them which do iniquity; And shall cast them into a furnace of fire: there shall be wailing and gnashing of teeth. Then shall the righteous shine forth as the sun in the kingdom of their Father."

The parable of The Draw Net: "Again, the kingdom of heaven is like unto a net, that was cast into the sea, and gathered of every kind: Which, when it was full, they drew to shore, and set down, and gathered the good into vessels, but cast the bad away. So shall it be at the end of the world: the angels shall come forth, and sever the wicked from among the just. And shall cast them into the furnace of fire: there shall be wailing and gnashing of teeth."

The third parable, of the Sheep and Goats, is the last one told in Matthew, shortly before the Passover and the Passion in Gethsemane. "When the Son of man shall come in his glory, and all the holy angels with him, then shall he sit upon the throne of his glory: And before him shall be gathered all nations: and he shall set the sheep on his right hand, but the goats on his left. Then shall the King say unto them on his right hand, Come, ye blessed of my Father, inherit the kingdom prepared for you from the foundation of the world: For I was hungered, and ye gave me meat: I was thirsty, and ye gave me drink: I was a stranger, and ye took me in: Naked, and ye clothed me: I was sick, and ye visited me: I was in prison, and ye came unto me."

The righteous ask when they did all these things: "And the King shall answer and say unto them, Verily I say unto you, Inasmuch as ye have done it unto one of the least of these my brethren, ye have done it unto me." But the unrighteous, those who withheld their succor, the goats, "shall go away into everlasting punishment: but the righteous into life eternal."

While the three parables tell us who shall be in the kingdom of God, they do not say what the kingdom is. The parables are both apocalyptic and eschatological.

Other parables are eschatological, such as the Ten Virgins. "Then shall the kingdom of heaven be likened unto ten virgins, which took their lamps and went forth to meet the bridegroom. And five of them were wise, and five were foolish. They that were foolish took their lamps, and took no oil with them: But the wise took oil in their vessels with their lamps. While the bridegroom tarried, they all slumbered and slept. And at midnight there was a cry made, Behold, the bridegroom cometh; go ye out to meet him." The foolish virgins were short of oil and asked to borrow some from the others, but they could not spare any. While the foolish virgins went to procure more oil, the bridegroom arrived for the marriage and shut the door. The foolish virgins asked the bridegroom to open for them. But he said, 'I know you not.' Watch, therefore, for ye know neither the day nor the hour wherein the Son of man cometh." Candidates for the kingdom of heaven must be prepared, be alert, and ever faithful. That parable is in Matthew. Mark has a parable of the Household Watching and Luke has a parable of the Watchful Servants.

The parable of the Vineyard and Householder is told in the three Gospels, but only in Matthew is it linked explicitly to the kingdom of God. A householder plants a vineyard, then rents it to tenant workers and goes away "into a far country." At harvest time, the owner sends his servants to collect what is due him. The tenants beat and kill the servants. The vineyard owner sends more servants, and they fare no better. "Last of all he sent unto them his son, saying, They will reverence my son." The laborers kill the son so that they can seize his inheritance.

The servants can be interpreted as the earlier prophets and the son, of course, as the Son of man. "When the lord therefore of the vineyard cometh, what will he do unto those husbandmen? They say unto him, He will miserably destroy those wicked men, and will let out his vineyard unto other husbandmen, which shall render him the fruits in their season."

In Mark and Luke, the parable leaves it at that — the vineyard will be given, to others. But in Matthew: "Therefore say I unto you, The kingdom of God shall be taken from you and given to a nation bringing forth the fruits thereof." The same ending as the parable with the paradox of the first shall be last and the last first.

On the same occasion, Jesus also told the parable of The Two Sons to the chief priests and Pharisees. A man had two sons. He tells the first to go to work in his vineyard. "He answered and said, I will not: but afterward he repented, and went. And he came to the second, and said likewise. And he answered and said, I go, sir: and went not. Whether of them twain did the will of his father? They say unto him, The first. Jesus saith unto them, Verily I say unto you, That the publicans and harlots go into the kingdom of God before you." When the chief priests and Pharisees "had heard his parables, they perceived he spake of them. But when they sought to lay hands on him, they feared the multitude, because they took him for a prophet."

The parable of The Wicked Servant illustrates the Golden Rule, which Jesus said is of the law and the prophets — in other words, not new in his gospel of the kingdom. Yet the parable begins: "Therefore is the kingdom of heaven likened unto a certain king which would take account of his servants." During the inventory, the king discovered one servant who owed him 10,000 talents. Each talent was worth a thousand dollars, so that it was a $10 million debt. Since the servant didn't have the money, his lord ordered that the servant, his wife and children be sold into slavery to help defray what was owed.

"The servant therefore fell down, and worshipped him, saying, Lord, have patience with me, and I will pay thee all." The king was affected by this display and forgave the servant's entire debt. "But the same servant went out, and found one of his fellowservants, which owed him an hundred pence: and he laid hands on him by the throat, saying, Pay me that thou owest. And his fellowservant fell down at his feet, and besought him, saying, Have patience with me, and I will pay thee all. And he would not: but went and cast him into prison, till he should pay the debt." Other servants, indignant and saddened by the imprisonment, went and told their lord. The king summoned the offending servant and said, "O thou wicked servant, I forgave thee all that debt, because thou desiredst me: Shouldest not thou have had compassion on thy fellowservant, even as I had pity on thee?" The servant was turned over to the authorities until the debt was paid in full. "So likewise shall my heavenly Father do also unto you, if ye from your hearts forgive not every one his brother their trespasses." Forgive us our debts as we forgive our debtors. Treat others as you want to be treated.

Like the parable of The Sower, the parable of The Talents has the same moral — "For unto everyone that hath shall be given, and he shall have abundance: but from him that hath not shall be taken away even that which he hath" — and a similar differential payoff. However, a quite different principle seems to be involved. "The kingdom of heaven is as a man traveling into a far country, who called his own servants, and delivered unto them his goods." The lord gives five talents to one servant, two talents to another, one talent to a third: "to every man according to his several ability." The first servant trades his five talents and earns an additional five talents. The second servant does the same and also doubles his two talents. The third servant puts his one talent into a safe place in order to preserve it.

After a long time, the lord returns. The first servant shows that he has increased the five talents 100 percent. The lord says, "Well done, thou good and faithful servant: thou hast been faithful over a few things, I will make thee ruler over many things: enter thou into the joy of the lord." The identical reward is given to the second servant. The third servant says, "Lord, I knew thee that thou art an hard man, reaping where thou hast not sown, and gathering where thou has not strawed: And I was afraid, and went and hid thy talent in the earth: lo, there thou hast that is thine. His lord answered and said unto him, Thou wicked and slothful servant, thou knewest that I reap where I sowed not and gather where I have not strawed: Thou oughtest therefore to have put my money to the exchangers and then at my coming I should have received mine own with usury. Take therefore the talent from him, and give it unto him which hath ten talents." The moral quoted above follows.

In the parable of The Sower, the sower must plant seeds for the possibility of a harvest. No reaping without sowing. Even if The Talents is interpreted as Jesus advising each person to make the most of his abilities and opportunities, the parable raises some puzzling and troubling questions. The "wicked" servant, after all, was an honest man. Is that the way honesty is rewarded in the kingdom of God? Usury, we know, goes counter to Christian ethics and for centuries was prohibited by the Catholic Church. How can God practice and praise usury? Above all that, is this harsh lord supposed to be the same loving Father who heeds his children's needs and forgives their sins?

At least we can discount the question about honesty by juxtaposing the parable of The Dishonest Steward. This one starts like the parable of The Wicked Servant. "There was a certain rich man, which had a steward: and the same was accused unto him that he had wasted his goods." The boss demands an accounting from his manager because his job is being terminated. The steward says to himself, how will I survive? I am not strong enough to dig and I am too proud to beg. Then he strikes on a solution to his dilemma. He decides to ingratiate himself with people who are in debt to the rich man. In that way, when he is out of a job, they will welcome him into their homes and employ.

So he quickly calls on the debtors and asks what they owe. The first man says 100 measures of oil. The steward tells him to make the bill for only 50 measures, and the manager gives his approval to the lowered bill. The steward arranges a series of such reductions.

When the lord finds out about these transactions, even though they were against his interests he has to admit that the manager acted shrewdly on his own behalf. The lord acknowledges that worldly people are better able to deal with their kind than are unworldly people. So it is smart to use your material wealth to make friends — but remember, when it is gone, you will have nothing and no one. Then Jesus draws the moral of the parable: "He that is faithful in that which is least is faithful also in much: and he that is unjust in the least is unjust also in much. If therefore ye have not been faithful in the unrighteous mammon, who will commit to your trust the true riches? And if ye have not been faithful in that which is another man's, who shall give you that which is your own?"

The kingdom of God also is described outside the parables, and some of these references are, if anything, even more difficult to decipher. "Woe unto you, scribes and Pharisees, hypocrites! For ye shut up the kingdom of heaven against men: for ye neither go in yourselves, neither suffer ye them that are entering to go in." "From the days of John the Baptist until now the kingdom of heaven suffereth violence, and the violent take it by force."

If being poor is a hard-to-fathom virtue, being rich is an equally difficult-to-understand flaw for candidates for the kingdom of God. Jesus tells his disciples: "How hardly shall they that have riches enter into the kingdom of God! And the disciples were astonished at his words. But Jesus answered again, and saith unto them, Children, how hard is it for them that trust in riches to enter into the kingdom of God! It is easier for a camel to go through the eye of a needle, than for a rich man to enter the kingdom of God."

On the theme of If I cast out devils, then the kingdom of God is come upon you: "If thine eye offend thee, pluck it out: it is better for thee to enter into the kingdom of God with one eye, than having two eyes to be cast into hell fire". And: "There are some eunuchs, which were so born from their mother's womb: and there are some eunuchs, which were made eunuchs of men: and there be eunuchs, which have made themselves eunuchs for the kingdom of heaven's sake. He that is able to receive it, let him receive it." It's not for everyone, but the saying seems to indicate that sexual intercourse is not a part of the kingdom of God or not an essential for entering.

There is one significant passage that tells us what is not a part of the kingdom of God, and the omission may come as a shock. In Matthew, the passage goes this way: "When the Pharisees had heard that he had put the Sadducees to silence, they were gathered together. Then one of them, which was a lawyer, asked him a question, tempting him, and saying, Master, which is the greatest commandment in the law? Jesus said unto him, Thou shalt love the Lord thy God with all thy heart, and with all thy soul, and with all thy mind. This is the first and great commandment. And the second is like unto it, Thou shalt love thy neighbor as thyself. On these two commandments hang all the law and the prophets." Mark carries the story a little further. "And the scribe (instead of the lawyer in Matthew) said unto him, Well, Master, thou hast said the truth: for there is one God; and there is none other but he: And to love him with all the heart, and with all the soul, and with all the strength, and to love his neighbor as himself, is more than all whole burnt offerings and sacrifices. And when Jesus saw that he answered discreetly, he said unto him, Thou art not far from the kingdom of God." Not far! But not *in* the kingdom of God. To love thy neighbor is not a part of the gospel of the kingdom of God. Perhaps this should not come as a surprise. Love thy neighbor was part of the law, and Jesus said the law and the prophets were preached until his new gospel. What was new about his doctrine was: love your enemies, love those who hate you and persecute you.

The passage introduces yet another problem. In Luke, the equivalent verses read: "A certain lawyer stood up, and tempted him, saying, Master, what shall I do to inherit eternal life? He said unto him, What is written in the law? What readest thou? And he answering said, Thou shall love the Lord thy God with all thy heart, and with all thy soul, and with all thy strength, and with all thy mind; and thy neighbor as thyself. And he said unto him, Thou hast answered right: this do, and thou shalt live."

On a number of occasions in the Gospels, the terms eternal life, life and the kingdom of God are used interchangeably. Just before Jesus tells his disciples how difficult it is for a rich person to enter the kingdom, this passage immediately precedes: "There came one running and kneeled to him, and asked him, Good Master, what shall I do that I may inherit eternal life? And Jesus said unto him, Why callest thou me good? there is none good but one, that is, God. Thou knowest the commandments, Do not commit adultery, Do not kill, Do not steal, Do not bear false witness, Defraud not, Honor thy father and mother. And he answered and said unto him, Master, all these things have I observed from my youth. Then Jesus beholding him loved him, and said unto him, One thing thou lackest: go thy way, sell whatsoever thou hast, and give to the poor, and thou shalt have treasure in heaven: and come, take up the cross, and follow me. And he was sad at that saying, and went away grieved: for he had great possessions." That was Mark. In Matthew, the passage begins: "One came and said unto him, Good Master, what good thing shall I do, that I may have eternal life? And he said unto him, Why callest thou me good? there is none good but one, that is God: but if thou wilt enter into life, keep the commandments."

In the three instances given above, it is the questioner who uses the term eternal life. On each occasion, Jesus, even though given the opportunity, declines to repeat the phrase. He appears, however, to promise an equivalent — life without the adjective or treasure in heaven.

In Jesus' replies, there is something strange and curious about the way he uses the word life. He employs it in a special sense. This is even more apparent in the following usages in Mark. "And if thy foot offend thee, cut it off: it is better for thee to enter halt into life than having two feet to be cast into hell." "And if thine eye offend thee, pluck it out: it is better for thee to enter into the kingdom of God with one eye, than having two eyes to be cast into hell fire". In the second instance, kingdom of God is substituted for life.

Life in this sense would seem to be the new spiritual life that Jesus offered to the man he advised to let the dead bury their dead, adding at that time, "but go thou and preach the kingdom of God."

In the famous passage about the lilies, there is still another equation of life and kingdom. The passage begins with this verse: "Therefore I say unto you, Take no thought for your life, what ye shall eat, or what ye shall drink; nor yet for your body, what ye shall put on. Is not the life more than meat, and the body than raiment?"

After counseling to observe the fowls of the air and lilies of the field, Jesus concludes: "Therefore take no thought, saying, What shall we eat? or, What shall we drink? or, Wherewithal shall we be clothed?....But seek ye first the kingdom of God, and his righteousness, and all these things shall be added unto you."

Another equivalency of the kingdom of God and life, but this time in addition, as seen in the opening verse of the lilies passage cited above, there is a provocative variation. Jesus first refers to life in the ordinary sense of the word and then to *the* life. *The* life would seem to be something different from what we commonly mean by the word life and would seem to reinforce what was indicated in the previous examples that this special usage is a coded term for the kingdom of God. "The" life in the lilies passage appears in the original King James Bible, but has been deleted from the new King James version. The passage in Luke begins, "Take no thought for your life, what ye shall eat; neither for the body, what ye shall put on. The life is more than meat...." The section ends with the same kingdom substitution for life. This time, the "The" is retained in the new edition of the King James Bible.

When it comes to the Gospel of John, the usage of terms reverses dramatically. The three Synoptic Gospels mention the kingdom of God more than 90 times. They use the word life in the special sense ten times and Jesus refers to eternal life four times. John mentioned the kingdom of God twice, uses the term eternal life ten times, life everlasting seven times, life in the special sense 15 times, and the life four times. That John believes there is an equivalency between eternal life and life is indicated by the fact that the terms are used in combination six times.

In the Gospel of John, for the kingdom of God substitute eternal life.

The eschatological interpretation gave prominence to the temporal question — when does the kingdom occur?

A future occurrence is indicated by the wish expressed in the Lord's Prayer: "Thy kingdom come." Schweitzer relied on that in advancing his eschatological theory, and also on a passage in Jesus' instructions to his disciples for their mission: "Ye shall not have gone over the cities of Israel, till the Son of man come." Schweitzer was convinced that Jesus thought of himself as the Messiah and this was a clear statement of his Second Coming.

The parable of the Wheat and the Weeds, appearing among the first extended parables in Matthew, has a similar eschatological content, supernatural as well: the separation of the good and bad at the end of the world. The promise to Peter and the other disciples distinguished between goods in the present world and the positions of eminence and eternal life they would inherit in the world to come. These two references indicate an event in the indefinite future. So does Jesus' prediction that non-Jews would inherit the kingdom.

The parables of the Ten Virgins, Household Watching and Watchful Servants have a timeless quality. Jesus is telling his followers to lead virtuous lives so that they will be ready for his Second Coming, an event that could happen at any time. Like the passage cited from the instructions to the apostles, Jesus' statement just before the Transfiguration presupposes an imminent occurrence: "There be some of them that stand here, which shall not taste of death, till they have seen the kingdom of God come with power." And there is the parable of the Fig Tree. After predicting dire events, Jesus says, 'Behold the fig tree, and all the trees. When they now shoot forth, ye see and know of your own selves that summer is now nigh at hand. So likewise ye, when ye see these things come to pass, know ye that the kingdom of God is nigh at hand."

The "at hand" in this late parable is reminiscent of the sentence that Jesus used to announce his ministry: Repent, for the kingdom of God is at hand. That would seem to say it is imminent. At the outset of his ministry, he said the time is fulfilled, so that the "at hand" could mean at any moment. At the Last Supper, the kingdom seems so close that: "I will not any more eat thereof, until it be fulfilled in the kingdom of God. And he took the cup, and gave thanks, and said, Take this, and divide it among yourselves For I say unto you, I will not drink of the fruit of the vine, until the kingdom of God shall come."

Shortly before the Passover, however, Jesus told his disciples a parable "because he was nigh to Jerusalem, and because they thought that the kingdom of God should immediately appear." It was the parable of The Ten Pounds, Luke's version of the parable of The Talents. In Luke, the eschatological element is given more prominence. The Talents begins: "The kingdom of heaven is as a man traveling into a far country, who called his own servants, and delivered unto them his goods." The parable immediately proceeds to the story — dividing his money among the servants and what each one does with his portion. In The Ten Pounds, "A certain nobleman went into a far country to receive for himself a kingdom, and to return. And he called his ten servants, and delivered them ten pounds, and said unto them, Occupy til I come. But his citizens hated him, and sent a message after him, saying, We will not have this man to reign over us. And it came to pass, that when he was returned, having received the kingdom, then he commanded these servants to be called unto him...." The parable then goes on to the judgment of the good servants and the unprofitable servant and the moral "unto every one which hath shall be given; and from him that hath not, even that he hath shall be taken from him." The Luke version adds one more verse: "But those mine enemies, which would not that I should reign over them, bring hither, and slay them before me." The eschatological addition competes with the point of the parable and seems to give it a double meaning, one explicit, the other allegorical.

The parable of The Talents is not talking about some future event or condition. It is giving information about the kingdom of God. So are the parables of The Mustard Seed, The Leaven, The Pearl and the Hidden Treasure. The kingdom of heaven *is* like.... "If I cast out devils by the Spirit of God, then the kingdom of God *is* come upon you." "Fear not, little flock, for it *is* your Father's good pleasure to give you the kingdom." "It is better for thee to enter into the kingdom of God with one eye" is talking about a means of access to the kingdom. So is: you must humble yourself as a little child. "Blessed *are* the poor in spirit: for theirs *is* the kingdom of heaven."

"And when he was demanded of the Pharisees, when the kingdom of God should come, he answered them and said, The kingdom of God cometh not with observation: Neither shall they say, Lo here! or, lo there! for, behold, the kingdom of God *is* within you." The statement seems to be saying here and now. While there are no other sayings by Jesus that indicate the kingdom is within a person, the only times the kingdom of God is mentioned in John could be interpreted to support such a view. Nicodemus, a Pharisee, "came to

Jesus by night, and said unto him, Rabbi, we know that thou art a teacher come from God: for no man can do these miracles that thou doest, except God be with him. Jesus answered and said unto him, Verily, verily, I say unto thee, Except a man be born again, he cannot see the kingdom of God. Nicodemus saith unto him, How can a man be born when he is old? can he enter the second time into his mother's womb, and be born? Jesus answered, Verily, verily, I say unto thee, Except a man be born of water and of the Spirit, he cannot enter into the kingdom of God. That which is born of the flesh is flesh: and that which is born of the Spirit is spirit."

Jesus is talking about spiritual regeneration. A person must undergo spiritual change in order to participate in the kingdom of God. This is the Gnostic view: resurrection takes place in the present world, within a person. The person must know whom he is, know himself in order to achieve perfection. Just because it is a Gnostic concept, however, does not invalidate it. Gnostics were fascinated by Jesus, obsessed with his mission, and devoted themselves to discovering his meaning. At the end in John, when Pilate questions Jesus, he answers, "My kingdom is not of this world." He could be talking about a spiritual kingdom. But he adds "if my kingdom were of this world, then would my servants fight." That would seem to make it another world.

When one turns to the efforts of experts to solve the riddle of the kingdom of God, one gets an even greater indication of how confusing Jesus' concept has been. The kingdom could not be ignored since it is so central to his teaching. Yet its meaning has eluded the most assiduous scholarship.

The *Encyclopaedia Britannica* says that although the phrase kingdom of God hardly occurs in pre-Christian Jewish literature, the idea of God as king was fundamental to Judaism and so must have formed some basis for the Christian concept. The Aramaic word *malkuth* refers to the rule of the king, his exercise of sovereignty. Jaroslav Pelikan, an eminent Yale University scholar of ecclesiastical history, writes in the *Britannica* that kingdom in this sense refers to the *reign* of God. It is not a realm, but a divine activity or relationship.

The Jews viewed their situation as so desperate that a supernatural intervention was necessary to set things right. A Messiah would, among other things, judge who was worthy to inherit the kingdom, indicating that this kingdom was not won by human achievement, but was a divine gift. So the dominant view of the time was that God's sovereignty would become fully effective in the future. The nationalistic and corporate attitude that forms the Jewish expectation, however, is absent in Jesus' teaching, which is addressed to the individual.

Scholarly opinion is divided on whether Jesus taught that the kingdom had arrived during his lifetime, but the probability is that while he recognized his ministry as a sign of its imminence he looked to its future arrival "with power." Professor Pelikan says Jesus appears as a herald, but also as a sign and bringer of the kingdom. Jesus brought the kingdom and the kingdom was bringing Jesus. When the kingdom did not arrive as expected, the belief developed that the Resurrection already had introduced many of the kingdom's blessings.

That was an earlier edition of the *Britannica*. The current one says that the nearness of the kingdom of God means that God already is working His will and ways upon the world. God is coming but is already present in the world. Jesus freed God from the exile of a pious tradition. Contradicting Schweitzer, the *Britannica* says it would not be accurate to interpret Jesus' doctrine in the Jewish apocalyptic sense of expectation nearly at the climax.

Chambers's Encyclopedia agrees that the essence of the kingdom is a new relationship between God and man. God is present among human beings, no longer is there an intermediary. The correct view of the kingdom must neglect neither present nor future aspects — we are somewhere between the beginning and completion of the kingdom.

Encyclopedia of Religion and Ethics points out that no one seems to have asked Jesus what he meant by the kingdom of God and he never felt it incumbent upon himself to explain what he meant. His attitude is not completely identical with the spiritual interpretation of the prophets, but is more like a force working from within. The parable of The Leaven makes it a self-propagating force while in the "Automatic Earth" it is a seed that the earth brings to fruition. Jesus does not appear to delineate any difference between the earthly and heavenly kingdom.

Baker's Dictionary of Theology says "The presence of the kingdom in history is a mystery. A mystery is a divine purpose hidden for long ages but finally revealed." Before the new age that is to come, the kingdom of God already is battling the kingdom of

Satan and bringing in advance the blessings of forgiveness, life and righteousness. Jesus said that since the days of John the Baptist the kingdom of God has been preached and men enter it with violent determination. The one who is least in the kingdom is greater than the greatest in the old order because of the blessings that were unknown to those who lived before the kingdom was revealed.

The Interpreter's Dictionary of the Bible says no one has been able to synthesize the futurist teachings and "realized" eshatology into a consistent whole, and it's best to allow for both aspects in Jesus' thinking. While the 'growth" parables can be cited to show the actual presence of the kingdom, each process ends in a climax, suggesting a future completion of the kingdom. As for saying that the kingdom of God is within you, the Greek expression can be translated in one of two ways: either "within you" or "in the midst of you." The former is a more natural meaning, "but several considerations make it likely" that the latter is the correct translation. "The idea of the kingdom as an inward principle of disposition in men suits neither the context of this saying nor the general tenor of Jesus' teaching on the subject". Professor Pelikan also believes "in the midst of you" is the correct interpretation: Jesus himself was the sign of the kingdom in the midst of the Pharisees.

"There is no saying of Jesus in which he explicitly connects the coming of the kingdom with his own death," says *Interpreter's Dictionary*.

In order to receive the kingdom means submitting to a discipline with absolute demands upon a person's devotion, as witness the parables of The Pearl and Hidden Treasure. Another indication of the supreme sacrifice required to enter the kingdom can be seen in the passage where the terms life and kingdom of God "are clearly synonymous. The service of the kingdom is to take precedence over even the most sacred and urgent of other duties".

In a Lenten lecture on "The Kingdom of God" at All Souls Unitarian Church in New York City, Dr. Walter Donald Kring, a Biblical scholar, said, "Scholars of all centuries have been puzzled by the idea of the kingdom of God and its coming." Many books have been written to explain why Jesus was wrong and the kingdom did not come. One common explanation was that Jesus meant a slow evolution — but there is nothing to indicate that he understood the eons-slow process. Another explanation, said Dr. Kring, is that Jesus had in mind an inner spiritual kingdom — but there is only the one such direct reference about being born again in John with the possibility of a second in Luke.

The ecclesiastical interpretation is that the church will rule until the Second Coming. The iconoclastic Emerson said that the kingdom is coming so that we don't need institutions. Those who preached a social gospel said the kingdom is humanity organized for God. Emmanuel Kant said it is the ethical political state.

Ignatius, a Christian leader early in the 2nd century, is reported to have told Emperor Trajan just before execution: "I have Christ the King of heaven....May I now enjoy the kingdom."

Eusebius, an influential Church Father whose career bridged the adoption of Christianity by the Roman Empire, believed the kingdom of heaven, like its counterpart on earth, was governed by the supreme King, God. Both were monarchies with a hierarchic structure. The Emperor was God's viceregent on earth.

Historian Edward Gibbon, who critically chronicled and examined the effect of Christianity from the 2nd century to the 15th century, reflected in *The Decline and Fall of the Roman Empire:* "It is incumbent on us diligently to remember that the kingdom of heaven was promised to the poor in spirit, and that minds afflicted by calamity and the contempt of mankind cheerfully listen to the divine promise of future happiness; while, on the contrary, the fortunate are satisfied with the possession of this world."

The most famous author of the 19th century struck upon his own interpretation of the kingdom of God and embarked on a new life based on his interpretation. Sifting through his own rational thought, as Jefferson did, Leo Tolstoy culled his pure gold of Jesus' teaching from the dross. Tolstoy found the linchpin of Jesus' gospel in the Sermon on the Mount, Matthew 5:39: "resist not evil." This became the heart of Tolstoy's doctrine of returning good for evil, universal love, moral self-improvement and nonviolence. This individual striving for perfection was expressed in his book *The Kingdom of God Is Within You.*

Tolstoy's new faith led him to condemn all forms of violence including war. People should not take part in the organized violence of the state, they should not own property because that was a source of violence, they should not live by the work of others, they should not eat the flesh of slaughtered animals. He preached charity and said the social order would become better only when all people learned to love one another. The aim of human beings is to achieve happiness, and this can only be accomplished by doing right, by loving everyone, and by freeing oneself from the appetites of greed, lust and anger. There was no personal immortality.

Tolstoy tried as well as he could to follow his own commandments, disdaining his money, trying to become as self-sufficient as possible, making his own boots, and working beside the peasants on his estate. This doctrine and behavior brought Tolstoy into conflict with the state, the Church and his wife. While the Czarist government was hostile to Tolstoy, he was too popular a figure to take action against. His followers, however, were persecuted — imprisoned and banished to Siberia, mainly for balking at military service. For his brand of Christianity, which discarded non-ethical elements, the Russian Church excommunicated him. Tolstoy wanted to renounce all his worldly possessions, but his wife persuaded him to sign them over to her. Eventually their marriage deteriorated into a tense, unpleasant estrangement.

At the time of all this domestic strife, Tolstoy was becoming possibly the most venerated man in the world. His fellow countrymen made pilgrimages to his estate and people from all over the world wrote to the pioneer of this new radical Christianity. One of his admirers was Mohandas Gandhi, who was just embarking on what would be the great task of his life — liberation of India from British rule. Gandhi already had rejected passive resistance as an effective tool for a new brand of militant nonviolence, what he called "force which is born of truth and love."

Tolstoy considered that Gandhi's form of nonviolence had universal significance. Gandhi had based his strategy on Hindu teaching, but his mind was open to ideas from everywhere. When Tolstoy sent Gandhi a copy of *The Kingdom of God Is Within You,* he was overwhelmed by what both men considered the authentic teaching of Jesus in contradistinction to what Gandhi had learned from Christian missionaries. *The Kingdom of God* infused and vitalized Gandhi's nonviolence. Where bloody Indian uprisings had failed, resist-not-evil, turn-the-other-cheek nonviolent resistance miraculously succeeded.

Another champion of oppressed people was inspired by Gandhi and the Sermon on the Mount. Martin Luther King said Gandhi was "the first person in history to live the love ethic of Jesus above mere interaction between individuals." What was new in history about Gandhi's movement, King said, is that it was a revolution based "on hope and love, hope and nonviolence."

In the most recent contribution to the subject, a Dutch Roman Catholic theologican, Edward Schillebeeckx, has written that "'kingdom of God' is the expression for the nature of God — unconditional and liberating sovereign love — in so far as this makes itself felt and is revealed in the life of men and women who do God's will." Schillebeeckx says, "The full content of this human salvation and happiness — the kingdom of God — transcends the power of our human imagination. We get only a faint idea of it....through human experience of goodness, meaning and love".

There seem to be as many answers as riddles posed by Jesus.

FOUR

New Knowledge

The definition in *Baker's Dictionary of Theology* that "A mystery is a divine purpose hidden for long ages but finally revealed" had two spectacular demonstrations in the mid 20th century.

One mystery concerned the Essenes. Three lst-century authors wrote about this shadowy sect. The Roman soldier-administrator-author-historian-naturalist-geographer Pliny the elder said the Essenes lived to the west of the northern end of the Dead Sea. Both the Jewish philosopher Philo and historian Flavius Josephus — a Jew who fought against the Romans, surrendered to them in order to save his life and then sided with them — said there were more than 4,000 Essenes. Those were the main sources, for there was not a word about them in the New Testament and they were ignored in orthodox Jewish writings.

Even though the Essenes were not mentioned in the New Testament, enough was known about them to suggest a tantalizing relationship to early Christianity. The Essenes had a prophet known as the Teacher of Righteousness. They called themselves children of light and condemned children of darkness, wicked people. The Essenes were critics of the Temple in Jerusalem. They lived in a communistic community, individuals owned no property nor possessed any money; they lived ascetic lives and were celibates: all that could be viewed as a forerunner of the Christian monastic tradition. And the Essenes practiced this super-good existence because they expected to inherit the kingdom of God. In the desert. And that made them suspiciously like John the Baptist. They acted on the same injunction in Isaiah referred to by John: "The voice of him that crieth in the wilderness, Prepare the way of the Lord, make straight in the desert a highway for our God."

The Essene connection to Christianity insinuated itself to Ernest Renan, the great 19th-century interpreter of Christianity and author of the most famous *Life of Jesus*. He was the only Frenchman in Schweitzer's gallery of German scholars. Said Renan: "Christianity is an Essenism that has largely succeeded."

But no one could be sure what the relationship was. There wasn't enough knowledge. Moreover, religious students believed that even if there had been information at the time of Jesus, it could not have endured for so many centuries. People of that era no longer were writing on clay tablets as did ancient Sumerians and Babylonians. Archaeologists had dug and tilled and sifted all over the Holy Land searching for documents, remnants of documents, in vain.

We know now that the information did exist and survive. It was hidden for 1,879 years. In the spring of 1947, a young Bedouin goatherd threw a stone into a cliffside cave just inland from the northwest shore of the Dead Sea. He heard the sound of pottery shattering. Later, the Bedouin youth and a companion screwed up enough courage to crawl into the cave. Inside were jars, some broken, some intact. The intruders took seven decaying rolls of leather, the first of the Dead Sea Scrolls.

After the Scrolls were authenticated, authorities wanted to go back to the cave, but it had been concealed by the Bedouin. In 1949, a systematic search was carried out by the Arab Legion of Jordan under the supervision of a Belgian officer with the United Nations Observer Corps. The cave was located and it yielded hundreds of manuscript fragments along with pottery, wood and cloth that indicated that the find was of great antiquity. The archaeologists still weren't sure what they had, and the deposits initially were thought to have come from the 2nd century B.C. A quick survey of the area located the remains of a small Roman fort from the 3rd or 4th centuries A.D. It was not until 1951 that a more thorough search of the fort area disclosed the ruins of Qumran, the major community of the Essenes. And it was right where Pliny had said it was by the Dead Sea eight miles south of Jericho, 15 miles east of Jerusalem. It went out of existence in 68 A.D. in the middle of the Jewish war with the Romans. As the Roman Tenth Legion bore down on Qumran, the Essenes saved the essence of their community, their library.

The artifacts in the cave perfectly matched those found at Qumran. Now the scientists knew what they had. A distinguished archaeologist of the day, William Albright, called it the greatest manuscipt discovery of modern times. A frantic race began between Bedouin and archaeologists to find more scrolls in the hundreds of caves that riddled the barren, eroded valleys of the area. Nine more cave depositories were discovered during 1952. The last Qumran cave — Number 11 — was uncovered in 1956.

Enough material was found in the caves of Qumran to keep Biblical scholars busy until the end of the 21st century. In one cave alone, the closest one to the Qumran site, more than 15,000 manuscript fragments were found. There were Old Testament texts a millennium older than anything in existence. And there were detailed descriptions of life in the Qumran community.

The information shows that some features of the Essene sect and primitve Christianity were parallel, held in common with the Judaic roots from which they both grew. Like Christians, Essenes believed they were a community of the elect. Both goups shared their meals and property. Both groups believed in a cosmic war of light and darkness. Eschatology figured prominently in both groups. Essenes and Christians believed fhey were living in the last days and awaited the judgment. The Essenes ate a "last supper" every evening. The Essenes awaited two Messiahs — a royal one of David's line and a priestly descendent of Aaron to usher in their kingdom of God. The Christians were waiting for the return of their Messiah who already had told them that the kingdom of God was at hand.

If Essenes and primitve Christians were close in many respects —the former were famous for their celibacy and the apostle Paul had said it is good for a man not to touch a woman — there is no obvious link between the Qumran sect and Jesus. There is no reason to believe the man from Nazareth ever went to Qumran. In all the Dead Sea material, there is no hint that the Essenes knew about Jesus. No mention of John the Baptist either.

Beyond that, the styles and much of the teaching of Jesus and the Essenes differed. Geza Vermes, writing in *The Dead Sea Scrolls,* says Jesus was "a Galilean charistmatic for whom a great deal of the Essene doctrine would have been repugnant." Jesus was not an ascetic like the Essenes, so much to the contrary that he said his detractors accused him of being a drunkard. The Essenes were such fanatics for physical cleanliness that they believed it a sin to defecate on the sabbath and carried around a little hoe to cover their droppings. Jesus, as noted earlier, did not consider it a sin to eat with unwashed hands. Jesus never extolled celibacy. He did recommend or suggest becoming a eunuch, but as an example of what some men must or could do in order to achieve the kingdom of God. Jesus devalued the inherent virtue of ritual: he condemned the hypocrisy of external show. He took his own independent view of the law. While Jesus did have his inner circle of disciples, he went out and preached to the people and confronted the powerful Establishment in the Temple. But above all his doctrine was new.

The essence of the Qumran sect was super-pietistic observance of the law of Moses. Where Jesus said the sabbath is made for man, the Essenes spent the sabbath in daylong prayer and meditation on the

Torah. They lived in seclusion, all details of their lives regulated by rules and officials. The extreme emphasis on the Torah and externals was the legacy of the austere Teacher of Righteousness. The founding Teacher of Righteousness is believed to have been of the line of Zadok, David's high priest and originator of the high priests in the Temple. The high priesthood was violated with the installation of a non-Zadokite in the 2nd century B.C., the time when the sect withdrew in disgust from Jewish society. Vermes says, "At the heart of Essenism rested elements of intolerance, rigidity and exclusiveness."

The kingdom of God that the Essenes awaited was an apocalyptic utopian society. It could be introduced only by God intervening in history. The good deeds of men were necessary, but the Essene kingdom was not a human product.

There is nothing to indicate that any of the Qumran materials reveals anything about the hidden doctrine of Jesus. Nevertheless, the discovery is not necessarily negative in this respect. A good deal of scientific investigation, probably most of it, produces similar results. Francis Bacon, the prescient herald of modern science, proclaimed in Elizabethan times that scientific inquiries could not fail. Those experiments that did not turn out positively had the merit of disproving a false lead or wrong theory, narrowing the focus by eliminating what was not germane, making the pursuit easier for the next investigators.

Incredibly, at about the same time the Bedouin goatherd was tossing his fateful stone into the Qumran cave, an almost identical kind of discovery — just as momentous — was taking place in Upper Egypt. In December 1945, two peasant brothers were gathering nitrate for their crop fields in a region that took its name from Nag Hammadi, the largest town in the area.

During the process of digging and loading nitrate into the saddle bags of their hobbled camels, the peasant brothers unearthed a buried jar. Muhammad Ali of the al-Samman clan would say later that at first he was afraid to open the sealed vessel, fearful that he would release a jinn imprisoned inside. But his next thought was that the jar might contain gold, and desire overcame fear. He smashed the jar with his pick-like mattock and found 13 papyrus books bound in leather.

Eventually the government learned of the books and confiscated them. The manuscripts were identified as Gnostic literature not known to have survived or even existed before.

How did the so-called Nag Hammadi library get there? What did the Gnostic writings signify? Scholars trace the find back to Pachomius, later St. Pachomius, who created the first Christian monastery in about 318 A.D. By the time Pachomius died in 346, he had established nine monasteries and two convents in the Nag Hammadi region. One monastery was little more than three miles from the site of discovery. These monasteries accumulated libraries. During the 4th century, the battle against the Gnostic heresy was being fought to its death. Orthodox Christian leaders now had Roman procurators and centurians to enforce their orders, and in 367 Athanasius, the powerful Archbishop of Alexandria, ordered the purge of all apocryphal books with heretical tendencies. His and similar moves were carried out so thoroughly that historians knew about the Gnostic texts mainly through the tirades written against them by the Church leaders. A few Gnostic articles finally did turn up at the end of the 18th and 19th centuries, but it was not until the 20th century that historians could understand Gnosticism as a coherent religion.

The theory is that before Athanasius' order could be executed, some monks, perhaps Gnostic in inclination, removed the targeted books from one of the monasteries near Nag Hammadi and hid them. Just as at Qumran, it was an effort to preserve something considered precious.

The Nag Hammadi books include one text, the Gospel of Thomas, that is startlingly reminiscent of the Synoptic Gospels. Professor Helmut Koester of Harvard Divinity School says the sayings collected by the apostle Thomas include traditions that may go back to the second half of the 1st century, raising the possibility that this Gospel could be as old or older than the canonized Gospels.

The Gospel of Thomas consists of sayings that appear in the Synoptic Gospels and sayings that do not. At least some of the sayings and parables that correspond to the New Testament appear to be in a more primitive and presumably more original form.

The Gospel of Thomas has no stories of Jesus' activities, no miracles, and nothing about the suffering on the cross. The Gospel is strictly a compilation of his sayings: dialogues between Jesus and the disciples or statements to the disciples. The sense of privacy, even esoteric nature of the Gospel is set with the first words: "These are the secret sayings which the living Jesus spoke and which Didymus

Judas Thomas wrote down."

The "secret sayings" of Jesus! Is this, then, the long-lost corpus of Jesus' secret teaching? Well, for one thing, it's not all secret. The authors of the Synoptic Gospels went public with a good number of the sayings. As for many of the others, there is a Gnostic cast to some but by no means all of them. Still, there is enough Gnosticism to see why the Gospel of Thomas was banned. About one half of the 114 sayings do not appear in the Bible. Exactly one in three corresponds closely to sayings in the Synoptics. Not quite 20 percent are part Biblical and part non-Biblical. One quarter of the sayings are, by my interpretation, Gnostic.

Of the dozen Biblical parables in Thomas, six are the same ones that appear in the three Synoptics — The Sower, The Mustard Seed, Lamp Under a Bushel, New Cloth-Old Garment, New Wine-Old Wineskins (in Thomas, they are called wineskins instead of bottles), and the Vineyard and Householder. This recurrence should serve to confirm the importance of these parables. Because of this consistency, the absence in Thomas of the seventh triple-appearing parable — Leaves of the Fig Tree — should have an opposite effect and cast doubt upon its authenticity. The blatantly eschatological parable appears in the suspect 24th chapter of Matthew, 13th chapter of Mark and 21st chapter of Luke where Jesus is made to prophesy the destruction of the Temple and Jerusalem (which took place some 35 year after his death but before the Gospels were completed). The parable is obvious and didactic, totally uncharacteristic of Jesus' parables.

The Vineyard and Householder also is rather transparent and this parable, too, appears late in the Synoptics. In the Bible, Jesus was talking to the Pharisees and scribes in Jerusalem not long before his execution. We can imagine that, unlike his other parables, Jesus wanted them to get the point immediately, which they did. The point, in the Synoptics, was that the lord of the vineyard would destroy the wicked workers who had killed his son and give the vineyard to other caretakers. Matthew has Jesus make it explicit he is talking about the Jews: "The kingdom of God shall be taken from you, and given to a nation bringing forth the fruits thereof." But in Thomas the moral is omitted. The parable ends with the statement that the workers killed the son because they knew he was the heir to the vineyard. Just that, and the reader is left to figure out the meaning of the parable. The meaning in this case would seem to be the sad facts of the assassination and not the punishment.

We see the same thing in the parable of the Wheat and the Weeds. In Thomas, the parable ends with the statement that at harvest time the grown weeds will be easily identified and destroyed. Gone is the long apocalyptic-eschatological explanation with the Son of man sending forth his angels. Similarly, the parable of The Draw Net in Thomas leaves out the eschatological moral appended in Matthew: "So shall it be at the end of the world: the angels shall come forth, and sever the wicked from among the just." The complete absence of apocalyptic eschatology distinguishes Thomas from the Synoptic Gospels.

The parable of the Hidden Treasure also is told differently in Thomas. In Matthew, the kingdom of God is compared to a treasure hidden in a field. A man finds the treasure, hides it, and sells all that he has to buy the field. Thomas also says it is a treasure hidden in a field, but the man does not know the treasure is there. The man dies and leaves the field to his son. The son, being equally ignorant of the treasure, sells the field to another man who plows it, finds the treasure and becomes rich. This formulation of the parable could be seen as a Gnostic theme — ignorance and discovery of the divine essence within one.

There are other sayings that give a sharper perspective to counterparts in the New-Testament Gospels.

Concerning Jesus' conviction that his doctrine was something entirely new: "I shall give you what no eye has seen and what no ear has heard and what no hand has touched and what has never occurred to the human mind."

He makes clearer that the passage about the lilies advises not worrying. "Do not be anxious from morning to evening and from evening to morning about what you will wear."

The code phrase "the Life" appears twice in the Gospel of Thomas and on one occasion is used as the equivalent of the kingdom of heaven.

As might be expected in a text that tends to be Gnostic, there is emphasis on light and enlightenment. On the search for knowledge. One saying illuminates Jesus' cryptic remark in Matthew that the Pharisees and scribes did not go into the kingdom themselves and blocked the way for others: "The Pharisees and the scribes have taken the keys of Knowledge and hidden them. They themselves have not entered nor have they allowed to enter those who wish to."

Knowledge figures crucially in the Recognition, which is entirely recast in the Gospel of Thomas. In the Synoptics when Jesus asks his disciples whom people think he is, they reply in religious terms. Peter speaks last and says Jesus is the Messiah. In Matthew, this answer so pleases Jesus that he gives Peter the keys of the kingdom of heaven and says he will found his church upon him. In Thomas, Peter speaks first and gives what might be accepted as the same answer. Peter says Jesus is like a righteous angel. Matthew, speaking second, likens Jesus to a wise philosopher. The climax this time is reserved for the author of the Gospel. Thomas says, "Master, my mouth is wholly incapable of saying whom You are like." This is the answer that pleases Jesus, but it is Jesus himself who supplies the revelation. "I am not your master. Because you have drunk, you have become intoxicated from the bubbling spring which I have measured out." Thomas, the pupil, has graduated to equality with the the teacher. In another saying, Jesus says, "He who drinks from my mouth will be as I am, and I will be he, and the things that are hidden will be revealed to him."

Jesus' confidence that nothing can remain hidden is emphasized in Thomas. "Know what is in front of your face, and what is concealed from you will be revealed to you." "His disciples asked him, 'Do you want us to fast, and how shall we pray, and shall we give alms, and what food regulations shall we keep?' Jesus said, 'Do not lie, and do not do what you hate, because all is revealed before Heaven. For nothing is hidden that will not be revealed, and nothing is covered that shall remain without being revealed.'"

There are conundrums in Thomas, too. "Jesus said, 'Blessed is the lion which the man eats, and the lion thus becomes man; and cursed is the man whom the lion shall eat, when the lion thus becomes man.'"

"The Kingdom of the Father is like a man who wanted to kill a powerful man. He drew his sword in his own house; he thrust it into the wall so that he would know if his hand would stick it through. Then he killed the powerful one."

Jesus tells his disciples: "If they ask you, 'What is the sign of your Father who is in you?' say to them, 'It is movement and repose.'" "His disciples said to Him, 'When will the repose of the dead come about, and when will the new world come?' He said to them, 'What you look forward to has already come, but you do not recognize it.'"

This last saying is suspiciously close to Luke 17:20-21 that ends with Jesus stating that the kingdom of God is within you. But there are others as well in Thomas. His disciples ask him, "On what day will the Kingdom come?" Jesus answers, "It will not come by expectation. They will not say, 'Look here,' or, 'Look there,' but the Kingdom of the Father is spread out on the earth and men do not see it." "Jesus said, 'If the ones who lead you say, There is the kingdom, in heaven,' then the birds of heaven shall go before you. 'If they say to you, It is in the sea,' then the fish shall go before you. Rather, the kingdom is within you and outside you."

Not a place, not a future event. These sayings led Elaine Pagels to write in *The Gnostic Gospels,* "That 'Kingdom,' then, symbolizes a state of transformed consciousness".

But after all is said, neither do the "secret sayings" of Thomas give any clear definition of the kingdom of God.

The presentation of Jesus' thoughts in a compilation of sayings as in the Gospel of Thomas or the sayings source used by Matthew and Luke tends to picture Jesus as a wise man or teacher of wisdom. That is how the disciple Matthew regarded Jesus in the Recognition in Thomas.

Is this a proper way to think of Jesus?

He was heir to an ancient wisdom tradition in the Middle East and a particularly strong one in Judaism. Wisdom is first heard of in Egypt soon after 3000 B.C. About 2450 B.C., a vizier to the pharaoh by the name of Ptahotep gained a reputation for his wisdom and set down his knowledge in a series of proverbial sayings. Being a high court attendant was a responsible position because the pharaoh was considered immortal, the giver of life and maintainer of order on earth. Ptahotep's writings were something like a manual to help his successors do an excellent job, but also something more because he undertook to explain how one could attain the good life, which was a moral life in a well-ordered society.

The flowering of wisdom in Babylonia took a different turn early in the 2nd millennium B.C. Babylonian civilization was reaching the zenith of its power and accomplishments. Paradoxically, success produced a spiritual crisis. People began to lose faith in their gods. The *Epic of Gilgamesh,* the first great epic, already had told the people not to expect immortality. Gilgamesh, the son of a goddess and human father, a superhuman hero king, went in search of immortality for himself and failed in his quest. The moral was clear: if such a one as Gilgamesh could not achieve immortality, who, then, could?

This wasn't the only blow to faith. Leading an exemplary life, doing everything possible to please the gods didn't necessarily bring desired effects. One complaint went so far as to charge it was impossible to figure out what the gods wanted of humans. For the first time, human beings began to perceive the transience of life, its impermanence, the vanity of human effort. This climate of despair, pessimism, even nihilism, is epitomized in the title of a well-known text of the time, "Dialogue about Human Misery." One speaker says that since childhood, he has behaved piously, prayed to the god, meditated upon the god, given sacrifices, but "the god brought me scarcity instead of wealth." No, it is the godless who become rich. Robbers and wicked men prosper. Evildoers are justified while just men are condemned. People "extol the word of a prominent man, expert in murder, But they abase the humble, who has committed no violence."

The despair stems from the unfairness of life and the fact that the gods have lost their efficacy in correcting human injustice. The historian of religion Mircea Eliade says similar spiritual crises would occur in India, Egypt, Iran, Greece, and Israel.

The Israelite spiritual crisis began with the incomparable success of King David and his son King Solomon at the beginning of the lst millennium B.C. Before this period of the United Monarchy, the Jews had been a group of scattered and struggling tribes. From relative obscurity and low status, Israelites suddenly commanded a kingdom on a par with other potentates. There was a royal court, visits from queens and princes. After the might achieved by David came the wealth and splendor of Solomon. He built a magnificent Temple for God and a royal palace for himself. His ships plied the Red Sea and Mediterranean, his subjects mined for gold in Africa. His astute policies for industry and trade brought fabulous riches that could hardly have been imagined by his countrymen. In order to consolidate the nation's peace and security, Solomon took to marrying foreign princesses. In their retinues were their gods. After the long struggle to retain purity from the gods of Canaan, the worship of Yahweh was threatened once again with pollution.

But this time the threat was symptomatic of a deeper problem. With the achievement of power and wealth, Yahweh no longer was so important or necessary. The emoluments of this world slackened the desire to know and appease Yahweh, enfeebled the fear of God's retribution. A death-of-God crisis infected part of Jewish society. Sure, the forms would be kept, but the passion of intense belief cooled.

This loosening of the grip of God meant that for the first time in Jewish society, Solomon was a ruler virtually without restraints. He could use people for his own ends. He introduced taxation and forced labor for the aggrandizement of the state. Secularization began with David, alienation with Solomon.

Jewish thinkers began to ponder the problem of human power without restraints. Without religious controls, a king can become a despot while other influential members of society can run roughshod over their less fortunate fellows, having the wherewithal to justify their transgressions. The retribution of God is not a deterrent to a person who no longer believes in that kind of punishment. To extol righteousness to a person who despises it is a waste of time. It was this dilemma — how to get the rich, the powerful, the arrogant who had lost their faith to pay attention — that gave birth to Israelite wisdom literature.

Great wisdom was attributed to Solomon. The Bible says he spoke three thousand proverbs. The Queen of Sheba, today's Yemen, was so intrigued by his reputation that she wanted to see for herself. An Arabic version of the story says she tested him with many riddles. The Bible says Solomon answered her every question and she was satisfied that he deserved his reputation. The proverbs of the Book of Proverbs are said to be Solomon's, and some may have come down from him. But more likely they are in the tradition that he popularized, created by thinkers concerned with the social inequities that Solomon spawned. The solution that these sages struck upon to solve their dilemma required a radical departure from Judaic tradition and Scriptures.

There is something that remains precious or even becomes more so to a person who no longer values honor or righteousness. And there is something that a person who has lost his fear of God then will fear more. They are life and death. The Jewish wisdom tradition turned its attention to finding how God's laws operate in nature, particularly human nature, in order to discover the rewards and punishments that the newly liberated would respect. In the new paradigm, life was God's blessing, death was God's curse. The way to life was through wisdom.

The Book of Proverbs constantly praises wisdom and contrasts it with its antithesis, folly. In the many examples that are given, wisdom becomes almost indistinguishable from virtue while folly is wickedness and vice. Pride, greed, plotting violence against innocent fellows, sloth, slander, deceit, bearing false witness will lead to death, that is, shortened life. Wise action — honesty, just conduct, industry, absence of hatred, kindness, mercy for the poor — will lead to life, and that means a constellation of good things: long life, good health, emotional and spiritual contentment, respect, prosperity, the well-being of the community and *shalom,* peace.

What this comes down to is the revolutionary concept that each person is responsible for his own destiny. Each person chooses his future. The inevitable decisions that must be made determine what will happen to the person. He or she will have to live by and with the decisions. Now it becomes clear that kings do not have absolute license to do as they please. Their freedom is circumscribed by accountability. Monarchs have to live with and be judged by their decisions.

Now these sages couldn't palm off their wisdom as coming from on high. They couldn't come down from the mountain with the commandments in hand. Their only authority was the authenticity of the statement itself. Life must validate their wisdom. The congruence or incongruence of wisdom with reality was there for all to see. This is a basic requirement for science: open experiments, openly verified, and available for retesting.

What these early teachers of wisdom were doing, had been forced to do, was to practice an early version of the scientific quest. They were seeking to discover the order in human life and in nature. There are two implications to this pursuit. One is that God is revealed through universal laws. The other is that God trusts human reason to discover what the laws are.

The wise person is the one who dedicates his life to finding God's ways. Moreover, this wisdom is attainable. The person who seeks can learn enough about God and his laws to ensure a fulfilling life.

Proverbs is an affirmation of wisdom, life and the goodness of creation.

Job and Ecclesiastes take different views of life and the quality of creation. Job, whose faith is tried by all kinds of horrible happenings, asks a question that is as contemporary to us as Rabbi Harold Kushner's best-selling *When Bad Things Happen To Good People:* If God is both omnipotent and good, why is there evil and why are innocent people allowed to suffer? Life is so miserable for Job that he does not regard it as God's blessing. Job can see death as a friend.

Ecclesiastes is reminiscent of the anomie that afflicted Babylonian society earlier. Similarities are so marked that passages in Ecclesiastes could have been lifted out of the *Epic of Gilamesh.* Like the

"Dialogue about Human Misery," Ecclesiastes emphasizes the indifference of God. As in Job, life is not regarded as God's gift for virtue. The same things happen to people whether they are good or bad. The sun sets, and also rises. "I....saw under the sun, that the race is not to the swift, nor the battle to the strong, neither yet bread to the wise, nor yet riches to men of understanding, nor yet favor to men of skill; but time and chance happeneth to them all." All is vanity. We strive to accumulate only to leave it to heirs who squander. Death awaits all. "Whatsoever thy hand findeth to do, do it with thy might; for there is no work, nor device, nor knowledge, nor wisdom, in the grave, whither thou goest."

Though Ecclesiastes may be disillusioned, its preacher is not despairing. "Cast thy bread upon the waters: for thou shall find it after many days." Like Proverbs, the book praises wisdom and denounces fools. "Wisdom is better than strength....Wisdom is better than weapons of war....Wisdom is a defence, and money is a defence: but the excellency of knowledge is that wisdom giveth life to them that have it." Ecclesiastes tempers its resignation to the injustice in life with advice to enjoy the things that can be savored. "I perceive that there is nothing better than that a man should rejoice in his own works....it is good and comely for one to eat and drink, and to enjoy the good of all his labor....live joyfully with the wife whom thou lovest all the days of the life of thy vanity, which he hath given thee under the sun, all the days of thy vanity: for that is thy portion in this life."

The prophets often criticized wisdom. What they were attacking was the high value that the state and professional sages placed on technological knowledge and management skills that could be used to serve the state and required no need to know Yahweh.

The deep division in Jewish society that began with David and Solomon went on for four centuries, rending the society's integrity. Each generation had to choose between the glory of Solomon and the righteousness of Moses. Wisdom, along with riches and might, served the state's power over the people. The covenant with God handed down from Moses and championed by the prophets demanded justice above all else. It was the divided kingdom that Jesus said could not stand.

The northern kingdom of Israel was the first casualty. Centuries later, the prophet Jeremiah charged that the kingdom of Judah was following false values that would lead to its death. History bore out Jeremiah's prophecy. After him, the deluge — the fall of Jerusalem and Babylonian Exile.

Deutero-Isaiah, who figured so importantly with his apparent role model of the Suffering Servant for Jesus and in initiating the eschatological movement, was no less pivotal in the wisdom dialectic. Confronted by the sweeping scepticism presented so persuasively in wisdom literature, this unknown prophet ingeniously combated the loss of faith in God by co-opting wisdom.

Second Isaiah said the real issue was whether a benevolent mind and righteous purpose were at work in the world. The mystery of God could not be penetrated, but God's purpose could be understood by interpreting events on a world-scale and in light of Israel's entire history. When this was done, it could be seen that God's purpose was universal justice. At that time, when the Jews were in exile, the purpose would be accomplished by breaking the power of Babylon and releasing the captive people. This was the unwitting role of Cyrus, the Persian conquerer.

As we have seen, the servant was willing to die for the truth of his teaching. His sacrifice won people's attention, but could not by itself win the day. Many martyrs have died for wrong causes. As in the substantiation of proverbs, the servant's mission and sacrifice had to be vindicated by the knowledge of God that he taught. The knowledge was verified by mighty events. Cyrus *did* topple Babylon. The Jews *were* freed. They *did* return to their homeland and start to rebuild. This is a world of reasonable order and goodness.

The prophet could only achieve this knowledge of God and the goodness of God's works through his faith. This combination was superior to the utilitarian wisdom accumulated for ulterior purposes. The Suffering Servant's ethical wisdom served the enlightenment and redemption of all humanity: "by his knowledge shall my righteous servant justify many."

This shift toward God-given wisdom developed further after the Exile. The most recent section of Proverbs was written following the return from captivity, but inserted as the first nine chapters. Setting this section at the beginning of the book tended to give new meanings to the older proverbs. In this new section, wisdom is elevated to a personified divinity. She, it, is regarded as so important that God created Wisdom before the Creation. God's first work was, in fact, a necessary instrument in the creation of the world and its order. Wisdom no longer is simply a human quality or achievement, but a universal reality inherent in but transcending the human scene.

Ancient proverbial themes are reinforced by this divine wisdom.

Kings reign and princes decree justice by wisdom. A theme that is explicit in Proverbs will reappear more enigmatically in the Sermon on the Mount. Wisdom speaks: "Riches and honor are with me; yea, durable riches and righteousness. My fruit is better than gold, yea than fine gold; and my revenue than choice silver. I lead in the way of righteousness, in the midst of the paths of judgment: That I may cause those that love me to inherit substance; I will fill their treasures." When Jesus advises to store treasure in heaven, he is talking about the kingdom of God.

This new strain of wisdom literature was continually nourished to the time of Jesus. Ecclesiasticus, an apocryphal book of Old Testament quality, was written about 185 B.C. The author also exalts a personified Wisdom: "I came forth from the mouth of the Most High." This metaphor is startlingly like Jesus' reply to Satan's demand to turn stones into bread: "Man shall not live by bread alone, but by every word that proceedeth out of the mouth of God." The saying was taken from Deuteronomy, but with the new awareness and later tradition, God's words are not simply commandments that must be obeyed without question or thought, but God's wisdom that is to be preferred to Satan's folly.

There are other themes that will be seen anew in Jesus. Ecclesiasticus attacks the rich, who encouraged the Hellenization of Palestine. Religious and conservative Jews regarded these pushers of cosmopolitanism as unprincipled opportunists and quislings, traitors concerned only with their own selfish welfare. In opposition to their secular wisdom, and that of the Greeks, Ecclesiasticus portrayed a teacher of wisdom who was devoted to the Scriptures, pondered the law, looked into the wisdom of the ancients, reflected on the prophecies, inquired into the hidden meaning of proverbs and tried to interpret the parables. Jesus could have sat for that portrait.

Still more Gospel themes emerge in The Wisdom of Solomon. This apocryphal wisdom book composed in the 1st century B.C. says flatly: "Wisdom is a spirit devoted to man's good". This spirit of God covers the Earth, sees into every person's heart, and knows every word said. "Hence no man can utter injustice and not be found out". Righteous Jews are contrasted with wicked, sinful and mundane Jews who persecute the righteous. Even so, the lot of the righteous is preferable to the condemnation and eventual sorrows of sinners.

The Wisdom of Solomon articulates a problem with which Jesus must have wrestled and is crucial to this inquiry, but upon which Jesus kept silent: "How can any man learn what is God's plan? How can he apprehend what the Lord's will is? The reasoning of men is feeble, and our plans are fallible....With difficulty we guess even at things on earth, and laboriously find out what lies before our feet; and who has ever traced out what is in heaven? Who ever learnt to know thy purposes, unless thou hast given him wisdom and sent thy holy spirit down from heaven on high? Thus it was that those on earth were set upon the right path, and men were taught what pleases thee; thus were they preserved by wisdom."

"And the child grew, and waxed strong in spirit, filled with wisdom: and the grace of God was upon him." "And Jesus increased in wisdom and stature, and in favor with God and man." "They were astonished, and said, Whence hath this man this wisdom....?" "Therefore whosoever heareth these sayings of mine, and doeth them, I will liken him unto a wise man". "John came neither eating nor drinking, and they say, He hath a devil. The Son of man came eating and drinking, and they say, Behold a man gluttonous and a winebibber, a friend of publicans and sinners. But wisdom is justified of her children." "The queen of the south shall rise up in the judgment of this generation, and shall condemn it: for she came from the uttermost parts of the earth to hear the wisdom of Solomon, and behold, a greater than Solomon is here."

Jesus spoke more memorable proverbs than Proverbs, made the parable his trademark, revalued wisdom themes with his own originality, pondered the law and knew the Scriptures by heart. He used wisdom as his sword, his scepter and his candle: to combat the religious Establishment, to confirm his mastery as a teacher and to discern the truth about life.

Albert Schweitzer came to the conclusion that Jesus' kingdom of God was something other-worldly and in the future. Schweitzer grasped the significance of the Suffering Servant for Jesus, saw the import of eschatological expectation in Deutero-Isaiah's message, and knew that a supernatural apocalyptic eschatology was a common fantasy at the time of Jesus. Schweitzer couldn't resist the logic of his insights and took the leap to his conclusion that Jesus adopted a contemporary popular belief. In order to reach this conclusion, however, Schweitzer had to disregard Jesus' explicit declaration that his concept was different from anything that had been held before. Schweitzer's conclusion implied to him that Jesus was a primitive man so consumed with eschatological imaginings that he could never be understood by the modern mind.

What Schweitzer didn't know was the important influence of the wisdom tradition. That is the product of recent scholarship. Nor did he have any idea that Second Isaiah could have had as great an effect upon Jesus within the wisdom tradition as in the other roles.

In any event, the existence of a powerful wisdom tradition that could have exerted great influence upon Jesus makes possible an alternative explanation for the kingdom of God, one that is related to life in this world.

If the kingdom-in-this-life possibility is valid, the German expedition to comprehend Jesus foundered not only because of its ignorance of the importance of wisdom, but also because it lacked requisite knowledge about life.

The scientific understanding of life really did not begin until 1859 when Darwin published his finely-reasoned evidence for the central role of evolution in the living process. The very next year, in 1860, Gregor Mendel made a second momentous discovery about life. His experiments with peas in a monastery garden beautifully revealed the laws of heredity. However, the leading scientists of the time were so arrogant and full of pride (sound familiar?) that they ignored Mendel's findings. How could these learned men do something so stupid and extraordinary, particularly since Mendel had found the very knowledge they were seeking? Mendel was not a member of the scientific Establishment, but an Austrian monk who did his science on the side. It was inconceivable to the experts that such knowledge could be uncovered by an outsider.

The laws of heredity were not rediscovered for another 40 years when the quest for the historical Jesus was winding down. With the exception of evolution, all the important scientific knowledge about life is the result of research in the 20th century. And it was not until the second half of the century, after Watson and Crick discovered the structure and function of DNA, that human beings began to understand life's secrets at the molecular level.

One part of the vast amount of knowledge amassed in the life sciences is especially pertinent because so many scholars have emphasized the gulf of 2,000 years between Jesus and us. The scholars have contended that this temporal remove is sufficient to make Jesus totally alien to us and thus beyond our apprehension.

It is true that there has been a tremendous accumulation of certifiable knowledge since the 1st century. People then did not know that the sun circling the Earth is an illusion caused by the Earth's rotation. Those people knew nothing about the interior of their own bodies, how the brain works, how the circulatory system functions, how emotions can produce physical effects. This lack of exact knowledge didn't prevent the most penetrating intuitions from making brilliant inferences. What people at that time could not do, however, is *prove* the correctness of their contentions.

In all other aspects, those people were biological¹y *identical* to us: physically, psychologically, emotionally, and in power of intellect. The basic cultural patterns had been set, too.

During the 20th century, we have learned a good deal about our distant ancestors. The final product of human evolution was a creature so intellectually superior to all other kinds of animals that it was labeled taxonomically *Homo sapiens,* intelligent man. In the last stages of this evolution, the species had to be divided into subspecies. One was *Homo sapiens neanderthalensis,* which came somewhat earlier than modern man, but had the same brain size. Neanderthal people disappeared perhaps 35,000 years ago, but by that time a creature exactly like ourselves, *Homo sapiens sapiens,* was on the scene. Like ourselves because, as far as we know, biological evolution stopped, presumably because Cro-Magnon man had all the genetic equipment needed for survival. Specifically, this meant that the species had sufficient intelligence to change social behavior and environment to meet the exigencies of existence: it no longer had to wait for the slower bodily modifications wrought by nature.

The wide-ranging and esteemed biologist Rene Dubos wrote in the preface to *Beast Or Angel?:* "My purpose here is to attempt to trace the origins of needs and yearnings which have always been those of humankind everywhere and always. In this search, I shall find it natural to express the same concerns and even to use the same words when speaking of the past, of the present, or of the future — the reason being that the biological and psychological characteristics of humankind have remained essentially the same for at least fifty millennia — in other words, since the time of the Cro-Magnon man."

Dubos says the "genetic constitution given us by the physical characteristics of our evolutionary cradle" is the reason why "our emotional needs still reflect Stone Age conditions of life. They explain many of our behavioral patterns."

Dubos discussed many of what he called human invariants in at least a dozen of his books. Human beings love the savanna terrain, where the species began, with its clumps of trees amidst open areas. Humans prefer a semitropical climate and create one wherever they live, even Eskimos with their well-insulated igloos and fur parkas. There is a subconscious human fear of dense forests where good vision is not much help against danger. Underlying human nutritional requirements are the same everywhere whether the diet is designed for meat-eaters or vegetarians, the savage or the effete.

Human beings are so basically similar that they can readily adapt to cultures that have been alien to their experience. Dubos says it is often emphasized how different the European explorers were from the Indians they found in the Americas. But what is far more remarkable is how alike they were, so much so that Columbus had no difficulty understanding and establishing relations with the natives of the West Indies. This was after hundreds of generations had evolved independently in cultures totally isolated from one another. Dubos cites the case of a Papuan raised in the Stone Age culture of New Guinea. When he was about 12 years old, he came into contact with American soldiers during World War Two. He went on to medical school and became a pathologist.

Hillsides in France where Stone-Age people developed their social habits are pocked with caves. "The Cro-Magnon site thus provides two aspects of the utilization and perception of space which have been associated with human settlements since the beginning of time — an enclosed area to serve as protection and an open vista leading the eye to the horizon." Today's high-storied apartment dwellers and all those seeking a room with a view are merely repeating the preference of long-distant forebears.

"Since human nature has been shaped by the conditions prevailing in tribes and villages, the genetic code which governs the responses of the human brain probably became adapted to social relationships involving only limited numbers of people." Biological limitations make it difficult to know really well more than a few hundred people. And these are the kinds of social groups — the family and extended family or clan, church groups, choirs, clubs, teams, fellow office workers, neighborhood associations — in which most people congregate. The people whom we deeply care about are few.

"We are still so like our Stone Age ancestors in fundamental needs and bodily structure that the best relics scientists have of early man are modern men," Dubos says. Young people crave adventure and sexual satisfaction. Adults are eager for achievement. Old people long for quiet and stability. Most humans feel revulsion at snakes and spiders. We are suspicious of strangers. The urge to control property and to dominate one's peers stems from animal territoriality and dominance.

"In view of the fact that human beings evolved as hunters, it is not surprising that they have inherited a biological propensity to kill, as have all animal predators. But it is remarkable that a very large percentage of human beings find killing an extremely distasteful and painful experience. Despite the most subtle forms of propaganda, it is difficult to convince them that war is desirable."

On the other hand, there is altruism, which got its start because of the biological and evolutionary advantages it gave to a species or group. But now human beings have made altruism a virtue regardless of practical advantages or disadvantages. "Whether or not the words altruism and love had equivalents in the language of the Stone Age, the social attitudes which they denote existed. The fact that the philosophy of nonviolence was clearly formulated at the time of Jesus and Buddha suggests that it had developed at a much earlier date."

Has anything changed basically in human affairs since Jesus' time? Is the betrayal of trust any less bitter? Has hypocrisy diminished, deceit gone away? Arrogance is just as obnoxious and virtue still as sweet. Today's thieves may wield computers and operate insider schemes from Wall Street, but they are what they always were, robbers. The parable of The Dishonest Steward is as up to the minute as those people in military procurement who do favors for the suppliers that become their future employers. On the other side, people who are persecuted for righteousness' sake are likely to be whistle-blowers in the Pentagon or employees of unscrupulous business firms. You will always have the poor with you, Jesus said. We still do.

There *is* a bridge across the chasm of time back to the teachings of Jesus. The bridge is life.

PART TWO

KEYS FROM THE LIFE SCIENCES

A. BIOLOGICAL
FIVE

By Their Fruits

The thesis of *The Immortality Factor,* published in 1974, was that only the brain of our species was powerful enough to perceive the awful truth that death is inevitable. Knowing of certain death brings with it knowledge of its antithesis, the possibility of ever-continuing life. Since never-ending physical life was obviously impossible, our distant ancestors believed that the soul existed immortally. This belief was founded upon some strong, but erroneous, convictions.

For one thing, as Freud pointed out, our unconscious mind believes it is immortal — this is an attribute of life, an irrational feeling deep within us. The young child cannot assimilate the knowledge of its finitude. Secondly, and most persuasively, deciduous trees and other vegetation appeared to die in winter only to be reborn in spring. With sympathetic magic, the kind of analogous thinking used by primitive people, what seemed to happen elsewhere in nature was transposed to the human situation. Similarly, a sleeping person resembles a corpse, but the sleeper awakens and resumes living.

The growth of knowledge undermined the assumption of life after death and made it for some people a less than satisfactory substitute for the real thing. At the same time, the irrational desire and drive to overcome death never slackened. The practice of medicine is, among other things, a concerted human effort to postpone the inevitable. The scientific effort to extend the human lifespan now is seriously underway.

The Immortality Factor, as noted in the Preface, mentioned some of the rational wisdom that Jesus had brought to his people, whose state of knowledge could not appreciate it. For example: "With the parable of the Sower he deciphered life's great principle of evolution — to them that have shall be given, from them that have not shall be taken away — nearly two millennia before Darwin." At the time, the juxtaposition of religion and science, Jesus and a biologist, seemed strange.

Two years later, during research for a book that essentially was addressed to the question "What is life?", the recollection of Jesus' insight into the principle of evolution prompted the thought that he might have made other discoveries about life.

Furthermore, as noted, my discovery of obscure interviews with hundreds of American centenarians revealed that more than a few of them said they lived by the Golden Rule and that they really did love their neighbors. A number said the key to living a long life is: Don't worry. This was the advice that Jesus gave in the passage about the lilies. Jesus may have been preaching about life in heaven, but his precepts brought added years in this world.

It was then the question occurred to me: Could it be that Jesus used life as a Rosetta Stone to decipher what God was about? After all, life is God's most exquisite handiwork. How can one properly serve God unless one knows God's designs and intentions?

That Jesus sought the discovery of God though observation of and meditation upon life became a hypothesis for the research on this book. The hypothesis rests on four premises.

First, that Jesus was a genius of the highest order. Jesus never has been regarded, to my knowledge, as a genius. Mention the word genius and the name that immediately flashes into most people's minds is Einstein. The German poet-writer Goethe also is said to have had an extraordinary I.Q. In the philosopher Arthur Schopenhauer's essay "On Genius," he mentions Homer, Plato, Aristotle, Horace, Petrarch, Tasso, Shakespeare, Goethe and Kant. But not Jesus even though the essay is a profile of Jesus!

"A man of genius," Schopenhauer wrote, is "one from whom we learn something which the genius has learned from nobody." It's as though the genius "were conscious of having by some rare chance and for a brief period attained a greater clearness of vision, and were trying to secure it....for the whole species." His work is "a sacred deposit and the fruit of his life."

Why the failure to recognize and acknowledge the remarkable intelligence of Jesus? For one thing, he did not distance himself from the common people, his constituency. He dined with tax collectors and other non-religious Jews, he liked to drink wine, he allowed a whore to wash his feet at, of all places, the dinner table of a Pharisee. He was no ivory-tower sage.

For another thing, there seems to be a popular notion that to be a genius means to be "secular." Secular is semantically opposed to sacred. Jesus is associated with the latter. But at the time Jesus lived many Jews considered wisdom to be God's greatest gift. Wisdom, therefore, was an appropriate mantle for and true sign of a son of God.

Luke says, "And the child grew, and waxed strong in spirit, filled with wisdom....And Jesus increased in wisdom and stature." Nor did

Jesus underestimate his genius. The wisdom of Solomon was the wonder of its time, he said, "and behold, a greater than Solomon is here." "And he turned him unto his disciples, and said privately, Blessed are the eyes which see the things which ye see: For I tell you, that many prophets and kings have desired to see those things which ye see and have not seen them; and to hear those things which ye hear, and have not heard them."

Second, the point made so emphatically by Rene Dubos: the essential human homogeneity for many thousands of years. Members of our species can think only as human beings. We are locked in by our psychological, nervous and other anatomical equipment. We cannot think like a snake whose dominant sense is the perception of heat. We cannot think like a bat that lives without vision in a world of sound. We cannot think like a wolf whose dominant perception of the world is its sense of smell. We cannot think like a bee whose 300,000 neurons are committed to instinctual circuitry. Our 10 billion or more neurons do give us the capacity to imagine how those creatures think, but despite our great mental plasticity, human thought has been grooved in a remarkable consistency and continuity.

After the long hunt by ancient Greek philosophers for the universal substance from which everything else came, they finally settled on four elements — air, water, earth and fire. What the Greeks had divined was the four states of matter. And there are only four: gaseous, liquid, solid and energy.

Empedocles back in the 5th century B.C. said there are two motivating causes for all physical occurrences. He called the causes Love and Strife. He said Love combines things and creates. Strife drives things apart and destroys. These dynamic forces correspond to what we today call attraction and repulsion. Not only do Love and Strife work against one another, Empedocles said, but they can operate in various combinations.

Twenty four centuries later, Freud said there are two basic instincts: *Eros* and the destructive or death instinct. Love and hate. Freud said the two instincts can work against each other or combine with one another in various ways. He said the instincts are analogues "of the opposing forces — attraction and repulsion — which rule in the inorganic world."

The ancients believed there are four basic bodily fluids or humors: blood, phlegm, yellow bile and black bile. The various ways that these mixed determined a person's characteristics and temperament. Predominance of blood made a person sanguine, the Latin word for blood, that is, ruddy, robust, confident, optimistic. Black bile, on the other hand, made a person melancholy. The phlegmatic person was slow moving. Yellow bile was known by the Greek word *chole* and the English equivalent, choler. A choleric person was yellow skinned, lean and mean, irascible, hot-tempered. We might smile at such quaint imaginings, but Hippocrates, the father of modern medicine, taught that good health depends upon the proper balance of bodily fluids. Physicians today know the truth of this belief: not only the narrow range of tolerances for blood constituents, including cholesterol which comes from the Greek *chole,* but the hormones of the endocrine system and secretions of the immune system.

Even the way we regard medicine is basically unchanged from the ancient Greeks. The chief protector of people's health was Asclepius, the god of medicine. Homer in *The Iliad* mentions Asclepius only as a skillful physician at the time of the Trojan War. Later he was honored as a hero and finally worshiped as a god. He had two daughters, Panacea (Cure-All), who fought illness with drugs, and Hygeia (Health), who represented living by the rules of health or what we call hygiene and preventive medicine. The physician remains a god today, panaceas are sold on television, and after two and a half millennia some people are beginning to live according to the wisdom of Hygeia.

Hippocrates' contemporary, Democritus, was no different in his conceptual thinking from today's particles physicist. Democritus said that everything is composed of atoms. He had no way of knowing absolutely that he was correct, no way of proving it. He had never seen an atom. He couldn't see one. He didn't have the cyclotrons that reveal the host of minute constituents of matter. But his intuition was so great, his hypothesis so correct that he even could explain why material things can have a different appearance from what they actually are. Democritus postulated that a stream of atoms emanated from the material — we would call them photons — so that what the person perceives is a subjective impression and not necessarily the intrinsic nature of the material.

When Nobel laureate Jacques Monod wrote a book in the 1970s about his philosophy of biology, he chose a phrase ascribed to Democritus — Chance and Necessity — for the title. Everything, according to Monod, is a consequence of chance and the determinism of nature. If a scientist at the forefront of molecular biology can reach back to antiquity for the apt phrase to denote his concept, is the contention that Jesus is an unfathomable stranger to us any longer tenable?

Third, Schopenhauer wrote in his essay on genius that "men of genius are those who have gone straight to the book of nature". Judaism was a sharp break from the religions of nature. Instead of pantheism and many gods immanent in nature, transcendental monotheism embraced one God who was other than nature even though operating though the mechanisms of this world. Judaism was anthropocentric. Aside from some passages in Song of Solomon, Job and Psalms, and a prominent vineyard parable in Isaiah, very little in the Bible is addressed to animate nature.

Jesus broke with this tradition to teach his doctrine. Consider the lilies, consider the ravens, the mustard is the smallest of seeds but grows into the greatest of herbs. He is observant of the behavior of nature as the parables of The Mustard Seed and The Sower show. He is sensitive to the mystery in the ways of nature as in the growth of a seed we "knoweth not how" and in the fact that trees and vines unerringly yield their specific fruit, that leaven always expands dough. He is particularly interested in the interaction of human beings and nature. He is well aware of what men do to their fruit trees that no longer give good yields. They are burned to make way for new trees that will produce. An enemy could try to destroy his neighbor's crop not by the arduous process of finding and removing planted seeds, but the the much simpler method of sowing worthless seeds. The sheep that is lost is the one most precious to the shepherd. The vineyard is an important place of employment, but also a model for what men and the nation do with the gifts God has given them. Foxes have their holes, but he is homeless. All of these examples reveal knowledge of nature at first hand.

This is not surprising in a man who grew up in Nazareth in Galilee. Galilee posed a vivid contrast to the desolation and austerity of Judea, the homeland of Jerusalem and the Essenes to the south. Galilee was verdant, and asceticism was not the way of the more joyful Galileans. Nazareth was a small town cupped in a ring of mountains and pleasant hills. From a rise beside the town, one could see Carmel by the edge of the Mediterranean Sea 20 miles to the west and the valley of the Jordan River about the same distance to the east. From the mountain tops, one was rewarded with a spectacular vista.

Renan, the French historian, said that in springtime the countryside was carpeted with flowers and "in no country in the world do the mountains spread themselves out with more harmony, or inspire higher thoughts."

This was the environment in which Jesus grew to maturity and spent his early manhood. The Bible says nothing of this period. But the fourth premise assumes that this silent period was a time of preparation for his mission. In addition to working as a carpenter for his livelihood, he went to those uplifting hills and mountains to think, meditate, observe and teach himself. We have the example of such preparatory meditations in Muhammed and Buddha, whose early lives are better known. For six years Buddha devoted himself to pondering the riddles of life and death, the existence of injustice and despair around him. When at last he found the wisdom he sought, he began his ministry.

Jesus announces the wisdom he has found in his encounter with Satan in the wilderness. His adversary could be understood as a devil's advocate who tests Jesus' knowledge. Or it could be a dialectic between Jesus and the principle of evil in abstract. Whatever, the kinds of questions asked and the answers given reveal the nature of Jesus' wisdom.

He had just fasted for 40 days and presumably was famished. "If thou be the Son of God," the tempter said, "command that these stones be made of bread." Jesus refuses to do so. He cites Scriptures that man lives by every word of God, and at the same time tacitly acknowledges that such a transformation is impossible. The choice of stones cannot be accidental. Jesus had recently heard John the Baptist preach that God could change stones into his elect to replace the Jewish heirs. John is saying that God is omnipotent enough to run the universe in any willy-nilly way that suits the deity. But Jesus, who declared that the law and the prophets were until John, is contradicting the ancient belief: Not so! God does not rule by caprice, but by law. The rule of God (man lives by every word of God) and the acknowledgment that the magical transformation is impossible are perfectly consistent and complementary.

This position is made even more explicit by the next question and answer. The devil's advocate demands that Jesus jump from a high place. God will protect him from harm. Again Jesus refuses. Again he cites Scripture to the effect that God should not be tempted. This time Jesus is talking about God's law of gravity that prevails everywhere, forever, and cannot be abrogated.

Jesus knows that God cannot intervene unnaturally because God doesn't work that way. God reigns through his universal laws. "It is easier for heaven and earth to pass, than one tittle [the smallest part] of the law to fail." This great and fundamental discovery by Jesus was made at a time when most of his contemporaries were expecting the direct intervention of God in unrealistic and supernatural ways.

For the final temptation, Jesus is taken to a high mountain with the kingdoms of the world spread out under him. It is not difficult placing him in a mountain eyrie near Nazareth imagining what he would do if he were offered all that his eyes could encompass to betray his beliefs. Just as he might have considered leaping from the location in order to test God's relation to him. He came to reject such an experiment and to understand why he should, just as he came to realize the ultimate fatuity of exchanging one's life or "the" life for all the world's wealth and power — which then could not be enjoyed. He gave his verdict on such a transaction when he asked "For what shall it profit a man, if he shall gain the whole world and lose his own soul?"

With all the interpretations possible, how could Jesus be certain what God was up to? The crucial problem was raised in The Wisdom of Solomon: "How can any man learn what is God's plan? How can he apprehend what the Lord's will is? The reasoning of man is feeble, and our plans are fallible....With difficulty we guess even at things on earth, and laboriously find out what lies before our feet; and who has ever traced out what is in heaven?"

This quest to understand how God works had been going on for a long time, since Jewish sages directed their attention away from Yahweh to try to decipher God's ways in this world. After nearly a millennium, The Wisdom of Solomon did not offer any answer to the problem except: "Whoever learnt to know thy purposes, unless thou hast given him wisdom and sent the holy spirit down from heaven on high?"

Jesus solved this problem in a world without proof through the sheer power of his logic and reasoning. God had to be revealed by God's works, according to the great law that Jesus expostulated: By their fruits you shall know them. Beware of false prophets, Jesus said in the Sermon on the Mount, and then immediately afterward told how they can be identified: by their works, by what they did, by the consequences that flowed from their words and deeds. "A good man out of the good treasure of his heart bringeth forth that which is good; and an evil man out of the evil treasure of his heart bringeth forth that which is evil."

To this day there is no better litmus test of human intentions and conduct. In today's world we are confronted with myriad decisions: Should we vote for candidate A or candidate B? Should we buy product 1 or product 2? Is this person truly a friend, is this person reliable enough to lend money, should I hire this applicant, should I work for this employer, should I invest because of this person's recommendations, is this person worthy to marry, can I trust my spouse? What should I believe? The questions and decisions abound through every phase of our lives. In modern life, in addition to falsehoods, there are the sophisticated arts of advertising, public relations, and skilled representations that can blend truth with omissions and hard-to-detect misrepresentations. But a person can cut through all that, if he has sufficient information, with Jesus' litmus test. "Not every one that saith unto me, Lord, Lord, shall enter into the kingdom of heaven; but he that *doeth* the will of my Father." Action, a later adage goes, speaks louder than words.

While Jesus' adage "By their fruits ye shall know them" usually is applied to human beings, the truth and necessity of the observation are taken from nature. "For every tree is known by his own fruit. For of thorns men do not gather figs, nor a bramble bush gather they grapes." The novelty of the saying was its application to human beings. If taken at its face value, the observation is such a truism that it is banal. Well, of course each kind of tree produces its own kind of fruit. So what else is new? Or, so what?

The fact that the vine produced grapes and the fig tree figs must have been just as obvious and unnoteworthy to people 2,000 years ago. But perhaps it is only the greatest genius who can perceive the fundamental principle in the commonplace. And recognize its value. The principle involved could be called the first law of biology, that which makes life possible: genetic invariance.

It so happened that Aristotle, the founder of biology, not only had noted the same phenomenon, but made it the cardinal principle of his philosophy. Has anyone ever seen an olive-headed vine? Aristotle asked, and commented, "An absurd suggestion." "For those things are natural which, by a continuous movement originated from an internal principle, arrive at some end....always the tendency in each is toward the same end, if there is no impediment."

Aristotle was the first Greek philosopher to study nature, and especially living things, assiduously. From his many observations, seeing the unvarying consistency of development from seed to adult, every organism always a reproduction of its parents, Aristotle believed he had discovered nature's deepest secret: that which causes all phenomena. The purposive final cause. His discovery was so new and different that he had to invent a word for it: *entelechy:* I have my goal within.

Today we know that what Aristotle discovered and Jesus perceived is DNA. The mechanisms of genetic continuity are encapsulated in the DNA molecule. The molecule's two helical strands twine about each other like a spiral ladder linked by millions of rungs on which are encoded all hereditary information. The molecule is ensconced within a chromosome, one of a complement of hereditary units within the nucleus of a cell, the basic entity of life. The complete genetic assemblage determines the individual's species or specific biological composition.

Theoretical biologists marvel at the stability of the DNA molecule and have no scientific way to account for it. Every arrangement of matter in the universe (that we know) tends to degenerate, but DNA has been reproducing itself for more than three billion years. Irwin Schrodinger, who won a Nobel prize for his work completing the revolution in quantum physics, wrote in his book *What Is Life?* before the discovery of DNA: "An organism's astonishing gift of concentrating a 'stream of order' on itself and thus escaping the decay into atomic chaos....seems to be connected with....the chromosome molecules, which doubtless represent the highest degree of well-ordered atomic association we know of". Biophysicist Howard Pattee told a conference considering the same question, "What is life?": "The only conclusion I have been able to justify is that living matter has distinguished itself from nonliving matter by its ability to achieve greater reliability in its molecular hereditary storage and transmission processes than is obtainable in any thermodynamic or classical system."

To be sure, the DNA molecule does undergo change. Individual molecules must be replaced through replication. While the pattern of the helical structure continues intact, constituent arrangements evolve, and so do species. Biological evolution is continuity with change. The beneficial changes are kept, the harmful changes self-destruct. In general, but not always, deleterious changes are eliminated by the inferior ability of the carrier organisms to survive and reproduce successfully. We can deduce that Jesus appreciated this principle, observing what happened to defective specimens and poor producers. "Every tree that bringeth not forth good fruit is hewn down, and cast into the fire."

Today we are beginning to see human intervention through biotechnology in the transmission of genetic information. The time may come when a person with a genetic defect will not have to pass it along with the rest of the sperm-egg inheritance to the offspring. Through genetic engineering the defective section of DNA will be removed or corrected. Drastic though this reformation may be, it is implicit in Jesus' teaching. "Either make the tree good, and his fruit good; or else make the tree corrupt, and his fruit corrupt."

The tree *must* produce its own kind of fruit, and genetic engineering does not in the slightest change the inviolable law of absolute invariance between the composition of DNA and the organism it produces. This correspondence remains sovereign. Says evolutionary biologist George Gaylord Simpson: "We really do not know why or how the specifications of a particular congeries of DNA molecules and a specific set of corresponding protein produce in one case a rosebush and in another case a man. That is the 'secret of life!'"

Only by their fruits shall you know the DNA molecules.

"Know what is in front of your face," Jesus said in the Gospel of Thomas, "and what is concealed from you will be revealed to you."

Jesus observed life in nature, then applied the principle he discovered to human nature, which is more complex, and to human affairs that are complicated by deceit, deception, disguise, dissimulation, duplicity, guile, hypocrisy, not to mention human emotions and motives. His doctrine is composed of two tiers. One level explains how life operates or how God operates through life. Since Jesus was not a biologist, but a fisher of men, mere knowledge is not an end in itself. It is a means to improve human well being.

If Jesus' penetration of life's secrets is the basis for his doctrine, then what Jesus learned about life is the key to his teaching.

SIX

Like A Mustard Seed

So impressed was Jesus with the regularity, reliability, and irresistible force of genetic invariance that he used it as the prime example for his disciples. If they could have faith — belief in themselves, in what they were doing, in their mission, in the kingdom of God — like a grain of mustard seed, they could accomplish anything. The famous passage is in Matthew when the disciples ask Jesus why they have failed in their efforts to cure a mentally ill boy. Jesus answers, "Because of your unbelief; for verily I say unto you, If ye have faith as a grain of mustard seed, ye shall say unto this mountain, Remove hence to yonder place; and it shall remove: and nothing shall be impossible unto you."

The growth of the mustard seed, because of the mechanisms that form or cause biological determinism, cannot be withstood. We see grass that pushes through asphalt, tree roots that split boulders, and the relentless encroachment of vegetation which is not kept in check by pruning and uprooting. While the faith of the disciples on this occasion was not strong enough to work a miracle, it was the faith of Jesus' followers — the apostles after his death, the primitive Christians, the martyrs, the early Church leaders — that enabled Christianity to prevail.

The parable in Mark of the Growth of Seed also features the phenomenon of genetic invariance — first the seed, ultimately the full corn in the ear. But the dominant phenomenon this time is the mystery of growth. The kingdom of God is like a man who plants a seed "And should sleep, and rise night and day, and the seed should spring and grow up, he knoweth not how. For the earth bringeth forth fruit of herself".

How can this happen? Why does it happen? Today, of course, we know that nutrients essential to the plant's growth are in the earth. The marvel of life, any kind of life, is the ability to absorb elements randomly dispersed in its environment, then assemble them in very precise arrangements.

It is not simply growth to which Jesus is calling attention, however, but what is referred to today as differentiation. First the seed....then the blade....the ear....the corn. How does this come about? To that question, modern biology still does not know the full answer.

All life starts from a single cell. In animals this cell is a fertilized egg. Within two hours and 40 minutes the fertilized egg of a sea urchin, a widely-studied organism, has divided, or doubled, seven times. There already are 128 cells. As cells divide and proliferate, they begin to form specialized cell lines, ultimately to form all the various materials that make up the body — the lens of the eye, rough covering of the tongue, elasticity of blood vessels, super-tough sinews of the heart, rigidity of bone structure, and on and on. There may be as many as 50 different kinds of cells in the retina alone.

Scientists now know how this is done. The complete genetic library for the human organism, exists in its entirety within each and every body cell. In other words, the total genetic information to reproduce another identical organism is present. But all the special-ized cells — that is, all bodily cells excepting the sperm and ova —have relinquished their capacity to activate all of the parts, or genes, of the DNA molecules to reproduce a new organism. Instead, only certain genes can be turned on. These genes manufacture the kind of protein required for whatever part of the body that the cell composes. The specialized cells are incapable of reproducing any cells but their own kind.

The mystery, despite the tremendous molecular knowledge we now possess, is essentially the same as it was in Jesus' time: how do we get from a single fertilized egg to an exactly-proportioned human adult, how is the genetic information contained in that original cell discriminatingly utilized to produce the variety and precise number of different cells necessary? How do cells know when to start and to stop reproducing? We still "knowth not how."

The sperm cell and the ova, which can reproduce another human being, each have only one half of the full complement of chromo-somes so that they must join in order to provide the requisite hereditary material. The germ cell of a plant that reproduces asexually does have the complete set of chromosomes. It is unisexual. In the Gospel of Thomas when the disciples ask Jesus how they can enter the kingdom of God, he gives this enigmatic answer: "When you make the two one, and when you make the inside like the outside and the outside like the inside, and the above like the below, and when you make the male and the female one and the same, so that the male not be male nor the female female...."

The Mustard Seed, one of the most important parables, told in the three Synoptic Gospels, as well as the Gospel of Thomas, emphasizes the power and accomplishment of growth itself.

"And he said, Whereunto shall we liken the kingdom of God? or with what comparison shall we compare it? It is like a grain of mustard seed, which, when it is sown in the earth, is less than all the seeds that be in the earth: But when it is sown, it groweth up, and becometh greater than all herbs, and shooteth out great branches; so that the fowls of the air may lodge under the shadow of it."

Garrett Hardin, one of America's foremost ecologists, said a fundamental difference between biologists and physicists is that biologists have a gut appreciation of the power of growth in the working of things. "Biological entities have the ability to multiply" and "the potential consequences are fantastic."

Hardin gave this example during a symposium at Brookhaven National Laboratory: "There could hardly be a more trifling physical event than dropping a single bacterium onto a human pharynx — the mass of one body is 18 orders of magnitude greater than that of the other. But if the bacterium is a living pathogen, and the pharyngeal membrane is susceptible to the disease, the consequences may literally be of world-shaking importance. A man may sicken and die, starting an epidemic that weakens an empire and changes the course of history. All this is possible."

An order of magnitude is scientific shorthand for ten times larger or smaller than. Anything that is ten times larger or smaller than something else is considered to be one order of magnitude different from its referent. So the human being is one quintillion — 1 followed by 18 zeros — times greater than the bacterium. Not much of a match-up.

But there is the deceptive power of growth in that word exponential. In mathematics, an exponent is the figure written to the right and above a number to indicate how many times that number is to be multiplied by itself. It is also called raising the number to the power specified. For example, 2 to the first power or 2^1 simply is the number 2. 2^2 would mean 2 x 2, one multiplication. The potential for expansion becomes apparent even with an exponent as low as five or six:

2^6 = 2 x 2 x 2 x 2 x 2 x 2 or
2 x 2 = 4 x 2 = 8 x 2 = 16 x 2 = 32 x 2 = 64

When the multiplication is carried several stages further, the size becomes almost impossible to anticipate. Let's add another half dozen doublings:

$$64 \times 2 = 128 \times 2 = 256 \times 2 = 512 \times 2 = 1024 \times 2 = 2048 \times 2 = 4096$$

The exponent 2 is the apt figure to use in this illustration because it represents what happens in cell mitosis, the process by which cells reproduce themselves. A cell fissions into two daughter cells and those two each become two more, and so on. In just 50 divisions, the single fertilized egg would become more than one quadrillion — one followed by 15 zeros — cells. With three more divisions, the total would reach close to 10 quadrillion cells, the number of cells in a human body. The multiplication by two is a phenomenon known as doubling, a useful one in keeping track of any kind of growth.

There is another characteristic of exponential growth that tends to mask its potential or ultimate power: it always starts slowly before it explodes. That is what ecologist Paul Ehrlich meant by the phrase The Population Bomb.

A popular example of this phenomenon is a hypothetical lily pond. Suppose you own a pond in which a lily patch is growing. The lily patch doubles in size each day and if allowed to grow, would cover the pond in 30 days, choking off all other life in the pond. You do not become aware of the danger until the water lilies have covered half the pond. That happens on the 29th day — you have one day to save your pond.

Population ecologists R.H. MacArthur and J.H. Connell gauged the power of biological growth at its theoretical limits. It is possible for certain bacteria to reproduce, or double, in 20 minutes. Conditions would have to be and remain optimal. After 20 minutes there would be two bacteria and after the first hour only eight of them. After 36 hours there would be so many bacteria that their mass would cover the entire earth to a height of one foot. And just one hour after that the mass would be over our heads.

Fortunately, explosive biological growth is governed by the environment. In real life, after any biological population grows to some unspecified size, it exceeds the environment's carrying capacity. The size becomes such that there no longer is sufficient space or food or water or sunlight or some other needed resource to support all the individuals. Or the crowding weakens the resistance of the organisms, making them susceptible to parasites and pathogens. Or the plenitude will offer the food to promote the growth of predators that proceed to decimate the supply until, in turn, their own population becomes insupportable and diminishes.

These checks and balances of nature and the orchestration of populations is a chief concern of ecologists. The phenomenon of biological growth is crucially important to human welfare in all kinds of ways. For example, the gypsy moth was deliberately imported into the United States in 1869 by an artist who hoped to get rich quick by developing a substitute for the silk worm. The scheme fizzled, some moths escaped, and because the species has no natural enemies in the United States it became an unstoppable plague. The disappearance of the chestnut tree is the reverse side of this phenomenon. The chestnut was a dominant tree species in the eastern deciduous forest when a fungus to which the tree was not resistant was accidentally released in 1904. By 1952, the parasite had wiped out all mature chestnut trees.

Monoculture — huge areas of one-crop agriculture — prepares a feast for one or several species of insects that normally feed on the farm plant. The concentration of a single plant species in one location, something that almost never happens in nature, sets the table for fast-reproducing insect populations. The farmer tries to blunt the power of insect growth in this simplified ecosystem with a chemical insecticide. But even with this intervention, the farmer is not always successful in keeping the uninvited guests from making pests of themselves and taking their tithe of the harvest.

The same phenomenon can be seen in human history. When human beings became numerous enough to congregate in cities, they unwittingly created the necessary condition for epidemic disease. In the Peloponesian War, totalitarian Sparta conquered democratic Athens after the city had succumbed to disease. Rome, with its huge population for the time of one million people, was repeatedly decimated by malaria. Every fourth European, 25 million of them in all, died in the ferocious bubonic plague in the 14th century. In 1918, 30 million people died in the world-wide pneumonia/influenza pandemic.

The biological growth that ecologists most fear today is that of the human species. At the time of Jesus, there were estimated to be 300 million human beings in an uncrowded world. It took more than 16 centuries for that figure to reach 500 million. But the Industrial Revolution was starting, and in 180 years the human population had doubled to one billion in 1830. In just one more century the population had doubled again to two billion. The accelerating growth rate, taking off like a rocket needed just 45 years to double the population to four billion. Now the doubling rate is down to 30 years.

What this means is that one species now is using for its own purposes nearly 40 percent of all plant production on the planet. These products from photosynethesis are what support all other non-vegetative life. Already the number of species extinctions is starting to increase and it is estimated that by the end of the next century more than half of all species of plants and animals existing today will be gone. Human beings will be living in the worst kind of poverty, the impoverishment of nature. The final tragedy will be what happens to our own species. In nature, whenever a population shoots past the carrying capacity of the environment, the population crashes. There is a huge die-off. That is the ultimate corrective for uncontrolled population growth.

So much attention has been paid to growth because it is such a central property of life. If you ask what evolution has been up to, George Gaylord Simpson wrote in *The Meaning of Evolution,* and take the long view over the past 500 million years, "the first and deepest impression is that of increase. Then there was little or no life on the lands or in the air; now there is hardly a handful of soil or a rod of the earth's surface or a bit of breeze in which life, small or large, does not exist."

That the central role of growth in life was grasped by Jesus can be inferred by the importance he attached to it in his teaching. The kingdom of God can or must grow from something that is infinitesmal like a mustard seed into something that is great and all-consuming. Growth is the mechanism by which life has overcome all obstacles — the harsh tests of the environment, the unpredictable challenges presented by chance, the temporary existence of all living units. Life must exploit every opportunity, use every advantage to grow and forever persevere in order to survive and prosper.

It is this characteristic that explains the parable of The Talents. This is what the lord meant by usury, by reaping without sowing —the expansion that is the natural process of living things. The servant who merely preserved but did not use and enlarge what was given him was wicked because he disobeyed a fundamental law of life —you must grow. Grow or die.

A tree must keep growing. Even when it reaches maturity it puts a new ring around its trunk each year unless the stored energy must be poured into a second growth of leaves to replace the ones eaten by gypsy moths. Human beings must keep growing, too. While we reach physical maturity at a relatively early age, we must keep growing intellectually, psychologically, emotionally, spiritually, socially, in talents or else start on the decline that leads to death. In this sense, the parable of The Talents could just as well be about what we mean today by the word talents. A person must use his talents, develop his abilities, practice his skills in order to keep them. In old age it is imperative for a person to exercise those faculties necessary for the enjoyment of independent life. Gerontologists know that there are two choices for old people: use it or lose it.

Actually this rule applies to people of all ages. And the law appears to be the point of the parable of the Hidden Treasure as it is told in the Gospel of Thomas. The kingdom of God is like a man who had a treasure hidden in his field, but he didn't know it. When he died, the field went to his son, who also was not aware of the treasure. He sold the field to a third man who plowed the field and in so doing found the treasure. He made use of the field and was rewarded.

Emerson, employing a metaphor too reminiscent of The Mustard Seed to be an accident, gave a variation of this thought in his essay on "Compensation." The death of a loved one seems like pure loss with no possible benefit, but "somewhat later assumes the aspect of a guide or genius; for it commonly operates revolutions in our way of life, terminates an epoch of infancy or of youth which was waiting to be closed, breaks up a wonted occupation, or a household, or style of living, and allows the formation of new ones more friendly to the growth of character....and the man or woman who would have remained a sunny garden-flower, with no room for its roots and too much sunshine for its head, by the falling of the walls and the neglect of the gardener is made the banyan of the forest, yielding shade and fruit to wide neighborhoods of men."

We see the principle everywhere in human society: people seek and build on advantage. They seize opportunity. If you're a young man, in good health and happen to be seven feet tall, you go out for basketball. It is true that this essential tendency of life can be abused. Some examples from nature already have been cited. We have a saying that the rich grow richer and the poor grow poorer. The Joint Economic Commmittee of Congress reported in 1963 that the top one-half of one percent of the American population possessed 25 percent of the wealth. Twenty years later in 1983 the top one-half of a percent controlled 35 percent of the wealth. We know that, just like the situation 3,000 years ago when Jewish sages first began writing Proverbs, the rich can afford the lawyers who will help them escape paying the legal penalties for their transgressions, hire financial advisors who show them how to enhance their wealth, pay for the best medical care to preserve their lives and thus provide more time to amass greater wealth, etcetera, etcetera, etcetera.

Jesus is not saying he advocates the system. He's not saying he likes it. He is saying: That's the way it is and you should know for your own welfare — those who have get greater abundance, those who lack something that is necessary stand to lose it all.

The parable of The Leaven, placed adjacent to The Mustard Seed in both Matthew and Luke, also appears to be about growth. But in addition The Leaven has a further interpretation, and will be dealt with later.

The miracle of The Loaves and Fishes, one of the few stories in all four Gospels, expresses the principle of biological multiplication perfectly. Jesus starts with two fishes that are made to feed five thousand people. Nature also needs only two fishes, one male and the other female, in order to produce a fishery that will feed a multitude.

SEVEN

Narrow Is The Way

"I love to see that Nature is so rife with life," Henry Thoreau wrote in Walden, "that myriads can be afforded to be sacrificed and suffered to prey on one another; that tender organizations can be so serenely squashed out of existence like pulp — tadpoles which herons gobble up, and tortoises and toads run over in the road; and that sometimes it has rained flesh and blood."

The philosophical Thoreau, an acute observer of nature, was an ecologist before the term was invented. Will and Ariel Durant, assiduous students of human history, came to a similar conclusion from their vantage point. After finishing the monumental 11-volume *History of Civilization,* they wrote in *The Lessons of History:* "Nature has no use for organisms, variations, or groups that cannot reproduce abundantly. She has a passion for quantity....she likes large litters, and relishes the struggle that picks the suviving few".

"The laws of biology are the fundamental lessons of history," the Durants said, and "the first biological lesson of history is that life is competition. Competition is not only the life of trade, it is the trade of life — peaceful when food abounds, violent when mouths outrun food."

The man most famous for recognizing and popularizing the downside of life was Thomas Malthus, a political economist in England. His father was a great admirer of two of the most fervid optimists in history — Condorcet in France and Godwin in England. Inspired by the French Revolution, they foresaw human progress advancing toward perfection. The Revolution was not so kind to Condorcet. He was executed in the Reign of Terror that followed.

As sons will do, young Malthus took issue with his father's position on the inevitability of human progress, saying there were great natural principles that constrained such progress. Malthus presented his argument with such persuasion that his father urged him to publish it. Thomas Malthus' *An Essay on the Principle of Population* appeared just before the start of the 19th century.

In the essay, Malthus said plants and animals have such a potential to expand that they could "fill millions of worlds in the course of a few thousand years." But lack of space and nourishment prevents this from happening. Population tends to increase geometrically while food production tends to grow arithmetically. "And the race of man cannot by any efforts of reason escape from" this circumstance. "Among plants and animals its effects are waste of seed, sickness, and premature death. Among mankind, misery and vice."

By vice, Malthus meant man's inhumanity to man — specifically, poverty and war. "But should they fail in this war of extermination, sickly seasons, epidemics, pestilence, and plague advance in terrific array, and sweep off their thousands and tens of thousands. Should success be still incomplete, gigantic inevitable famine stalks in the rear, and with one mighty blow, levels the population with the food of the world."

There can be no doubt that Jesus fully grasped this principle of life. "Enter ye in at the strait gate," he said in the Sermon on the Mount, "for wide is the gate, and broad is the way that leadeth to destruction, and many there be which go in thereat: Because strait is the gate and narrow is the way, which leadeth unto life, and few there be that find it." In Luke, as noted, this image is applied to human beings with regard to the choices they make in terms of religious doctrine. As Jesus said on many occasions, he offered the way to life (or the life). But in Matthew, the saying is unadorned by any doctrinal reference: it is a blunt statement about the nature of life, the way it works.

Life, in the shutter pictures of isolated moments, appears to be stable and static, but it always is dynamic, changing and an unremitting elimination procedure. Not all the same people who are alive today will be so tomorrow: some will be substracted, some new ones will be added.

Probably the most dramatic illustration of an elimination contest going on all the time in nature is that employed to insure conception. The process is the same for all species, but we probably know the most about our own, and it is of the most interest to us. The following example is not given to contend that Jesus was familiar with the details of modern biology and human anatomy, but to illustrate a fundamental principle of life that he did understand and for which he used a very suggestive term.

Strait, as noted, is an archaic word meaning tight, closely fitting, constricted, as is the channel for procreation which becomes the birth canal. This is for our species the preeminent strait gate and narrow way and in either direction they lead to life.

The odds in the fateful rendezvous that will create a new life are fantastic. The woman's two ovaries each has some 370,000 egg cells at birth. From this supply potential of 740,000, she will use little more than 400 eggs in her entire lifetime. About every 28 days, an egg, the largest human cell about the size of a grain of sand, is discharged from one or the other ovary. It slowly moves down the fallopian tube, which is about twice the thickness of a single strand of hair, toward the uterus, or womb. The time window is about 24 hours. After that, the egg distintegrates.

In order to find this precious pearl of life, the male propels up to 300 million sperm into the vagina with one ejaculation. The sperm cell consists mainly of a head and a tail. In the head of each sperm is the full array of the man's genetic composition, contained in a single set of 23 chromosomes. Another 23 chromosomes reside in the egg. If the two are joined, there will be the complete complement of 46, the heredity, heritage and inheritance of a new human being. The long tail, which lashes from side to side, has a single mission: to deliver the genetic payload to its destination.

There is a good reason for the huge population of entrants at the start of the race. As many as 20 percent of the sperm can be defective because of infection, cigarette smoking, chemical pollution in the air and water, tight clothes, a slight elevation in temperature or stressful living conditions for the man. The vagina is acidic to protect the woman from bacteria and infection, but that makes a hostile and dangerous environment for the sperm. About one quarter of them die immediately. Then the woman's defense system goes into action; after all, the sperm are foreign invaders. So getting through the vagina is running a gauntlet, although there is a degree of success in numbers.

With the result that hundreds of thousands of sperm survive the ordeal of the narrow way to reach the strait gate to the uterus, the cervix. Many sperm cannot find their way through the cervix so that the total number of sperm swimming into the womb is further reduced. These surviving sperm now are confronted with a cruel choice. In the wall of the uterus are the entrances to two corridors, the fallopian tubes. It is like the story of the lady and the tiger —behind one door awaits a beautiful woman, behind the other death.

Half the sperm make the wrong choice. They enter the empty tube. Of the 200 to 300 million sperm that started out, no more than 50 reach the egg, and only one will fertilize it — the one that has successfully passed through the strait gate and narrow way to find *life!*

The final test for the last competing sperm is to burrow through the outer layers of the egg. The first one that penetrates the egg's membrane is drawn inside and the membrane immediately undergoes biochemical changes that make it impermeable to other sperm.

Obviously, nature has a method to this madness. The successful sperm proves it is the strongest, and the most viable, but this does not guarantee it is genetically unflawed.

But as soon as fertilization takes place a new elimination procedure commences. The entering cohort for this challenge is made up of all the human beings conceived on the same day or in the same week or, and this is the most common tabulation, in the same calendar year. The attrition starts in the uterus. It is estimated that one in every five pregnancies aborts spontaneously. The highest incidence of infant deaths occurs with the trauma of birth. The toll stays relatively high during the first four years of independent life. Then children pass through the healthiest, lowest-mortality decade of their existence. As individuals venture out into life on their own, the death rate begins to climb.

Past the age of 40, people everywhere die at a virtually uniform rate. The number of deaths doubles every seven to eight-and-a-half years. This means that the chances of dying are 100 times greater at age 85 than at 35. Slightly past the age of 70, half of the cohort is dead. "The days of our years are threescore and ten," said the 90th Psalm, "and if by reason of strength they be fourscore years, yet....it is soon cut off, and we fly away." After a century, very few of the starters, fewer than one percent, still cling to the life that was found by the two cells that sought it.

Again the model for Jesus is life. Again he uses it as an apt and valid framework for spiritual salvation. If the saying in Matthew is a statement about the way life is, in Luke it becomes a moral for the way to conduct one's life. "Strive to enter in at the strait gate: for many, I say unto you, will seek to enter in, and shall not be able. When once the master of the house is risen up, and hath shut to the door, and ye begin to stand without, and to knock at the door, saying, Lord, Lord, open unto us; and he shall answer and say unto you, I know you not whence ye are: Then shall ye begin to say, We have eaten and drunk in thy presence, and thou has taught us in the streets. But he shall say, I tell you, I know you not whence ye are; depart from me, all ye workers of iniquity."

You had your chance and did not take it. You had your choice and did not pick correctly. That's the way life is. Once you have committed yourself, there is no going back. You wind up where your choices and fitness have taken you.

In *The Lessons of History,* the Durants wrote: "The second biological lesson of history is that life is selection. In the struggle for existence some individuals are better equipped than others to meet the tests of survival."

Jesus, too, believed there was a method to the winnowing process that separates winners from losers, the wheat from the chaff, the saved from the lost, the successful seed from the failures. He explained it in his greatest parable.

EIGHT

The Sower

With the parable of The Mustard Seed and the apothegm of the Broad Way to destruction, Jesus showed he had a deeper understanding of life than Aristotle.

From Aristotle's studies of how precisely the parts of animals are made to accomplish designated tasks, he concluded, "Nature never makes anything that is superfluous." He scoffed at the proposal by an earlier philosopher, Empedocles, that nature experiments with all kinds of forms. Where are Empedocles' bizarre chimeras? Aristotle wanted to know, for he refused to accept Empedocles' explanation that the reason nature's mistakes are never seen is that they are unable to survive. In fact, Empedocles had found the mechanism of evolution long before anyone knew what that was.

Jesus perceived the irresistible force of life's growth and unblinkingly accepted the inevitable consequences: enormous losses. Many are called, but few are chosen. These two basic laws of life were not specifically articulated until Malthus wrote his famous essay on population. Malthus was proclaiming an unpleasant dilemma and it was vigorously rejected by a young humanitarian movement. Christians of the time were intent upon improving the lot of the poor. Malthus was saying that if you make things a little better for the poor, the result will be more poor. No matter what you do, there will always be a great number at the bottom of the pile and just a few at the top.

From a biological point of view, life needs surplus in order to select the best specimens that can survive, that are fit to survive, and by this process better ensure the preservation of life. Charles Darwin already was pondering such problems after his return to England from the voyage of The Beagle. He had begun to search for the way that species originated. Starting in July 1837, he collected facts (just as Francis Bacon had recommended, Darwin says) with no theory in mind. He concentrated on domesticated animals since they were most readily observable, interviewed breeders and gardeners, and read voluminously. "I soon perceived," Darwin writes in his autobiography, "that selection was the keystone of man's success in making useful races of animals and plants. But how selection could be applied to organisms living in a state of nature remained for some time a mystery to me."

Fifteen months after Darwin began his investigation, he happened to read Malthus "for amusement." When Darwin saw the first two laws of life clearly presented, he saw the solution to his problem. "Being well prepared to appreciate the struggle for existence which everywhere goes on from long-continued observation of the habits of animals and plants, it at once struck me that under these circumstances favourable variations would tend to be preserved and unfavourable ones to be destroyed. The result of this would be the formation of new species." Nature, or you could say God, selects through the environment. The obverse is that the superior individual, the one with the most perfectly suited endowment or behavior (and for humans, attitude) for his particular environment, is the one that prospers.

"For he that hath, to him shall be given: and he that hath not, from him shall be taken even that which he hath." Jesus' great law of life is the product of the two preceding principles: the necessity for growth and the inevitable reduction of excess. This law tells *how* the elimination occurs, *why* it takes place in the way it does. It contains the secret of the selecting process.

We have to be careful to remind ourselves that such a term as selection, or natural selection as it is called in the parlance of evolution, is a modern designation for a biological mechanism. Jesus knew nothing about this. The science of biology was non-existent. No one can imagine that he could have known about the eons-long process of evolution without the requisite amassing of knowledge. Nevertheless, selection as a phenomenon of life, as a process of life operated as surely in Jesus' time as it does today. It was there for him to detect. With his knowledge of these and other laws of life, can it be any wonder that he so esteemed his doctrine that he said there never had been anything like it?

That Jesus placed great importance on the hath-hath not principle and used it as a widely-applicable law can be seen from the number of times and variety of contexts in which it appears. It is given as the moral of the parable of The Talents in Matthew and Luke. It follows slightly separated from the parable of the Lamp Under a Bushel in Luke and is the moral of that parable in Mark. The saying is the moral of the parable of The Sower in Matthew. And in the Gospel of Thomas, two separate versions appear by themselves, isolated, free-floating.

The real wonder is how Jesus was able to divine the principle of selection because it is not so readily apparent in human affairs. Yet the specific linkage to survival is made in the Gospel of Thomas. If you express or realize what you have in you, it will save you. But if you don't have it within you, that deficiency will kill you.

If we turn to nature with the knowledge we have today, we are able to see that it operates like a law of mathmatics. For example, when farmers sprayed DDT for the first time, they grossly altered the environment in a way that was unprecedented for the target insects. Upon first use, the lethal insecticide probably killed all but an infinitesmal fraction of the insect population. But nature is so provident that a few insects possessed the genetic ability to survive the poison. These were the "haves," and over thousands of generations, the survivors expanded the protective genes in the insect population until DDT, eventually began to lose its effectiveness. The process of diminishing returns coincides with the build-up or what is called the development of resistance. The same phenomenon can be observed with penicillin and the pathogens it kills.

The rule is: the species with the genetic endowment and behavior that best suits a particular environment is the one that survives in that situation. In ecology's first milestone laboratory experiment in the 1920s, Russian biologist G.F. Gause put two closely related protozoan species in the same environment, feeding on a bacteria culture. When either species was placed in the culture separately, the population grew to the size allowed by its food resource and leveled off. When *Paramecium caudatum* and *Paramecium aurelia* shared the same environment, each population grew normally for the first six to eight days. Then *P. caudatum* began to diminish while *P. aurelia* continued to grow. At the end of 16 days, only *P. aurelia* survived.

Why? What happened? Neither species attacked the other, but *P. aurelia* was less sensitive to the bactera's waste products. Thus that population took ever more of the limited food, a process that inevitably had to end the way it did — the species that had, grew more abundant; the one that lacked, lost even what it had.

Under those circumstances, in that environment! When Gause pitted *P. caudatum* against *P. aurelia* in a non-bacterial culture medium, *P. caudatum* became the surviving population, again by means of differential reproduction. The environment this time favored — selected — *caudatum*.

This surprising all-or-nothing outcome led to Gause's law: competing species that exploit the same environment in the same way cannot coexist in the same place at the same time. The second surprise is that this exclusionary principle does not lead to a reduction of species, but just the opposite. The hath-hath not law leads to a diversity of niches — sets of living conditions — and species.

Darwin, in fact, had seen this phenomenon on the isolated Galapagos Islands, 600 miles west of South America. Uninhabited by humans, the islands were a natural laboratory for the study of exotic life forms. On those islands, Darwin found 14 different kinds of finches, many of which he had never seen before. There were ground finches, tree finches, a warbler finch, even a woodpecker finch — a finch that could use a spine or stiff twig plucked from a plant and held in its beak to probe for insects. The beaks of the different finches were of varying sizes and shapes best suited to the procurement of the food sought.

This is how ecologists explain the diversity of finches. A group of the birds left the mainland and, carried by the wind, found a home in the Galapagos. Food was plentiful, there was ample room and no predators. The finches did what comes naturally under such circumstances. They reproduced an ever larger population until they became a plague like the gypsy moth. Then hard times for the finches. The available food no longer was sufficient. The struggle for existence intensified with many casualties. Competition for food was fierce and a premium came with any ability to exploit new food supplies — foods different from that used by competitors. Small differences in behavior or size and shape of beak resulted in small improvements in survival and in the all-important ability to produce more young. The successful traits thus were passed on and amplified in the population until ultimately here was a subgroup of finches quite different from the others.

Darwin wrote in his autobiography that even after he had discovered the principles of selection and variation leading to species formation, he still didn't understand why there was this pressure to change into new species (some scientists today estimate there may be 30 million species). Then one day, like the proverbial scientist, Darwin shouted the proverbial "Eureka!" "I can remember the very spot in the road whilst in my carrriage, when to my joy the solution occurred to me....The solution, as I believe, is that the modified offspring of all dominant and increasing forms tend to become adapted to many and highly diversified places in the economy of nature."

Gause's niches! Each species must take over or carve out its own niche in the world. Life's never-ending inventiveness in finding new ways to exploit the environment is what has made possible the saturation of the earth with living things. Grazers eat grass, browsers eat leaves, carnivores eat meat, squirrels eat nuts, flycatchers eat insects, chickadees eat seeds, cedar waxwings eat berries, robins eat grub and worms, mosquitoes ingest blood, termites eat wood, crows eat carrion, different microorganisms finish the remaining dead organic matter — all living side by side. Millions of species in millions of niches.

It is amazing that Jesus grasped this principle of life as well. "In my Father's house," he said, "are many mansions." This saying is life's credo for successfully colonizing the planet.

The parable of The Sower is Jesus' manifesto of the survival of the fittest.

A sower went forth to sow, and some seeds fell by the wayside where birds ate them. Some seeds fell upon stony places and withered. Some fell among thorns and were choked. But some fell on good ground and brought forth fruit "some an hundredfold, some sixtyfold, some thirtyfold."

Jesus then turns this literal tale into a metaphor, which he explains to his disciples. The seed is the word of the kingdom of God and the environment is the minds of human beings. The person who does not understand is like the seed that fell by the wayside, and the wicked one devours him. The seed falling on stony places is likened to the person who gladly receives the word but it does not take root, he doesn't value it and will not act according to it or stand up for it when adversity comes. The seed among thorns is like the person who hears the word but it is overwhelmed by his involvement with cares and the deceitfulness of riches in this world. The seed on good ground is the person who understands the word, acts according to it, and has a fruitful life.

To begin with, the parable showed Jesus' comprehension of the interdependency of heredity and environment. There was an old debate inside and outside of biology that the relationship was either/or — either nature governs or nurture determines. The opposition of false alternatives has been pronounced dead, but has taken an unconscionably long time in dying, as the mid-20th century psychology of Behaviorism and the more recent Sociobiology show. The extremes of these contrasting interpretations can be judged from two books published in the 1970s. This is the way the publisher trumpeted behaviorist B.F. Skinner's book, *Beyond Freedom & Dignity:* "He tells why, instead of promoting freedom and dignity as personal attributes, we should direct our attention to the physical and social environments in which people live. It is the environment that must be changed rather than man himself if the traditional goals of the struggle for freedom and dignity are to be reached." And this was the publisher's announcement of *The Selfish Gene:* "Richard Dawkins introduces us to ourselves as we really are — the throwaway survival machines for our immortal genes. Man is a gene machine: a robot vehicle, blindly programmed to preserve its selfish genes."

Seeds are capsules of heredity, and Jesus knows that they can express themselves successfully only when they arrive in a congenial environment. That would seem to make environment the determining factor. But there must be something to express, something to start with in the seeds. In the first telling of the parable, Jesus recognizes qualitative differences in the seeds that reach good ground. Each one produces fruit according to its potential (the parable of The Talents also made a point of differential potential). In the explanation, not every mind is conducive to the growth and blossoming of the kingdom of God: only those sensibilities that can understand and nourish it. The end product results from the interaction of both heredity and environment. They are inextricably interwoven as is every organism and its environment.

The parable illustrates broad is the way to destruction, narrow is the way to life. There are many ways that the seeds can fail, but only one where they can succeed.

The parable further shows Jesus' appreciation of something discerned by few observers — the third element in what Voltaire called the "holy trinity of destiny": heredity, environment and circumstance. The seeds are sown indiscriminately, just as they are in nature. And with wasteful prodigality to improve the odds that at least one will find life. As any householder with trees in the area knows, only those seeds that find open and fertile soil, not already occupied by grass, can take root.

The word of the kingdom is broadcast in similar fashion....without the sower knowing where it will find a fertile resting place, a receptive mind and heart. Chance, an unreliable instrument, is made a means to promote success. Fruitful dissemination — that is, fruitful reception — of the word is accomplished through chance. "Chance," said Louis Pasteur, "favors only the prepared mind."

Life and chance are intimately involved in many different ways. We have seen the fantastic lottery that is the origination of an individual. Every one of the 300 million human sperm possesses a different genetic composition. If each one of that donor's sperm could fertilize an identical egg, there still would be 300 million dissimilar individuals. But when the 300 million are multiplied by the original 740,000 egg possibilities in the mother's ovaries, the odds for the selection of any particular human being become incomprehensible to our minds.

Chance is just as operative in the progression of living things that we call evolution. Evolution is a subtle and sophisticated process, but all its manifestations rest on two mechanisms — chance or randomness interacting with adaptation, the adaptation brought about by natural selection.

Chance, the ruler of the inanimate world, is the arch enemy of life. The deepest perception of the ancients was that chaos is the inhospitable, lethal opposite or opponent of the order and harmony of the cosmos. These are the two principles of non-life and life. In inanimate nature, according to the second law of thermodynamics, everything — matter and energy — tends to disintegrate into a total randomness that no longer can be useful for any purpose. After death, without the unifying force of life, the body disintegrates.

Life is locked in a mortal contest with chance. Chance must be overcome, tamed, used, exploited. Jesus gave an explicit example of one way this is accomplished in the parable of The Sower. In another example given, the roulette of conception is made to serve the quest for quality, the selection of the most deserving.

In another struggle with chance, life loses almost all the battles and yet triumphs magnificently. The replication of DNA in the division of cells is not always perfect. Every once in a while, but with enough regularity that its periodicity often can be calculated, there is a reproductive mistake in a certain section of the DNA strand. One or a certain number of genes that existed in the parent are replaced in the daughter cell. This alteration, when important enough to produce some substantial structural or behavioral change, is a mutation. Most mutations are deleterious. If the handicap is serious enough, the individual dies before reaching the age of reproduction and the harmful trait is erased. Even if the individual survives long enough to beget offspring, the disadvantage will be so limiting to the heirs that it eventually will be eliminated from the population.

If, on the other hand, the mutant change is beneficial, then its possessor will prosper and pass on the advantage, which will enhance the survival and thus reproductive capabilities in successive generations. Relatively more people will be born with the trait than those without it so that it spreads to an ever larger proportion of the population. Differential reproduction is what evolution is all about. Jesus gave this principle its due in the parable of The Sower both in the seeds that failed and those that succeeded. The seeds that fell on good ground brought forth fruit "some an hundredfold, some sixtyfold, some thirtyfold."

This phenomenon is what makes possible the marvelous mechanism of adaptation. Life, in effect, ignores the failures and keeps adding up the successes. With this kind of scorekeeping, life has been able to defeat chance, the great leveler, and populate the earth. Not only that, but life has converted the mortal danger of mutant mistakes into a requisite device for survival. Mutations give life an opportunity to be dynamic. Life forms need to change when environmental conditions change. Mutations, occurring as they do on a chance basis, provide the escape from determinism — the freedom — to evolve into new forms.

This leads to still another aspect of the parable. Modern science says that evolution is strictly a deterministic process. Whatever the environmental challenge presented by chance, living things can only — that is, *must* — respond according to their genetic repertoire. Indeed, Jesus was so impressed with this unbreakable and irresistible invariance that he advised his disciples to emulate it in their faith.

Scientists acknowledge that indviduals, and this is particularly evident in the human species, act purposefully with goals in mind. Our legal system is based on the assumption of freedom of will. If the system were based on determinism, then no one would be responsible for his actions and could not be held accountable. Society would be reduced to chaos.

When one goes much below the human level, however, it becomes difficult to distinguish voluntary, purposeful actions from involuntary determinism. Birds mating, nest building, calling, migrating all are purposeful acts. But they can equally be explained as repetitions of instinctual patterns set off by environmental and innate instinctive triggers. Plants respond to light, temperature, seasonal change and other environmental occurrences automatically. Microorganisms have chemoreceptors that enable them to find food and avoid noxious materials. In other words, behavior programed for survival. The correct decisions of the past are preserved by their beneficial effects and imprinted in the genes of successors.

Biological evolution is held to be solely the product of determinism, that is, determinism interacting with randomness, what molecular biologist Jacques Monod meant by *Chance and Necessity.*

The determinism/free will puzzle may be older than the nature/nurture debate. The relationship between determinism and free will was an issue for debate at the time Ecclesiasticus was written about 185 B.C. and must have remained a vital concern at the time of Jesus. It still has not been laid to rest. "Determinism and free will," Rene Dubos said during an interview "are crucial to an understanding of life. They are at the core of the life dilemma. I accept both. Just as a physicist accepts both waves and particles, even though incompatible, as necessary to explain physical phenomena."

Dubos cited another eminent biologist, C.H. Waddington, to show that evolution has been affected by purposeful actions as well as chance. Waddington said that some mammals, descendants of amphibians that came out of the oceans onto land, deliberately decided to return to the seas so that today we have air-breathing whales and porpoises.

It has been a mystery how the human species was transformed from ape-hominids to what we have become today. Dubos, in his book *Beast or Angel? Choices That Make Us Human* argues persuasively that the mechanism of this transformation was choice. "Throughout history and prehistory humankind has had to choose repeatedly between opposite tendencies which seem to be inherent in human nature." The weight of the decisions in the long series of choices brought us along the road to civilization. Terrible episodes in recent and current history show that we have not completed the transition from our animal heritage, and the importance of choosing remains as urgent as ever. "To be human is, first and foremost, to be able and willing to choose among the options that are offered to the human species by the natural order of things." Sound familiar? That was the conclusion of the Jewish sages who created Proverbs: choice is the pivot to life or death, good or evil, happiness or sorrow.

Choice, no matter how it is operated, is life's decisive weapon in the war against circumstance. Dubos was alerted to this early in his career as a bacteriologist. For ten years The Rockefeller Institute for Medical Research had been seeking a way to break down the capsule that shielded the bacterium of lobar pneumonia from the human defense system. Dubos' first assignment was to find the magic bullet to pierce the bacterium's armored sheath, a polysaccharide. He knew from his experience as a soil bacteriologist that there must exist some organism to destroy this substance. If this were not so, polysaccharide matter would collect and grow like a New York City dump.

After one year of experiments, Dubos found a microorganism that could produce an enzyme that would attack the polysaccharide. The microbe did this only when the bacterium, not a preferred or usual food source, was the alternative to starvation. The enzyme was not ordinarily produced and would not have appeared under normal conditions. Dubos realized that the unicelled organism has an array of biochemical options that are called forth by the demands and opportunities presented by the environment.

The mechanism of choice is presented beautifully and simply in the parable of The Sower. In the first telling, on the level of seeds and vegetation, choice does not involve free will. Seeds fall by the wayside where they are vulnerable, easy targets for birds. Seeds fall on stony places and therefore are unable to take root. Seeds fall among already prevalent thorn bushes which keep the young newcomers fom developing. But the seeds that reach fertile ground must take root and grow and produce.

When the parallels are translated at the human level, choice graduates to the realm of mind and motivation. Free will emerges. The outcome is not automatic. It could have been different. The person who receives the word of the kingdom of God but does not understand it loses it. The knowledge and wisdom are stolen by the devil. Like seeds on stony places, the message does not take root in the person who receives the word with joy, but then doesn't value it. It doesn't last long. The message won't become part of his life. He won't act on it and if it causes any trouble, he becomes irate. The third person, like seeds among thorns, receives the message, but it is crowded out of his thoughts by the cares of life and the allure of worldly riches. "But he that received seed unto the good ground is he that heareth the word and understandeth it" and therefore elects to accept the kingdom of God. His life is fruitful.

This parable on the necessity, importance and unpredictability of choice reveals further deep insights that Jesus had into life.

In order to gauge how deep, the parable can be compared to

another body of modern knowledge. In 1948, Claude E. Shannon developed what has come to be known as Information Theory, first presented in "The Mathematical Theory of Communication" in *Bell System Technical Journal*. This was followed by and to some extent enlarged upon by other communication theories. In the postwar, mass-media world, communication theories became essential and effective tools for broadcasters, telephone-telegraph-teletype services, publishers, manufacturers, advertisers, politicians, public relations firms — anyone who wanted to convey, purvey or manipulate information.

Shannon turned the communication of information from an art into a science. He did this by quantifying information into units or what he called bits. The basic idea was that information could be quantified like physical entities such as mass or energy, atoms or acres. He even used a term that until then had a meaning specific to thermodynamics. Entropy in the context of heat is energy that no longer can be used to do work. Heat energy degenerates into randomness, a basic equilibrium that is the irrecoverable end of mass-energy. The end of the cosmos would be total entropy, chaos.

In Information Theory, entropy means uncertainty. If entropy mounts beyond a certain point, if a message becomes too garbled, the receiver cannot understand it. Entropy can be guarded against by redundancy. If the sender puts in more information than is needed to grasp the message through excess repetitions, then even if some of the information is lost or distorted in transmission, the message still can get through.

This is exactly the strategy life uses to thwart the entropy brought about by chance and is the reason that Aristotle was dead wrong when he said that nature makes nothing superfluous. Redundancy of individuals ensures survival and guards against extinctions. The analogy between information and life can be carried much further. The DNA molecule is regarded today as a library of information. Entomologist and wide-ranging biologist Edward 0. Wilson writes, "In a purely technical sense, each species of higher organisms — beetle, moss, and so forth — is richer in information than a Caravaggio painting, a Mozart symphony, or any other great work of art." Each of the four strands of DNA in the ordinary house mouse, for example, has about one billion pairs of nucleotides coding for 100,000 structural genes. "The full information contained therein, if translated into ordinary-sized letters of printed text, would just about fill all fifteen editions of the *Encyclopaedia Britannica* published since 1768."

Great redundancy is built into DNA, certainly in the human chromosomes, presumably for the same reason nature makes an excess of individuals. Every time a cell divides the genetic message must get through. We know that life has carried out this communication with unexcelled faithfulness for more than three and a half billion years. The reason the immune system can cope with virtually all illnesses except those aided and abetted by advancing age is that it has retained the information from the experiences of countless organisms over eons. (One of the important reasons for the growth of cancer is that the genetic system has not had time to become acquainted with all the exotic materials that we now dispense into the environment.)

While Information Theory can be complex or abstruse, it breaks down into easily understood components. An information source sends a message to a transmitter that converts the message into a signal. The source could be a man talking into a telephone or a woman performing before a television camera. In one case, the man's voice is transformed into electrical impulses that go through a wire. In the other, the woman's image and voice are transmitted by radio waves through the atmosphere. Next, the signal must be picked up by a receiver which decodes it back into the original message so that it can reach its destination, the mind of another human being.

Information is the content of the message intended for its destination. However, extraneous information can become involved with the message at any stage. This unintended information, known as noise, can compete with or distort the message. This is the entropy that reduces the integrity of the message. The noise frequently is absorbed during transmission as audio static or visual "snow," but it could be competing sounds at the scene of the transmitter or a flaw in the receiver. It could be a hole burned by a cigarette in a newspaper page or a can of paint spilled on a book. Or the message itself might be faulty from the start: it sends conflicting signals or not the right ones. All communicators give much thought to making the message compelling to the target audience. Expressing an idea persuasively is a problem faced by all kinds of pioneers and leaders through the ages. One of the essentials, and therefore a basic strategy, is to adapt the message so closely to the dominating values and aspirations of the audience that it eagerly welcomes the message. Companies spend billions of dollars in marketing surveys in an attempt to find out if their messages are coming through effectively to potential customers.

In still another variation, the flaw could be in the mind of the intended recipient. This is what is known as psychological entropy. He doesn't get the message for all sorts of reasons: he is distracted by other concerns, his prejudice or lack of knowledge causes him to reject or not understand the message. Or he is not within earshot when the telephone rings or he has gone to the refrigerator when the commercial goes on or the set is turned off.

Communication was the life blood of Jesus' mission. The message was his doctrine, the transmitter his mouth, the signal his words. We have every reason to believe that he was a superb communicator. He spoke aphorisms, stories so memorable and thoughts so compelling that even after a generation or more of oral transmission they could be written down with sufficient fidelity to become one of our supreme treasures. He used words well enough to debate lawyers and outwit Pharisees. He must have been eloquent in his preaching because audiences flocked to him.

That leaves the other half of the communication system. The eyes of the receivers to see the healing performed, their ears to hear the words that he spoke, their minds to understand the message he conveyed. The parable of The Sower shows how well Jesus understood the communication system. In particular, he comprehended that the state of the receiver was just as critical as the message sent. In fact, Jesus puts all the emphasis on the minds of the receivers. The person who does not have the wit or knowledge to understand the message will reap none of its benefits. It is totally lost upon him. Neither can the message move and produce its good effects upon the person who is predisposed against it. Nor will a person who desires worldly possessions buy what he is selling. The message won't appeal to those consumed by lust or distracted by worries. Only the person who has the kind of character and knowledge to understand the message will act upon it. "Only that day dawns," said Henry Thoreau, "to which we are awake."

Was Jesus living in a pre-dawn when people were not yet awake to his message? "Therefore speak I to them in parables: because they seeing see not; and hearing they hear not, neither do they understand. And in them is fulfilled the prophecy of Isaiah, which saith, By hearing ye shall hear, and not understand; and seeing ye shall see, and shall not perceive: For this people's heart is waxed gross, and their ears are dull of hearing, and their eyes they have closed; lest at any time they should see with their eyes, and hear with their ears, and should understand with their heart".

Only in Matthew, where the message of Jesus often is expounded the most clearly, is the reader told explicitly in the parable of The Sower that a specific reason for exclusion from the kingdom of God is lack of understanding. And only in this version of the parable is the reader told explicitly that the person who can and chooses to enter is one who understands. This parable with its explanation by Jesus does not describe the kingdom of God, but The Sower leaves no doubt that one of the keys to this kingdom is understanding what it is.

There is one further stage in communication theory. The reaction of the receivers to the message often enough comes back to the sender, completing the feedback loop. Positive feedback is reinforcing, of course, encouraging. The applause and shouts of "Encore! Encore!" elicit more of the same. Negative feedback can have a more powerful effect upon the originator than the original message did upon the intended audience. The candidate who cannot persuade voters is not elected, the program that fails to win ratings disappears from the air, the product that does not sell is discontinued. Of course, choice is involved with the outcome. The manufacturer could choose to persevere with the product in hopes that it will catch on or modify it or change the message.

Sometime after the parable of The Sower was spoken the gospel of the kingdom was de-emphasized. Its place was taken by the Messiah. The audience was given what it wanted.

B. PSYCHOLOGICAL and NEUROBIOLOGICAL

NINE

Out Of The Mouth

The mouth as an organ of communication was a powerful and often-used image in the Old Testament. This shouldn't be surprising since the word directly spoken face to face was the main medium of social intercourse. A man's word, not his signature, was his bond. The injunction against speaking blasphemy was one of the Ten Commandments. God could hear.

The first time the word mouth is used in Genesis is when the Lord asks Cain where his brother Abel is. How should I know? Cain replies, "Am I my brother's keeper?" And the Lord says, "What hast thou done? the voice of thy brother's blood crieth unto me from the ground. And now art thou cursed from the earth, which hath opened her mouth to receive thy brother's blood from thy hand".

Early in Exodus when the Lord is summoning and encouraging Moses to be a leader of his people, Moses says, "O my Lord, I am not eloquent, neither heretofore, nor since thou hast spoken unto thy servant: but I am slow of speech, and of a slow tongue." God replies: "Who has made man's mouth, or who maketh the dumb, or deaf, or the seeing, or the blind? have not I the Lord? Now therefore go, and I will be thy mouth, and teach thee what thou shalt say."

Late in Jesus' ministry, when he is instructing his disciples about the future, there is a repetition of this passage. Jesus tells his disciples not to worry about what they will say and how well they will say it when the time comes, "For I will give you a mouth and wisdom, which all your adversaries shall not be able to gainsay nor resist." In computerese, the wisdom is the software, the mouth is the hardware. In modern parlance, a mouthpiece is an instrument to transmit the spoken word or it can be one's spokesman at law, in which case the attorney combines the message and its transmission.

With the invention of the printing press, the mouth was supplanted as the principle instrument of mass communication by journals, books and newspapers. Radio restored the spoken word to a position of eminence in mass influence. But it was not until after World War Two with television that the mouth could regain some of the importance it had at the time of Jesus.

Of course, in alluding to the mouth as an instrument of communication, Jesus was advancing nothing new. But he also refers to the mouth in a way that had no Biblical precedent. This new usage is presented with the greatest detail in the paradoxical saying about what defiles a person. The incident is reported in both Matthew and Mark. In Matthew, the word mouth is mentioned four times. In Mark, the mouth is omitted but obviously intended. Mark, however, includes a meeting of Jesus with some Pharisees and scribes that contributes to an understanding of the episode. So the following paraphrase amalgamates the two versions.

The Pharisees and scribes see that some of Jesus' disciples are eating their bread with unwashed hands. The passage explains that Pharisees and all Jews do not eat without carefully washing their hands. In the tradition of their elders, they go to great lengths to keep themselves physically pure. So they ask Jesus why his men don't follow tradition and instead eat with impure hands. Unquestionably, the sanitary laws rigorously observed by Jews contributed to the control of infections and epidemic disease and were especially important for the conditions under which the nomadic mass of people had to exist in the early days. Strict adherance to these laws was obtained by equating cleanliness and holiness, with a natural enough implication that holiness resulted from cleanliness. Jesus attacked that notion. He responds to the Pharisees and scribes by saying that Isaiah was talking about hypocrites like them when he said, "This people honoureth me [God] with their lips, but their heart is far from me. Howbeit in vain do they worship me, teaching for doctrines the commandments of men."

Jesus says that the dietary rules, which they slavishly obey, come from men and are inconsequential, but at the same time the Pharisees and scribes violate one of the Ten Commandments from God: to honor your father and mother. Jesus says the Pharisees and scribes get around this commandment through a loophole they have devised. They stretch a law in Leviticus governing offerings to the Lord to avoid giving anything at all to their parents. And, Jesus says, they have contrived many such legal trickeries. (On another occasion he said that they had created a bill of divorcement to subvert the injunction in Genesis that what God had joined together could not be separated by men.)

Following his confrontation, Jesus delivers a sermon to the people in which he says: "Not that which goeth into the mouth defileth a man; but that which cometh out of the mouth, this defileth a man."

Afterwards, the disciples tell Jesus that the Pharisees and the scribes were unhappy with what he said. Jesus tells his disciples not to be concerned. The self-appointed religious leaders are the blind leading the blind. Then the disciples say they don't understand what he meant and, in private, he explains. What is put into the mouth goes into the belly and then passes out of the body. What comes out of the mouth comes from the heart, and he mentions evil thoughts, murders, adulteries, fornications, thefts, false witness, blasphemies, covetousness, deceit, pride, foolishness. These are things that defile a person, not eating with unwashed hands.

People at the time of Jesus still believed that the heart was the organ of thought, consciousness, decision making, feelings, attitudes and emotions. This was believed all through antiquity. When Egyptians meticulously prepared their dead pharaohs for the immortal voyage, the embalmers carefully removed the organs and placed them in jars to remain with the body in the sepulcher. The heart was left in the body, however, because Egyptians believed the heart was the seat of thoughts and emotions and that like a flight recorder it kept a record of the person's acts for the gods to judge. The pharaoh's brain, believed to be worthless, was removed through the nostrils and thrown away.

No less an authority than Aristotle taught that the heart is the central abode of life, thought, soul and source of natural heat. Hippocrates made a notable dissent to the general belief. He asserted that the brain was the site for consciousness, thinking, pain, judgment and feelings. More than anything, the misconceptions and conflicting theories pointed up what a baffling mystery the body's interior was at that time. Actually, location of the site was inconsequential and irrelevant to Jesus' teaching. What he taught in this instance was a pioneering insight upon which much of his doctrine was based.

Food and drink entering through the mouth go into the alimentary canal, but what comes out of the mouth originates in an entirely different source. It emanates from the person's mind. Jesus believed that he had found a sure-fire way to perceive the human mind. His reasoning was perfectly consistent with and logically stemmed from the invariance he saw in the fruits of trees. Words are the fruits of the mind. The mouth is the faucet through which flows the person's beliefs, attitudes, precepts, values, judgments, prejudices, desires, intentions — every nuance of mind. "O generation of vipers," he said another time, "how can ye, being evil, speak good things? for out of the abundance of the heart the mouth speaketh."

The saying in Deuteronomy that man does not live by bread alone, but by every word out of the mouth of God offered another route to the same perception. The precept in the book of Moses was laid down as a commandment. It had been preceded by the other two references that Jesus cited in The Temptation — "Thou shall fear the Lord thy God, and serve him" and "Ye shall not tempt the Lord thy God". And the chapter begins two verses earlier with "All the commandments which I command thee this day shall ye observe to do, that ye may live, and multiply". Following a reference to the trials during the 40 years in the wilderness, the full verse reads: "And he humbled thee [the Hebrew people], and suffered thee to hunger, and fed thee with manna, which thou knewest not, neither did thy fathers know; that he might make thee know that man doth not live by bread only, but every word that proceedeth out of the mouth of the Lord doth man live."

In the Old Testament context, the precept says that only God knows many alternative means of subsistence and that is another reason to believe in God implicitly and obey God's commandments. Jesus gives the saying a new connotation: man does not live by material things alone, but the spiritual as well. Through the wisdom tradition, the words out of God's mouth could be interpreted as the wisdom of God. It is but one more step to deduce that what comes from the mouth of God reveals the mind of God.

From the mind come not just words. Words are heralds of behavior. The thought is father to the act. Desires, lusts, hatreds, love both precede and produce various kinds of conduct. Where your treasure is, there will be also your thoughts, concerns, protection, sacrifice. "A good man out of the good treasure of the heart bringeth forth good things: and an evil man out of the evil treasure bringeth forth evil things."

Everything proceeds from the mind. There was just one precedent for this concept in the Old Testament. Proverbs 23:7: "For as he thinketh in his heart, so is he". That saying stands alone whereas Jesus magnified and elaborated the principle throughout his doctrine.

Jesus was enabled to arrive at this concept by the Hebrew belief that body and mind are inseparably fused. Jesus carried the conviction one step further. Body and mind are together, but not equal: the mind governs the body.

Democritus believed that the soul, like the body was composed of atoms which dispersed after death. Aristotle believed the soul was the form of the body. These philosophies of body-soul fusion led to an unpleasant but unavoidable deduction: death meant the complete termination of the individual (although Aristotle hedged a little bit by saying the intellect was separable). Plato's philosophy, which poetically articulated an ancient conviction that body and soul are totally different and separate things, offered a way out of the dead end. Not only are the body and soul distinct, but the soul — that is, the sentient, thinking, feeling, conscious part of the person — could continue a noncorporeal existence after the death of the body. That is what Socrates meant when he said that philosophy is a preparation for death.

Jews rejected any possible immortality of the soul alone because they were convinced that a person could not be divided that way. But many Jews clung to a hope of survival after death through resurrection of the integrated body-mind. The Hellenic world rejected resurrection because the reassembling of bodies offended Greek rationality. By the time of Jesus, even Jews felt that resurrection had to take place before disintegration of the body, or within three days.

The good news of Jesus' Resurrection spread by Christianity served to reinforce the faith in an afterlife inculcated by Platonism. The dualism of body and soul, or mind, became the accepted doctrine in the Western world, explaining and confirming what the senses perceived to be true in this world and holding open the portals to the next one. With Gnosticism the separation of the different entities was taken to its extreme. Body and soul were antagonistic, body and mind were alien.

By the 17th century, the birth of science and revival of philosophy provided modes of thought powerful enough to challenge the dogmas of religion. Almost at the outset, a brilliant philosopher-mathematician-physiologist, Rene Descartes, reaffirmed the body-mind dualism, setting the norm for the following centuries of thought. Descartes said mind is the expression of God and although linked to the body during life cannot be understood by science. The body is a machine that is totally within the realm of human knowledge and can be explained by science. The next great philosopher, Spinoza, born 36 years after the birth of Descartes, strengthened Descartes' dichotomy. Spinoza regarded physical nature as one closed system and psychic or mental nature as another. Spinoza said there could be no causal connection between what was totally disparate.

The physical sciences progressed the most quickly, but even biology and medicine benefited from the division, at first. Investigators could concentrate on the physical structures and operations of the living machines. The more advanced discoveries in chemistry, physics and mechanics could be applied to the workings of bodies. Gradually the split hardened into absolute realms in medicine. If something was wrong with your body, you went to a physician. If you were mentally ill, you saw a psychiatrist, psychologist, psychoanalyst or psychotherapist.

But at the same time, scientists were beginning to discover physical-mental linkages. Ivan Pavlov's study of conditioned reflexes at the beginning of the 20th century was the first systematic investigation to show biological mechanisms involved in mental processes. At about the same time, Walter Cannon in the United States was tracking hormonal reactions to keep the body adjusted to environmental stimuli. It was found that the hormonal endocrine system was controlled by the hypothalamus in the brain. Biochemist Hans Selye showed that psychological stress could induce atrophied adrenal glands, duodenal peptic ulcer, heart exhaustion and death in experimental animals. From the psychological side, Sigmund Freud was finding what a profound effect childhood experiences, subconscious memories and mental activity could have on behavior.

Growing out of these findings, psychosomatic medicine tried to bridge the institutional gulf between treating mind and body. But this unorthodox medical approach for many years was unable to win many medical practitioners. Stress theory received a similar cold shoulder. These models of reality were difficult to understand, to substantiate and to utilize. The dazzling successes in the "hard" sciences, in identifying specific microbial causes of disease, in drugs and antibiotics appeared to most physicians to be the proper ways to go.

In psychology, Behaviorism seemed to be solving the mind-body problem by eliminating mind. Mental processes really were biological processes, physically conditioned reflexes that were reinforced or dissipated by environmental influences. In philosophy at mid century, the mind-body problem was a mess. There was a parallelism school a la Spinoza. The epiphenomenal school contended that since physical nature is a closed system, mental events cannot be considered as causes of changes in the human body. The interactionist school held that mental events can both cause and be caused by physical events. The 1965 *Encyclopaedia Britannica* said this belief made the most sense, but added that some philosophers have maintained there "is no intelligible or necessary connection between cause and effect."

Nevertheless, the scientific evidence and consensus for the mesh of mind and body grew in the second half of the 20th century. As early as 1951 in a popular self-help book, *The Will To Live,* psychotherapist Arnold Hutschnecker declared unequivocally that mind and body are one. This oneness holds the secret of health or illness, he said. Anxiety predisposes to physical illness. Depression is a partial surrender to death. Emotions are the first line of defense in health. "To prolong life, therefore, we ought to regard the whole person, his interest in living and his adjustment to life, instead of devoting ourselves exclusively to his physical symptoms."

In the 1960s, Rene Dubos was writing that "Cartesian dualism, useful as it has been, is leading medicine into a blind alley precisely because it is philosophically unsound....all manifestations of human disease are the consequences of the interplay between body, mind and environment."

In the 1970s, anthropologist Vernon Reynolds could write in *The Biology of Human Action* that "body and mind are inseparable and both locked within society." "In the last analysis, it is what we think that counts, and to deny this is to deny the unique feature of human evolution, the conceptual mind, which sets us apart from other species." "As Reynolds shows," anthropologist Ashley Montagu commented on *The Biology of Human Action,* "people are — to a great extent — the makers of their own nature. They are not the creatures, but the creators of their destiny."

The science of neurobiology was born and developed during this period. Scientists began to discover and document the relation between brain and mind....how the brain through the central and peripheral nervous systems and the endocrine system galvanizes actions....the biochemistry of emotions....the dominating positions of thoughts and experiences in the formation of character and behavior.

In the 1980s, a book entitled *The Brain* by Jack Fincher begins: "Every cell of the human body is ruled by the brain. Its commanding presence orders sensation, movement, thought, a lifetime of memory and dream." And neuroscientist Eric Kandel begins the definitive textbook *Principles of Neural Science:* "The key philosophical theme of modern neural science is that all behavior is a reflection of brain function. According to this view — a view that is held by most neurobiologists and that we shall try to document in this text — the mind represents a range of functions produced by the brain." Kandel defines behavior as "the manifestation of mind in the physical world."

After some two millennia, after four centuries of science, after the sedulous efforts of tens of thousands of investigators, human beings finally caught up to the insight of Jesus.

"Blessed," he said, "are the pure in heart." A pure heart is better than pure hands. Hands soil quickly, but a clean mind ensures a clean body. When you make the inside like the outside and the outside like the inside, Jesus said in the Gospel of Thomas, then you will enter the kingdom of God.

"Another parable spake he unto them: the kingdom of heaven is like unto leaven, which a woman took, and hid in three measures of meal, till the whole was leavened."

This was a great mystery at the time of Jesus. Why did the bread rise? How did it rise? It was a question of central importance. Bread was the main article of food in Palestine as it had been for human beings in the Middle East since the beginning of agriclture and long before that. Bread, in fact, sparked the agricultural revolution some 10,000 years earlier. Humans had discovered they could make a paste out of wild grains by grinding the seeds between stones and adding water. The paste was cooked on a hot stone into flat biscuits. Because this source of food offered security against hunger, people began to cultivate the wild wheat and barley growing luxuriantly in the Fertile Crescent, an arc of land that extended from east of the Tigris and Euphrates Rivers, north through the southern part of what is now Turkey and then south along the eastern Mediterranean into Palestine and Egypt. Sizeable harvests required the organization of mills for grinding. Bread was our first manufactured food.

Thousands of years later in Egypt, it is believed, a batch of flour became contaminated with airborne wild yeast, a unicelled plant organism. This time when the meal was cooked, the dough expanded. It was lighter, fluffier and tastier. Because this new bread inflated, it could not be satisfactorily heated just from the bottom but had to be baked on all sides, necessitating development of the oven. Egypt was famous for its baking industry and varieties of bread.

The ancients discovered that they could perpetuate the leaven, the agent of expansion, by saving a part of the batter and then adding it to the next lump of meal. When the people of Israel fled from Egypt, they left without taking a supply of leaven and had to eat unleavened bread in the wilderness.

The ancients had no idea that by transfering the leaven to the next batch of dough they were introducing yeast cells into the new flour. What then took place was a form of fermentation. It was not understood that fermentation was an organic process until the work of Louis Pasteur in the middle of the 19th century. He concluded: no fermentation without life. His discoveries led him to the germ theory of disease. What does happen is that sugar occurring naturally in the wheat is consumed by the yeast and in the process chemically transformed into alcohol and carbon dioxide....the same bubbles that cause effervescence in beer and wine. When the fermented dough is heated, the gas bubbles expand to make the bread porous and give it greater size. The leaven causes the meal to "grow," and growth has been shown in this inquiry to be associated with the kingdom of God.

But leaven, as Jesus uses it, has a meaning that is more important in explaining the parable. The answer unfolds in each of the three Synoptic Gospels. In Mark, after Jesus has miraculously fed the five thousand and four thousand, he is confronted by Pharisees who demand that he show a sign from heaven for his credentials. This is where he says no sign shall be given. He leaves the Pharisees and with his disciples boards a boat on the Sea of Galilee. The disciples forget to bring bread for the trip.

Jesus, still thinking about his unpleasant interview, addresses the disciples. "Take heed, beware of the leaven of the Pharisees, and of the leaven of Herod." The disciples misconstrue his remark, believing that he is angry at them for forgetting the bread. When Jesus discovers what they are talking about, he berates them. How could they possibly think he was refering to the lack of bread? Didn't they see him feed a multitude from a few loaves and fishes? "And he said unto them, How is it that ye do not understand?" The episode abruptly ends there with no further explanation.

In Luke, there is just one verse, but in it Jesus tells what he means by the leaven of the Pharisees. "In the mean time, when there were gathered together an innumerable multitude of people, insomuch that they trode upon one another, he began to say unto his disciples first of all, beware ye of the leaven of the Pharisees, which is hypocrisy."

Matthew gives the same sequence as Mark: feeding the five thousand and four thousand, the confrontation with Pharisees and this time also Sadducees. The same answer, but this time there is an addition to no sign shall be given: "but the sign of the prophet Jonas." Again Jesus departs with his disciples, they forget the bread, they misinterpret what he means about the leaven, and he criticizes them for their lack of comprehension. However, in Matthew the episode ends this way: "How is it that ye do not understand that I spoke it not to you concerning bread, that ye should beware of the leaven of the Pharisees and of the Sadducees? Then understood they how that he bade them not beware of the leaven of bread, but of the doctrine of the Pharisees and the Sadducees."

Leaven in human beings is *doctrine!* Leaven is what a person thinks, believes and advocates. It infuses and permeates every inch of his being. The germ of an idea, of an ambition, of a lust or discovery of the kingdom of God grows until it becomes all-consuming. It transforms the person, molds him, makes him what he is. There could not be a more perfect contrast between the doctrine of Jesus and our present materialist attitude. We say: You are what you eat. He said: You are what you think.

The science of nutrition is showing how important diet is to physical size, health and disease, and how poor nutrition can curtail energy, intelligence and, ultimately, life. Yes, sufficient and proper food is necessary for a healthy existence. There is justification for the saying.

But the adage is inadequate and misleading because man does not live by bread alone. In the most important ways, the human animal thrives or declines, prospers or fails, lives or dies by what goes on in his mind. Thoughts, beliefs, and consequent behavior determine the quality, and even the length, of life. They sculpt the individual.

A Renaissance humanist, Pico della Mirandola, stated this concept beautifully. God, he says, made man at the close of creation to know the laws of the universe, to love its beauty and to admire its greatness. God bound man to no fixed place, to no prescribed work and by no iron necessity. God says to Adam: "I have set thee in the midst of the world, that thou mightest be free to shape and overcome thyself. Thou mayest sink into a beast, and be born anew to the divine likeness. The brutes bring from their mother's body what they will carry with them as long as they live; the higher spirits are from the beginning, or soon after, what they will be for ever. To thee alone is given a growth and a development depending on thine own free will."

Each person, as Reynolds and Montagu said, creates himself, his nature, his destiny.

The science of neurobiology shows how this is accomplished, and in so doing corroborates the uncanny accuracy of Jesus' insight.

The broad overall structure of the brain, as other parts of the body, is constructed from the genetic blueprint. This specificity applies to all species and gives them their particular physical characteristics. Of course, there are minor variations within species because of the individual parental heredities.

In the scientific study of phyla, the broadest groupings of organisms in the animal kingdom, certain trends can be seen in the development of nervous systems as one moves up the evolutionary scale. Unicelled microorganisms, the most primitive in the sense that they are the earliest of the life forms on earth, have no nervous systems. Nerve nets first appear in coelenterates, such as coral, sea anemones and jelly fish. Flat worms have a primitive ganglion, the first cluster of nerve cells or neurons that is the prototype for a brain.

By the time we get up to the molluscs and arthropods — crustaceans, insects and arachnids — ganglia dispersed through the body are connected to a central ganglion located in the gut. In insects, space was a limiting factor for brain size. The stomachs of spiders are so reduced by the nervous system that they can only digest their prey as a liquid. These nervous systems are almost entirely programed — genetically "hard-wired" nerve connections — with the instinctual repertoires of behavior that have proved successful for the species to survive for millions of years. The choices available to these creatures are between or among set behavioral patterns that are the best responses to environmental stimuli. Individuals do not think for themselves. Their capabilities for learning are minimal.

It is only with the first vertebrates, fish, that a true brain has a chamber of its own in the head. The brain architecturally was given the room to grow and evolve in complexity through amphibians, reptiles and birds. In mammals, a feature of the brain that has negligible or only minor importance in these other classes attains ascending prominence. Not only does total brain size increase from rat to cat to chimpanzee to human being, so does the proportion of the brain known as the cerebral cortex, the outer layers of grey matter. In a human being, the neocortex, as it is also called, forms two-thirds of the mass of the brain, five-sixths of its weight and covers most of the older brain.

What has happened is that these enlarged outer layers have taken over or filtered or controlled almost all of the functions once carried out by the more primitive parts of the brain. The neocortex has taken charge and performs all the higher functions such as thinking and remembering. Not the least of the achievements of neurobiology is to verify what a fantastic instrument the human brain is. There are somewhere between ten billion and 100 billion neurons. From conception until birth an average of 20,000 neurons must be formed *every minute.*

As impressive as the population of neurons might seem, the real measure of the complexity of the human brain lies in the fact that each cell is connected to from 1,000 to 100,000 other neurons. That means anywhere from ten trillion to ten quadrillion interconnections by which neurons can send and receive information. Each synapse, the juncture between nerve connections, is a go-no go decision gate that can send or block impulses, suggesting the enormous potential for mental flexibility. In fact, neuroscientists are coming to believe that intellectual capacity rests on the number of neuronal inter-connections, the channels open for cortical communication. Native intelligence may be the ability or limits of individual neurons to form links with other brain cells.

There is still another progression in the development of the cerebral cortex in mammals. The neocortex of a rat is almost entirely filled with areas that direct the animal's sensory and motor functions and with instinctual behavioral characteristics. Very little of the rat's cortex is left unassigned at birth. This open or association area increases from rat to cat to dog to monkey to chimpanzee to human being. What the association area is for, neurobiologists have discovered, is learning that does not by genetic necessity have to be related to some bodily function.

By many painstaking investigations mapping the brain, scientists have made the startling discovery that most of the human cortex is composed of association areas. To be sure, the human child starts out with some necessary instincts at birth. It knows how to find the mother's nipple and to suckle. Its prehensile grip is prematurely strong, a holdover from the time when it had to cling for its life to its tree-borne mother. The top central part of the human cortex is assigned to the body's motor and sensory functions. A small section at the back governs visual processes. The auditory area is in a low central spot and not far away is the speech center — the structure of language is built into our neocortex, what we learn is a local variation.

The size of association areas is a physical explanation for

gradations in mammalian learning capacities. On the evolutionary scale, the dog is a highly intelligent animal. Now we can make a presumption why you can't teach an old dog new tricks. The learning space is totally hard-wired and/or the aging neurons have lost the ability to forge new channels.

In human beings, the cortical area available for learning and the storage of unspecified information is, comparatively, vast. No one knows how long a human being would have to live before exhausting this capacity, but it appears to be more than ample for the human lifespan.

The way that any brain learns anything is by arranging the information in neuronal connections as a response to environmental stimuli. For instance, as soon as a cat's eye neurons are exposed to light they quickly form the nerve associations that fix that cat's vision for life. Under natural conditions the visual system will be normal. However, if the neurons in a cat's eye are deprived of visual stimulation for a certain period after birth, they develop abnormally. Scientists have rigged early exposures so that one cat could not recognize vertical lines, another horizontal lines. These defects cannot be corrected. Once set, the visual apparatus is locked in for life.

Before the environmental impingement, the neuron is uncommitted. This uncommitted state is known as plasticity. It is the plasticity of the human brain that is the marvel of creation and is the reason for the uniqueness of humans among all living things. As Pico della Mirandola said, God bound humans to no ecological niche, to no particular way to earn a livelihood and by no instinctual absolute.

At birth, most neurons in the human brain are not committed and most areas of the cerebral cortex are uncommitted to any particular type of learning. What the uncommitted neurons in the uncommitted areas *are* programed to do, however, is to respond to environmental influences. To learn whatever, one way or another. They learn from what they are exposed to, from what we experience. We learn from experiences. That's why an enriched environment, one with lots of beneficial stimulation, is advised for infants and young children —because that is precisely the way to achieve optimal development of their mental capabilities. An enriched environment is just as important for old people to keep their minds functioning and growing. Neuroscientists and gerontologists believe that far too many people are warehoused in impoverished environments where they sink into senility.

The plasticity of the human brain means that it is as susceptible to negative as to profitable influences. An abused child is likely to develop into an abuser. An unloved and cruelly mistreated child often turns into a walking time bomb, needing just some small social slight to trigger an act of violence. Research has found that the sense of hopelessness from a shattered childhood can turn into the rage and psychological preparation for the making of a cold-blooded terrorist.

These are blatant examples of the way the process works and they involve early childhood experiences when the person still has little power over his destiny. With a normal childhood, the individual gains increasing control over selecting the influences that will form himself. "We shape our buildings, and afterwards our buildings shape us," Winston Churchill declared in explaining the importance of rebuilding the House of Commons the way it had been before World War Two bombings. We choose our vocations, our friends, our ways of life, what we will believe and then these environmental influences mold our brains. We form our brains and then our brains shape our minds, our behavior and our lives.

Neurobiologist Steven Rose in *The Conscious Brain* explained how plasticity of the brain can have double-edged consequences even under benign circumstances. A scientist is taught to recognize in nature what is important for his specialty, to think in certain disciplined ways based upon what his predecessors already have learned in order to perform the kinds of experiments that will add to that knowledge. "By the time the scientist is through his socialization process, it is very difficult for him to think, select and remember out of the experimental rut which the plasticity of his brain has dug during his training."

The philosopher Alfred North Whitehead observed that for all the virtues of specializing, and this may be the only way we now can cope with the enormous range of knowledge today, specialists lose their capacity to think in terms of the whole. Dubos noted that scientists act and write as if their own narrow discipline affords the only or best access to reality. This attitude isn't confined to scientists, of course. Different points of view go with the territory, whether one is a priest, a prince or a prostitute. An environmentalist, painter, civil engineer, duck hunter and developer looking at the same marsh will see different images because of the differences in their perceiving minds produced by their training.

Whether or not this mental diversity is desirable, it is unavoidable.

It is the product of plasticity, but also a sign that this plasticity becomes more circumscribed by experiences. The brain becomes more wired whether the person chooses his social circumstances deliberately or by default. Rose defines the self as the sum of the experiences to date and the individual's reactions to the experiences stored in the brain. Physicist Erich Harth in *Windows On The Mind: Reflections on the Physical Basis of Consciousness* says there are two selfhoods, the physical uniqueness of our bodies recognized by the immune system as self and "that other selfhood which is largely experiential and is expressed in our central nervous system."

All of this new knowledge is implicit in Jesus' teaching of the primacy of the mind. What a person thinks and chooses to do, in the parable of The Sower, determine what he becomes and what happens to him. What is in his mind inevitably rules his behavior and is revealed by his words and acts. What he believes, his doctrine, leavens his entire being and makes him what he is. Even the two selfhoods, the physical and the spiritual, are acknowledged by his saying that man lives by bread and by the word of God. In Jesus' value system, we know which one takes precedence. "Seek ye first the kingdom of God, and his righteousness; and all these things shall be added unto you."

This information still doesn't tell what the kingdom is, but it does disclose where it is. The kingdom of God is in the mind.

TEN

The Finger Of God

Jesus saw the primacy of the mind in operation every time he performed an act of healing. He knew that a requisite for his success was that the other person had to believe without reservation in Jesus' ability to cure him. Jesus' appreciation of the crucial role of faith — of the power of the mind — was described in Chapter One.

In order to show the point beyond any doubt, two of the incidents reported in the first chapter will be examined further. The first is the case of the palsied man. That occurred in Capernaum where Jesus was highly esteemed. He was preaching the kingdom of God from a house and was surrounded by a crowd of listeners. Four men arrived at the scene carrying a bed with a man suffering from palsy. This pathological condition causes uncontrollable tremors with partial or complete paralysis. Seeing the multitude of people, the four bearers realized that they never would be able to get through to Jesus. But they were determined. They somehow managed to get onto the roof of the house with the bed, probably no more than a cot. Then they somehow lowered the bed with its sufferer to a position beside Jesus. "When Jesus saw their faith, he said unto the sick with palsy, Son, thy sins be forgiven thee." Some scribes who were present objected to what Jesus said as blasphemy because only God could forgive sins. Jesus retorted that they were quibbling over a technicality. "But that ye may know that the Son of man hath power on earth to forgive sins, (he saith to the sick of the palsy,) I say unto thee, Arise, and take up thy bed and go thy way into thine house. And immediately he arose, took up the bed, and went forth before them all."

The coupling of disease with sin was a belief that went back to the ancient tribes of Israel. Soon after the escape from Egypt in Exodus, God tells Moses: "If thou wilt diligently hearken to the voice of the Lord thy God, and wilt do that which is right in his sight, and wilt give ear to his commandments, and keep all his statutes, I will put none of these diseases upon thee, which I have brought upon the Egyptians: for I am the Lord that healeth thee."

Jesus said his acts demonstrated God's power. However, the healing power of diety was shared by many people. Priests in Egypt were the mediators of faith healing as were priests in ancient Greece.

Sick people came to temples of Asclepius where religious rites were performed along with purifying baths, anointments and fasting. The immense number of offerings left by patients in these sanctuaries indicated the efficacy of faith healing. The connection between faith and cure goes far back in human prehistory to witch doctors and shamans who were able to inspire the sufferer's belief in their healing powers.

"When Jesus saw their faith," he saw the signal that he could succeed.

The necessity of belief was shown with absolute clarity by Jesus' negative experience at his home town of Nazareth where his neighbors knew him too well as Mary's son the carpenter to trust him as a healer. Because of their disbelief, he was unable to do any mighty works as he had at a synagogue in Capernaum. Jesus said to them, "Ye will surely say unto me this proverb, Physician, heal thyself: whatsoever we have heard done in Capernaum, do also here in thy country." It may seem strange for Jesus to allude to himself as a physician. This is the only place in the Gospels where he does so, and even here it is someone else's saying and is used in a generic sense. He preferred to regard his healing work as part of his role as a prophet. He said at Nazareth that prophets were not honored in their own country and town and family. But in the Gospel of Thomas, Jesus makes his meaning very explicit: "A prophet is not acceptable in his own village; a physician does not heal those who know him."

That faith healing still works miracles and still is connected with religion are testified to by the crutches, wheelchairs and eyeglasses at Lourdes in France, Ste. Anne de Beaupre in Quebec, the practice of Christian Science and the achievements of some evangelists and charismatics. Nothing has changed except that we are learning much more about how the mind exactly does rule the body.

At the time of Jesus, people still held an ancient belief that disease was an outward sign that the victim was inhabited by a demon. Many people today — familiar with stress, viruses, bacteria, genetic defects and other such causes of illness — might be uneasy at Jesus commanding unclean spirits to leave bodies. Such an old-fashioned understanding of the actual situation could raise doubts about his track record.

Reason why such fears are unnecessary was given by molecular biologist and Nobel laureate Francois Jacob in a discussion of how modern science began. First of all, Jacob says that "it is probably the structure of the Judeo-Christian myth that made modern science possible." Western science is founded on "the doctrine of an orderly universe created by a God who stands outside of nature and controls it through laws accessible to human reason."

Before science could begin, humans needed a new vision of their world, Jacob says. This was furnished by the invention in art of perspective and depth, light and shade. Painting was transformed from symbolizing to *representing*. A series of other substitutions followed: action for prayer, history for chronicle, drama for mystery, novel for tale, polyphony for monody, and scientific theory for myth. Myths and scientific theories operate on the same principle. "The object is always to explain visible events by invisible force, to connect what is seen with what is assumed....A disease can be viewed as the result of a spell cast on the patient or a viral infection."

What is fascinating is that the scientific approach is not always more effective, still another affirmation of the overriding importance of the particular mind and the degree of confidence in the prevailing social concepts. In 1981, *The Journal of the American Medical Association* reported the story of a 28-year-old Philippine-American woman who was diagnosed as having systemic lupus erythematosus, a serious autoimmune disease in which the immune system attacks rather than defends the body's organs. The woman was given various drugs to no avail. She sought a second opinion which confirmed the first diagnosis and was told to start using even more powerful drugs to suppress the immune response. The woman instead decided to go back to her native village in a remote part of the Philippines. She went to a local witch doctor who removed the curse put on her by a former suitor. Three weeks later, after returning to the United States, the woman had no symptoms of lupus and remained free of the disease thereafter.

The phenomenon of voodoo death involves just such a curse. Dr. Walter Cannon, the discoverer of the body's homeostatic mechanisms, cited the case of a native tribesman who worked on a sugar plantation in Queensland, Australia. The man said he was going to die because a spell had been put on him and nothing could be done about it. The medical doctor at the plantation examined the man and found him to be normal. Yet he grew weaker, and there was nothing the physician could do, until the man died. How could pointing a bone with an incantation kill? The autopsy revealed no obvious cause of death.

Dr. Cannon came to the conclusion that the curse was deadly because the victim *believed* it. The fear triggered the body's defense mechanisms, but there was nothing to fight. No germs, no cuts, no enemy who could be physically overcome. The wound was in the mind. The terror could not be alleviated. The body's chemical and nervous defenses could not be turned off. They raced like a car engine with the brakes locked, until something burned out.

Dr. Herbert Benson in his book *The Mind/Body Effect* says, "The success of such practices is dependent upon both the victim's awareness of the spell cast and the victim's strong adherence to his society's belief systems." These factors lead to the conviction that any hope of escape is impossible. The imagination, the mind, does the rest.

Benson cited a modern equivalent of voodoo death. A 45-year-old professional man found himself in an intolerable situation which required him to move to another town. Just before his departure, other difficulties arose to make the move as repugnant as staying. Still, in a state of high emotion, he went ahead with the change even though the life he was going to was as impossible as the one he was leaving. About half way on his trip, the train stopped at a station and he went outside to pace on the platform. When it was time to reboard the train, the man knew he couldn't go on. But neither could he go back. His solution: he dropped dead.

Dr. Benson, an expert on the heart-nervous system complex and pioneer of the stress-reducing Relaxation Response, says sudden deaths from intense psychological states in healthy people almost certainly are due to circulatory failure and disruption of normal heart functioning.

When I was working at a New York television station during the turbulent 1960s, there was a dedicated cameraman in his early fifties who was assigned with his crew and reporter day after day to cover unrest and street fighting in Brooklyn. The assignment was particuarly hazardous for a cameraman because with the camera lens pressed to the eye, he could not see thrown bricks and missiles that came hurtling in his direction. Several of our crewmen had been hurt or experienced near misses. It was nasty work. On this particular evening, as the cameraman left for home, he was heard to say, "I'm not going to do that any more." Yet he could imagine what his assignment would be in the morning. His code was not to shirk an assignment. The cameraman died during the night from a heart attack.

George Engel, a professor of psychiatry and medicine at the University of Rochester Medical Center, found the sense of powerlessness to be strongly associated with sudden death. Feelings of helplessness and hopelessness lead to a giving up.

These powerful negative attitudes also are involved in other disease states. Arthur Schmale Jr., also at the University of Rochester Medical School, interviewed 51 women who were undergoing examinations to see if they had cancer of the cervix. Previous Pap tests showed that each of the women had some irregular or suspicious but not cancerous cells. The interviews disclosed that 18 of the women had experienced some profoundly distressing life situation within the preceding six months. Dr. Schmale and a co-investigator predicted that the 18 women would have developed cancer while the other 33 would not. Eleven of the 18 did have cancer as did eight of the other 33. The predictions were 70 percent accurate.

A rigorously controlled study conducted at King's College Hospital Medical School in London arrived at strikingly similar results. A group of women with breast cancer was examined from 1974 to 1984. At the end of the ten-year period, 70 percent of the women who displayed aggressive determination to conquer the disease still were alive; only 25 percent of the women who felt fatalisic or hopeless survived.

The list of psychological factors predisposing to cancer compiled by O. Carl Simonton and Stephanie Matthews-Simonton, two innovative therapists in the field, was:

1. A great tendency to hold resentment and a marked inability to forgive

2. A tendency toward self-pity

3. A poor ability to develop and maintain meaningful, long-term relationships

4. A very poor self-image.

Since the mind plays such an important role in the onset and progress of neoplastic disease, the Simontons strive to improve the patient's self-esteem, and to recruit the patient's suggestible mind in the fight for recovery. The Simontons teach their patients to conjure mental images of their white blood cells knocking out cancerous cells. The tactic has proved to be beneficial.

Nicholas Hall, Allan Goldstein and their colleagues at the George Washington University School of Medicine have been measuring this technique physiologically. Along with relaxation therapy, patients imagined that their cancer cells were being crushed by the legions of the immune system. A pilot study showed that such imagining actually did rally the immune system: cancer-fighting lymphocytes were mobilized at an accelerated rate.

So, again, the mind is a two-edged sword. It can cut either way, depending on how it is employed. Dr. Kenneth Pelletier couldn't have made this phenomenon any plainer in his book on holistic medicine than in the title he chose: *Mind As Healer, Mind As Slayer.*

This mental influence on health, disease and recovery first was suspected in modern times through the placebo effect. A placebo traditionally is an inert pill that was given to subjects in tests of the effectiveness of proposed drugs. One group of people would be given the drug, a second group given placebos, and then the results compared. Time after time, researchers discovered that a certain number of subjects benefited from the placebos which produced no organic effect. "It is a remarkable fact," Rene Dubos writes, "that the percentage of success is the same whatever use placebos are put; approximately 35 per cent of all treated cases exhibit a placebo effect." The percentage probably reflects a combination of the persons most receptive to suggestion and those suffering from ailments that are psychosomatic.

"When Jesus saw their faith," he proceeded to cure the palsied man. When two blind men asked him to cure them, Jesus replied, "Believe ye that I am able to do this?" They said, "Yea, Lord." And he touched their eyes, saying, "According to your faith be it unto you." And they could see. On many occasions Jesus emphasized the necessity of belief. This does raise the possibility that he exercised some kind of selection and thereby increased the odds for his success. What would he have done if the two blind men had answered, "We're not sure, Lord"? A prudent surgeon is very reluctant to operate on a patient who does not believe he will survive the operation.

On the other hand, there is the physician as placebo effect. Jesus had the ability to inspire the confidence that Hippocrates knew to be extremely important in the healing art. The Greek father of modern medicine emphasized the importance of the physician's demeanor and bedside manner. At the beginning of the 20th century, the most influential physician in the United States was William Osler who attributed his phenomenal success as a healer precisely to the confidence he could inspire. Dr. Osler extolled "The Faith that Heals....Faith in the gods or the saints cures one, faith in little pills another, hypnotic suggestion a third, faith in a common doctor a fourth."

One other element is involved. "Certainly the physician's sympathy for the human condition is one basic ingredient of the art of medicine," Dubos writes in *Man, Medicine, and Environment.* "Numerous writings, from Hippocrates on, express how fundamental and long-standing is this need for compassion in the physician." When Jesus cured the demented man tormented by a legion of devils, a man who was an outcast, living naked in a graveyard, and violent, Jesus showed compassion as well as courage. The man was undyingly grateful to him. We are told on many occasions that the poor sufferers asked for mercy and he had compassion on them. That was his business, saving lives, physically and spiritually.

Dubos expressed his belief in the importance of faith healing in a book that he wrote about a colleague, Oswald Avery, at The Rockefeller Institute for Medical Research (later to become The Rockefeller University). Avery with two colleagues made the initial discovery that the hereditary material was in DNA in the chromosomes, opening the entire field of molecular genetics. In *The Professor, The Institute and DNA,* Dubos wrote that in the original text he had "included some 10 pages devoted to the place of the various practices of faith healing (self healing) in medical history. However, the four persons who read the typescript felt that this subject should be deleted because it had no 'obvious relevance'...I have reluctantly followed their advice and shall publish these pages elsewhere. But I must at least state my opinion that, although the relevance of psychological aspects of healing to scientific medicine is not obvious, it is nevertheless extremely important, and may become even more so in the near future."

The passage reveals the status of the mental component in scientific medicine in 1976 and the prophetic vision of Dubos.

In the brief period since then Dubos already has been vindicated. The very next year Roger Guillemin and Andrew Schally won Nobel prizes for their work detailing how the brain communicates biochemically with the endocine system. Before and since then, an enormous amount of research has shown how stress — caused more often psychologically than physically — can cause disease. Stress now is linked with every major killer disease in industrialized nations and the biggest crippler, arthritis.

The way psychological stress works is that the brain recognizes a situation that is potentially dangeous or in some way unpleasant. An assessment is made whether the predicament can be avoided, remedied or coped with. Coping or the belief that one can cope blunts the stress response. A negative interpretation starts a cascade of stress-related mechanisms. The hypothalamus in the brain alerts both the sympathetic branch of the autonomic nervous system and the pituitary, the master gland of the endocrine system. The sympathetic system triggers one part of the adrenal glands to pump adrenaline (epinephrine) and noradrenaline (norepinephrine) into the blood stream to mobilize the body for action, the famous flight-or-fight response. The pituitary secretes the hormone ACTH to elicit from the adrenals a variety of steroid hormones that provide long-term defenses against stress.

These pathways of internal response are known as the psycho-neuroendocrine system. The existing literature on these phenomena is voluminous. More recently, researchers have been finding the link between mind-stress-brain-nervous system-endocrine system with the immune system, thus completing the entire network of the body's defenses and their intimate relationship with mental influences.

In the 1960s, investigators were under the impression that the immune system functioned independently of the rest of the body. Now research is showing that the immune system is inextricably meshed with the brain, endocrine and autonomic nervous systems. Acute stress can suppress activity of the thymus gland's production of lymphocytes that constantly roam the body on search-and-destroy missions for foreign intruders. This provides a very good model for how cancer can get started. A chemical or some other kind of carcinogen causes one or more normal cells to become malignant. Normally, lymphocytes will recognize these indigenous rogue cells as foreign and eliminate them. If, however, the body's corps of scouts and sentinels has been reduced, the cancer cells may escape detection. Once a colony of cancer cells is established, it may be able to resist even an immune system that has returned to normal. The loss of surveillance could account also for the onset of pneumonia and other infectious diseases.

It has been discovered in recent years that the rate of morbidity and mortality is abnormally high after the death of a spouse, a powerful cause of stress. Now studies have shown that during the time of bereavement lymphocytes are less able to react to intruders.

Hall and Goldstein say that as recently as the beginning of the 1980s the medical community viewed the connection of mental states and immunity "as a mixture of pseudoscientific hocus-pocus, self-delusion and dumb luck." Now we are seeing the beginning of a new integrative science, psychoneuroimmunology. "The discovery of pathways that bind the brain and the immune system rescues the behavioral approach to disease from the shadowy practices of witch doctors and places it squarely within the rational tradition of Western medicine."

Behavior as used here is exactly in the sense given by neuroscientist Eric Kandel: "the manifestation of mind in the physical world."

Herbert Benson, another champion of behavioral medicine, says that Western civilization "seems unable to reject" Descartes' dichotomy between the mind and the body whereas the strength of primitive medicine and religion derives from the unity of life and thought.

Another name for behavioral medicine is holistic medicine — health depends upon the proper and integrated functioning of the whole person, body and mind. Modern medicine is being forced to accept the Hippocratic concept that illness means the whole person is sick and the whole person must be taken into consideration and treated.

This, too, was the profound understanding of Jesus: the indissoluble union of the body and mind, of the spirit and health. He saw health precisely in terms of wholeness.

To the woman who touched his garment and was cured of her hemorrhaging, he said, "Thy faith hath made thee whole." To blind Bartimaeus upon restoring his sight, Jesus said, "Thy faith hath made thee whole." To the leper that Jesus healed: "Thy faith has made thee whole." Jesus knew that a house divided cannot stand, and that a divided person is sick. In the three Synoptic Gospels, Jesus is quoted as saying, "They that are whole need not a physician."

On one occasion, Jesus suggested a new dimension to the act of healing. "If I with the finger of God cast out devils," he said in what is accepted by modern scholars as certainly one of his authentic statements, "no doubt the kingdom of God is come upon you."

In addition to the primacy of the mind, Jesus preached the necessity of the unity of the mind.

If Thine Eye Be Single

One evening Jesus and his disciples were sitting down to dinner in a public house when they were joined by "many publicans and sinners." That is, non-religious Jews and other persons of low status and ill repute. These people obviously felt comfortable with Jesus and wanted to be with him. One can imagine a big table at which there is a certain amount of camaraderie, raucous laughter and crude talk. After all, this is the social milieu from which the disciples were drawn.

A group of fastidious Pharisees, the socially elite, come upon this scene — catch him at a supposed indiscretion. Indignant and never missing an opportunity to score a point, the Pharisees ask the disciples why Jesus, a purported prophet, is associating with these kinds of people. Jesus, soon aware of the indictment, tells the Pharisees, "They that be whole need not a physician, but they that are sick." Then he asks if they know what the prophet Hosea meant by his saying that God wanted to see compassion in his people rather than sacrifice and burnt offerings. "I am not come to call the righteous," Jesus says, "but sinners to repentence."

But who are the sinners? The Bible says the traditional sinners are sitting at the table with Jesus. He announced at the synagogue in Nazareth, reading from Isaiah, that the spirit of the Lord had appointed him to preach to the poor, set free the downtrodden, minister to the sick. When he tells the Pharisees that not healthy but sick people need a physician, Jesus seems to be answering their accusation by ostensibly referring to his dinner associates. But is he? He immediately follows that statement by reminding the Pharisees that a truly religious person would have compassion on those less fortunate than himself instead of deceiving himself with empty religious forms. He follows that statement by saying he has not come to call the righteous — seeming to mean the Pharisees — "but sinners to repentence."

However, the doctrine in that passage is addressed to the Pharisees. We have no idea what he taught the publicans and sinners at the table. We are not told. Presumably, Matthew, Mark and Luke did not consider that part important. That is not the point of the story. The point is that Jesus, like the Suffering Servant, is calling to repentence sinners *who do not know they are sinners.* He ministers to people who are suffering from a fracture of the mind. The ailment he seeks to cure is hypocrisy.

A significant portion of Jesus' teaching is directed against the evils of hypocrisy. The most frequent target was the hypocrisy of the Pharisees and scribes. They scrupulously obeyed the letter of the law while, in Jesus' eyes, committed the more serious crime of violating its spirit. The Sadducees and lawyers came in for blame, too. They all looked to find faults where others erred. They were forever righteously judgmental. "Judge not," Jesus admonished in the Sermon on the Mount, "that ye be not judged. For with what judgment ye judge, ye shall be judged." "Why beholdeset thou the mote that is in thy brother's eye, but considerest not the beam that is in thine own eye?"

"Not everyone that saith unto me, Lord, Lord, shall enter into the kingdom of heaven, but he that doeth the will of my Father which is in heaven." Doeth is as far from professeth as righteousness from sin. It is not a matter of theology or morality. Because of the way the brain is formed, what the person does is the antecedent for what he becomes. A person is what he has done and does what he is.

Dennis Garvin lost the last relative he had to care for him when he was eight years old. Alone in the world, he had to survive on his own — "root pig or die," he put it. Not an easy task for a lad so young in the devastated South after the Civil War, especially for a black boy. More than 90 years later, when a Social Security agent visited Garvin, the centenarian was bedridden. But the windows in his room were wide open, he enjoyed what he could see of the outside world, and his conversation was animated. When the visitor asked him to what he attributed his longevity, Garvin replied with reverence, "The Lord. Seek ye first the kingdom of God." Then he paused, searching for the rest of the answer. "Ask and ye shall receive." Another pause. Then with all the assurance of conviction he proclaimed: "But you have to live it."

A person must practice a sincere righteousness in order to enter the kingdom of God, Jesus said. The sham righteousness of the scribes and Pharisees wouldn't do it. In fact, Jesus said, they were so hopelessly confused and lost that they could not possibly find the kingdom. Unfortunately, they were misleading many other people who sincerely wanted to discover the kingdom for themselves.

As noted in Chapter Four, the fabulous wealth acquired by Solomon for the Jewish state produced the severest challenge to the Jewish religion. The allure of riches competed with the righteousness of Yahweh, causing the divided kingdom that Jesus said could not stand. The affluent despised the poor, the powerful ruled the devout. Wisdom gained a bad reputation because it was used exclusively to serve the state, as were riches — both producing the apparatus and structure of force needed to control dissent.

The prophets accentuated the split society. Isaiah condemned the people's wickedness, and saw God's punishment in Assyrian iron. Stricken Israel fell. Jeremiah saw the division in the people as a corporate sickness. He said the nation was dying. Stricken Judah fell.

The secular wisdom in Ecclesiastes, a wisdom book written after the Exile, was that both the material and spiritual were needed for existence. However, the spiritual no longer was justice — Ecclesiastes couldn't find much of that — it was wisdom. Money is a defense against the threats to survival, Ecclesiastes said, and so is wisdom: "but the excellency of knowledge is, that wisdom giveth life to them that have it."

The Second Isaiah liberated wisdom so that it could assume its normal role of providing for the betterment of all people. The Suffering Servant allied wisdom with righteousness. Wisdom was the discoverer and proclaimer of God's universal justice.

Rich men gained bad reputations during the Greek domination of Palestine. Not only were the wealthy often apostates from the religion as of old, but they wanted to Hellenize the nation, threatening the very existence of Jewish identity.

With Jesus, the division that for so long was viewed as national and societal was internalized. It was the fork in the road for each person's journey through life. The dilemma confronts each of us today and how we solve it molds our lives. We need income to put bread on the table, to clothe and educate our children, to pay medical bills, to buy a car and television set, to take a vacation, to buy a second home, to start a new business, to invest for future security, to expand the business, to buy an airplane, to buy an estate, to buy a yacht, to pay for an improved public image, to buy other people to serve our ends, to corrupt justice — where does it end? Where should it end?

There is a Spanish song that reflects the human condition — *Todos queremos mas,* We all want more. Rising expectations, the American dream, Horatio Alger, becoming Number One, fame and fortune, hard-earned success, to win at all costs. They all are mixed up in our culture. Millionaires are a dime a dozen. Today the billionaires are admired. Wealth appears to be all gain and no loss. Wealth confers all the advantages, all the benefits, all the rewards in life's competition: public respect, self-esteem, comfort, luxury, security, and with economic security peace of mind.

Yet Jesus said the poor are blessed and the rich are damned. One of his most famous sayings is that it is easier for a camel to go through the eye of a needle than for a rich man to enter the kingdom of God. The saying was preceded by the story of the rich young man who asked Jesus what he must do to gain eternal life. Jesus said to him, "If thou wilt enter into life, keep the commandments." Which ones? the young man asked. Jesus said: Do not murder, nor commit adultery, nor steal, nor bear false witness, honor your father and mother, and love your neighbor as yourself. The young man said he always had done all those things. What else? "Jesus said unto him, If thou wilt be perfect, go and sell that thou hast, and give to the poor, and thou shalt have treasure in heaven; and come and follow me. But when the young man heard that saying, he went away sorrowful: for he had great possessions."

Jesus coined the term treasure in heaven which he opposed to inferior material wealth that is vulnerable to moth and rust. In the parable of The Dishonest Steward, the lord tells the manager who has cheated him that if he could not be trusted with money, "who will commit to your trust the true riches?"

What are these precious things? A surprising answer was to be found in *The New York Times.* The newspaper gave extensive coverage to the murder in Central Park of an affluent teenage girl by a wealthy 19-year-old boy. Both habituated East Side bars that were hangouts for the elite sons and daughters of rich people. These privileged youngsters went to the finest preparatory schools and most prestigious universities, expected to take European vacations, expected to go on to high-paying jobs, had plenty of money to spend with easy access to glamorous night life, and said they wanted to continue the good life that money can bring.

They seemed to enjoy the best of everything with no deprivation. Well, not quite. *Times* reporters kept digging into the social situation, and a drastically different picture began to emerge. Wealth actually was impoverishing these young lives. John Levy, the director of the C.C. Jung Institute, explained how this could be possible. Dr. Levy said the environment of wealth tends to lead to psychological maladies that he calls "affluenza." The symptoms of affluenza include boredom, guilt, low self-esteem, and lack of motivation. Boredom because there is no challenge in their lives. Guilt and low self-esteem because they haven't earned anything and have no achievements in which to take pride. Lack of motivation because their futures already are economically secure. Dr. Levy says the family wealth insulates the children from challenge, risk and consequence — the very and vital ingredients they need to achieve significant, fulfilling lives and to experience what probably is life's greatest satisfaction, to make it on your own. It is no surprise, then, that the scions of family fortunes rarely achieve anything notable.

Not only does the wealth rob the children of the best part of their lives, it deprives them of their parents. The young people spent all their evenings and nights in the chic cafes because they, in effect, had been banished there by absentee parents. It was simpler and certainly no burden to give the child a 20 or 50 dollar bill for the evening than to provide the time, effort, guidance and responsibility in a home environment. One of the young people complained that it was hard to know your father when he worked 20 hours a day to make money.

"If you choose to spend your time making money and being on the fast track," said psychologist Bernice Berk, "that is a choice. And the children know that. When a parent spends 90 percent of their time making more money than they could possibly spend and five percent of their time with the family, those values are passed on to the kids. It tells them families are not important. Making money, having money, spending money is."

The economist John Kenneth Galbraith has written that much attention is paid to the stratospheric salaries, perquisites, stock options, golden parachutes, and economic security of corporation executives. More attention should be paid, Galbraith says, to what they give up in return. Their total, 24-hour devotion to the organization is made at the expense of family, friends, sex, recreation, and sometimes health and effective control of drinking alcohol. The executive relinquishes the right to personal thought and expression, slavishly abiding by whatever is the corporate line. Increasingly, the sacrifice includes personal identity, even public recognition of the executive's achievements. Galbraith says people once knew the heads of great corporations. Now they are disappearing into a corporate anonymity. Considering all this along with the renunciation of a wide range of enjoyments, Galbraith concludes that the modern executive should be paid well "to give up so much....of one's only certain life."

Jesus made the same point in the parable of The Rich Fool. There was a landowner who was inundated with the bounty of his produce. He asked himself what he was going to do. "And he said, This will I do: I will pull down my barns, and build greater; and there will I bestow all my fruits and my goods. And I will say to my soul, Soul, thou hast much goods laid up for many years; take thine ease, eat, drink, and be merry. But God said unto him, Thou fool, this night thy soul shall be required of thee."

"I went to the woods because I wished to live deliberately," Henry Thoreau wrote in *Walden*, "to front only the essential facts of life, and see if I could not learn what it had to teach, and not, when I came to die, discover I had not lived. I did not wish what was not life, living is so dear." Don't let the mirage of security, Jesus advises, steal your birthright to experience a full life.

There is another lesson in the parable of The Rich Fool. It could be called the Evolution of an Entrepreneur. We see it happen all the time with American corporations. A firm starts out making a certain product. The company learns how to manufacture the best product in the field. As a result, the corporation starts making good profits. Not only does the industrial growth ethic prod the firm to strive for greater profits, but a subtle change of emphasis takes place. Whereas the making of an excellent product initially was the goal with profits a consequence, the making of profits assumes the highest priority with the product becoming a means to achieve the new goal. Under this alignment, the importance of making the product is demoted while the importance of making money is enhanced. Profits can be increased further under this new priority system by reducing the quality of the materials that go into the product and the number of skilled workers making the product. The descent from excellence to shoddiness proceeds until it no longer is tolerated by consumers. Sometimes, however, the deception is concealed until the discovery of jeopardy to consumers, whether they be astronauts, takers of risky medicines or drivers of dangerously-flawed automobiles. The decline in standards includes the fall from rectitude to dishonor.

The mutual exclusivity of serving God or mammon is awesome in its workings. Because of the law of misplaced emphasis or displaced goals or serving the wrong master, we see the metamorphoses of some of our most cherished institutions.

A New York City high school student grasped the point perfectly. Some years after Albert Shanker and his teachers union waged the first strike against the deteriorating school system, the student told me that a school is not a place where students learn, but "a place where teachers make money." The Cox Commission report on the 1968 riots at Columbia University warned that education and commerce don't mix: "A university is essentially a free community of scholars dedicated to the pursuit of truth and knowledge....Any tendency to treat a university as a business enterprise with faculty as employees and students as customers diminishes its vitality and communal cohesion." Today *students* are employed to fill stadiums and guarantee lucrative television contracts. The students' education is beside the point. Hypocritical officials plead they are victims of their institutions' servitude to mammon.

As soon as the trade book industry decided the only line of consequence is the bottom line, the desire to maximize profits quickly led to the manufacture of non-books for non-readers. Perhaps the sharpest way to etch what has happened to the medical industry is through sarcasm: imagine the kind of fees Jesus could command if he were practicing today! Even science, the professional search for factual truth, is finding, now that money has become so essential to its functioning, that it no longer is immune to the virus of dishonesty.

On the level of the individual, the law of two masters is just as inexorable. Most of us, other things being equal, will choose the job paying the top dollar. As long as standards are maintained, as long as the person keeps trying to do his best, as long as the person takes pride in his skill, then the integrity of the work remains uppermost. Whenever acquisition of wealth is given the highest priority, it follows that in order to maximize results the person is willing to compromise principles, act unethically, resort to dishonesty, behave dishonorably, mistreat his fellows — these are subordinate considerations.

The inversion of values, however, bars the person from the kingdom of God: "....the deceitfulness of riches, choke the word, and he becometh unfruitful." J. Paul Getty was the richest man in the world. He was dull, greedy, ungenerous, cheap, begrudging and mean. A biographer wrote that the oil tycoon took great pleasure from being mean. He was married five times, but never invited his parents to any of his weddings. He did not know his offspring. His oldest son committed suicide. The youngest son died at the age of 12 after many operations. Getty never visited the boy in the hospital. The multibillionaire believed his family was plotting to take his money so that when his grandson was kidnaped, Getty refused to pay any ransom and relented only after the kidnapers sent the youth's severed ear in the mail. His wealth bought him unlimited sex, but always suspicious and contemptuous of people, his life was loveless and joyless. Did J. Paul Getty live in the kingdom of God?

It does not *have* to be that way, of course. "Seek ye first the kingdom of God, and his righteousness" and all the worldly things you need will be added. Put first things first. It could hardly be coincidence that in my study of 1,200 American centenarians for the book *Living To Be 100* none of them mentioned the accumulation of wealth as a goal in life. A few of them were quite wealthy, but most lived in modest comfort or at least without want. Intuitively and probably for some of them consciously, they had followed the advice of Jesus. All of them, including a few who were on welfare, were content. A Social Security represenative wrote of Charles Steurer, who gained enough wealth from his cabinet-making business to become a philanthropist: "Happiness, he believes, is not something to be found anywhere; it is a state of mind. Unlike the poetic Browning, the practical Steurer believes that the grasp should never exceed the reach. Grasping for too much is a symptom of an incurable disease. Getting one thing means wanting another and contentment is never attained. Contentment and happiness have been attained by Mr. Steurer because, as he says repeatedly, 'I have the God-given gift of peace of mind.'"

When Jesus said how difficult it is for a rich man to get into the kingdom of God, his disciples "were exceedingly amazed, saying, Who then can be saved? But Jesus beheld them, and said unto them, With men this is impossible, but with God all things are possible."

> As Jesus passed through Jericho on his way to Jerusalem, behold, there was a man named Zacchaeus, which was the chief among the publicans, and he was rich. And he sought to see Jesus who he was; and could not for the press, because he was little in stature. And he ran before, and climbed up into a sycamore tree to see him: for he was to pass that way. And when Jesus came to the place, he looked up, and saw him, and said unto him, Zacchaeus, make haste, and come down; for to day I must abide at thy house. And he made haste, and came down, and received him joyfully. And when they saw it, they all murmured, saying, That he was gone to be guest with a man that is a sinner. And Zacchaeus stood, and said unto the Lord;

Behold, Lord, the half of my goods I give to the poor; and if I have taken any thing from any man by false accusation, I restore him fourfold. And Jesus said unto him, This day is salvation come to this house, forsomuch as he also is a son of Abraham. For the Son of man is come to seek and to save that which was lost.

Many scholars, theologians and Christian lay people have found Jesus' ethics to be the most difficult part of his doctrine. The meaning of the injunctions is clear enough. What is puzzling is their character. His ethics are at odds with our human nature. Some are virtually impossible for an ordinary human being to carry out. Some appear to be downright unwise and imprudent. Turn the other cheek to Hitler and he put you in an oven. "Blessed are the meek: for they shall inherit the earth"? It wasn't the meek who subdued Hitler. The Beatitude goes counter to our instincts and experience. We know that the physically strong win contests, the intellectually daring conquer ignorance, the powerful run things, and the bold suitor wins fair maiden. It is the rich who inherit the earth, for they own the land.

Love your *enemies?* That's asking too much of any person. The old reptilian parts of our brain were not preserved over eons for nothing. The law of survival is fight or flight. Hans Selye, the biochemist who discovered the stress syndrome, says even to love one's neighbor as oneself is not biologically possible.

Rape is a heinous crime. Society does not countenance it and severely punishes those who are unwilling or unable to restrain violent impulses. But not to lust, even fleetingly, after a woman? After all, it is nature that makes the pretty flowers to attract the bees so that there will be pollination. The latest research shows that sexual fantasy is almost universal in human beings of both sexes. Being angry with a person is one thing. Acting upon that anger and killing him is something totally different, ethically as well as in the eyes of society. But not in Jesus' doctrine, for he said: "Be ye therefore perfect, even as your Father which is in heaven is perfect."

There have been various interpretations of what Jesus meant. One was that the counsel of perfection could be achieved only by monks and hermits. This led to the double standard of behaving one way in church on Sunday and following the more practical rules of the world the rest of the week. Johannes Weiss, the theological scholar, said at the end of the 19th century that Jesus' ethics showed that he was talking about a transcendental kingdom of God. The ethics were meant to detach people from this world and prepare them for the next. "That is why His ethic is of so completely negative a character; it is, in fact, not so much an ethic as a penitential discipline!"

Albert Schweitzer, following up on Weiss, believed the ethical principles were to be taken literally, but that Jesus had laid down such harsh rules of conduct only for what he thought would be a brief interim until the arrival of the heavenly kingdom. That's one of the interpretations that Professor Frederick Grant of Union Theological Seminary was referring to when he wrote: "There are certain modern theories which tend to reduce the severity of Jesus' 'heroic' ethics, for it is thought that his teaching is impracticable or impossible to follow." The other theory is that Jesus was proclaiming the pure will of God without any concession to weak human nature "to force men to admit their sinfulness and recognize their total dependence upon divine mercy and grace."

Dr. Grant comments, however, that Jesus never said a word about either theory and most Christians always have assumed "that Jesus' teachings were meant to be obeyed, with the result that many have achieved sainthood by the help of divine grace."

Joseph Klausner in *From Jesus To Paul* writes that "the ethical teaching of Jesus, which in spite of its impracticality, charms us by its loftiness and perfectionism." But, Klausner goes on, "Judaism will never allow itself to reach even in theory the ethical extremeness characteristic of Christianity; this extremeness has no place in the world of reality."

But who said Jesus was talking about ethics? It is a natural assumption to make because the Judaism which was his matrix is a religion concerned with ethical monotheism. And, it's true, Jesus is recommending ways to think about and behave toward one's fellows.

Why not look at what Jesus did say? Most of the inferred ethical precepts are in the fifth chapter of Matthew, although they are supported and appended elsewhere in the Gospels. In the verse introducing the rules, he is very specific about what he means: "Whosoever therefore shall break one of these commandments, and shall teach men so, he shall be called the least in the kingdom of heaven: but whosoever shall do and teach them, the same shall be called great in the kingdom of heaven."

Jesus is talking about guidelines to the kingdom of God. The kingdom of God, we have decided, is in the mind. "The light of the body is in the eye: if therefore thine eye be single, thy whole body shall be full of light. But if thine eye be evil, thy whole body shall be full of darkness. If therefore the light that is in thee be darkness, how great is that darkness!" That is a fascinating metaphor. The eye is an extension of the brain. The eyes are the part of the brain that comes directly into contact with the external world. We find eyes to be the most expressive part of the body because they offer direct access to what a person is thinking and feeling.

What the brain thinks, Jesus says, permeates the entire body. If the thought is father to the act, if concept is precedent to and cause of behavior, if the ear of corn grows out of the stalk that grows out of the seed, if there is inevitability to the process — then it is logical that codes of conduct deal with behavioral antecedents in the mind. One must go to the source of the process to deal with originations. Make the tree good in order to bring forth good fruit.

This accounts for the equivalence of thought and conduct in Jesus' teaching. Don't think it in the first place. If you do, suffer the consequences. Coveting your neighbor's wife can only lead to adultery. Either that or torment. Lusting after women can only end in immorality, violent coercion or else frustration. Lust for wealth can lead to crime. Anger is the fuel of violence. Jesus knew that once the desire is set, the person will go for it because "where your treasure is, there will your heart be also." So keep your eye single.

All of this flows consistently from Jesus' understanding of the primacy of the mind, but it still looks like ethics. In order to see that he is getting at something quite different, we must turn again to stress theory.

Technically, stress is the term used to cover the functions continually taking place from minute to minute to keep the body finely adapted to whatever environmental situation it is in. Stress not only is normal but essential for continued life. These homeostatic functions are performed largely by the autonomic nervous and endocrine systems. The autonomic nervous system is like an automatic pilot that runs the body without the conscious direction of the brain. We wouldn't have time for much else if we had to monitor and regulate blood flow or supervise digestion. But just as an automatic pilot can be overriden by the human pilot, the autonomic system is directed how to behave by thoughts, conjectures, assumptions, conclusions, assessments, feelings about what the actual situation is.

The autonomic nervous system has two branches, the sympathetic and parasympathetic. These systems work in conjunction, and if they get out of sync, which is suspected to be a cause of voodoo death, the person is in big trouble. The parasympathetic nervous system takes the lead in running things when the body is at ease and when the person is asleep. The parasympatheic system responds to pleasurable stimuli such as the stroking of skin and the smell of food; it evokes good feelings.

The sympathetic nervous system takes over when an emergency arises. It can arouse the body for action almost instantaneously. I vividly remember one time when I was driving to a tennis match, I raced a long freight train to a railroad crossing in order to save three or four minutes. I was a safe distance in front of the locomotives, but what I didn't count on was that the crossing gates started to come down as I approached the tracks. I had to make a split-second decision whether to jam the brakes and hope I stopped in time or risk pushing through and possibly hitting the crossing bar. I pressed down on the accelerator and just made it under the descending bar. Safely on the other side, my heart was pounding and I could feel the surge of adrenaline. I was so energized by that one instant of emergency that I handily defeated a tennis player who more often beat me.

The adrenal glands, situated just above the kidneys inject adrenaline and noradenaline into the blood stream to stimulate heart action, raise blood pressure, pour sugar into the blood, constrict blood vessels to the digestive area. In addition, the sympathetic nervous system orchestrates a constellation of changes to prepare the body for either of two kinds of action: flight or fight. You know the feelings. The heart beats faster and more violently, the hands become clammy, cold feet, knot in the stomach, tight throat, tense neck and upper back. There are dozens of changes in musculature, blood vessels, organs and biochemistry in this mobilization for action. The person becomes so intensely alert he "can hear a pin drop." There is an "adrenal rush." Many people find this to be an intensely unpleasant sensation. Yet some of us are attracted to it, which explains the popularity of "spine-chilling" (still another of the syndrome's characteristics) horror movies. Some people become so addicted that they regularly put their lives on the line in high-speed auto races and risk their worldly goods on the deal of a card.

Researchers have found that constant tripping of the alarm system in our civilization — resentment at an overbearing boss, chronic bickering at home, encounters with hostile drivers on the highway, failure and frustration in career ambitions, insults and feelings of inferiority, the wear and tear of the rat race, financial pressures and indebtedness — can lead to hypertension, cardiovascular disease and most other modern ailments. Nearly three-quarters of Americans suffer from headaches, more than half from back and muscle pains. The reports of pain came most often from people who also reported much stress in their lives.

Most, but not all, of the stressful psychological states are grouped around the flight-or-fight reaction. Selye says one of the most destructive of all emotions is the desire for revenge. In the category with vengeance are hatred, hostility, resentment, disdain, wrath, anger, internalized anger, and self-hatred which leads to depression. On the "flight" side are fear, worry and anxiety. In between are two other feelings that Selye also ranks at the top of the destructive list: indecision, when one isn't sure which course to take, and frustration, when one is caught between conflicting principles and needs or between competing desires. Another division that can tear a person apart is ambivalence, experiencing strong love and hate for the same person. Other emotions that become destructive when held chronically are guilt, remorse, regret, grief, sorrow, sadness, bereavement, self-pity, distrust, envy, jealousy, despair, depression, hopelessness.

Selye calls these negative emotions distress.

On the positive side, which Selye calls good stress, are emotions that promote a person's health, well-being and happiness. They are the good feelings we get when we are among people we love and trust, family and friends, employers who believe we are doing well and praise us, when we can take pride in solid achievement and succeed in matters of principle. These positive feelings can be grouped under the rubric of love. Selye says a feeling of gratitude is among the most important of them. In addition to the varieties of love, there are trust, respect and protectfulness; whatever puts us at ease as opposed to being uptight and tense.

If we return now to Jesus' "ethics," it will become apparent that his rules of ethical etiquette deal with the powerful emotions that produce good or bad stress and have everything to do with our well-being. In other words, he wasn't commanding superhuman efforts in order to benefit other people, but was giving his listeners advice primarily aimed at helping themselves. As evidence of his reasonableness and astuteness, he was appealing to his listeners' self-interest and addressing their own welfare. But they had to have the wit to understand what he was talking about in order to act in their own interests.

The importance of "if thine eye be single" was illustrated by the story of Flora Whisenand, one of the 1,200 centenarians studied for *Living To Be 100*. My conclusion in that study was that these people were able to live to an extreme old age because of a combination of being able to avoid harmful stress, being able to cope with it when it was unavoidable (for instance, a number of them went back to work at advanced ages when the Depression destituted them), and promoting the positive attitudes that are life-supporting.

A Social Security representative visited Mrs. Whisenand who was confined to a nursing-home bed in rural Indiana. She was so frail and weak that the government man couldn't be sure whether or not she was blind. Five other women were in the room — two sisters-in-law, two neighbors, and a nurse — all of whom took it upon themselves to answer questions put to Mrs. Whisenand by the Social Security agent. There was one question that really intrigued him, but he doubted that the old lady could give him the answer. Why had this particular woman been able to live so long? There was nothing extraordinary about her. Quite the contrary, her life seemed no different from other lives. She was a church-going farm wife who, as far as he could tell, had lived a routine existence.

At the end of his report, he conjectured that the secret of her longevity was "living her entire life in a rural atmosphere, she nurtured flowers, crops and farm animals instead of the frustration and boredom of forced retirement in our industrial society." He offered that conclusion without paying any attention to the reason that Mrs. Whisenand herself gave. On this point she would not settle for the replies given by others, but insisted on speaking for herself.

"She made no comment when I inquired if she had an explanation for her long life. The nurse and other ladies in the room volunteered that she came from a long-lived family. A cousin, John Fields, came striding into her room last summer, at the age of 97, for a visit from his home in Indianapolis. He has since died. Her brother Calvin died at age 99 two years ago. Mrs. Whisenand offered the following, which I presumed had some bearing in her mind on the point: 'Nothing has transpired in my life that I'm ashamed of."

The righteousness that exceeds the righteousness of scribes and Pharisees obviates the corrosive emotions of hypocrisy, shame, guilt, remorse and makes possible peace of mind, contentment, pride and self-esteem.

Jesus' teaching concerns the polar opposites involved in bad and good stress, the negative fear/hate and positive love/joy emotions.

The beautiful passage about the lilies is both a prescription against worry, anxiety, fear of the future and a reassurance that things will turn out all right. Don't fritter your life away on petty matters. Don't worry about what you will wear or that you won't be able to put food on the table. Can all your concern add an inch to your stature? If God takes care of the birds and flowers, why can't you have faith that you will be provided for? Material things cannot give you what matters: peace of mind, wholeness of mind, good feelings about yourself. If you set your life straight in the fundamental ways, the rest will grow out of that. Then you'll have it all.

John Tuggle was a rugged fullback for the New York Giants in 1983. In October 1984, he told a sports reporter: "If I actually sit down and think about it, I've been through a lot in the last year — my divorce proceedings began in January, then the knee, and now this." The professional football player rubbed his head. Tuggle seriously injured his knee during summer practice, threatening to end his career. The 'this" he referred to was a bald head, his hair removed by chemotherapy. First the divorce, then the job injury, then cancer.

The impact upon health of marital separation — whether due to death, divorce or other reason — was revealed through pioneering research done by Thomas Holmes, a psychiatrist at the University of Washington School of Medicine, and Captain Richard Rahe of the Naval Health Research Center in San Diego. They devised a scale to measure the intensity of stresses we face in life by quantifying 43 of the most common stressful events. The severity of stress impacts is rated numerically. The researchers found that as a person accumulates points from any combination of these events during a time span of a year or less that person's likelihood of becoming ill increases proportionately.

At the top of the Holmes/Rahe list is the death of a spouse, which they assigned a value of 100. In second place is divorce with a point rating of 73. Marital separation is third with a 65. Tied for fourth are a jail term and death of a close family member, each with a value of 63. The three most stressful events in some way involve the loss of a wife or husband.

Divorces have increased spectacularly in the United States, from about one divorce for every four marriages in 1960 to about one divorce for every two marriages in the 1980s. Divorce has become so common in the American lifestyle and lost so much of its social disapproval that one would suspect a corresponding reduction of the emotional toll involved. If people seem to marry and divorce more casually, splitting up no longer is the crisis it once was. Unexpectedly, the more scientific research that is done on the subject, the more scientists are coming to believe that divorce is even more stressful than the death of a spouse.

Recent studies, expanding on earlier research, show that compared to the married, the never-married and widowed, divorced adults have higher rates of emotional disturbance, accidental death and death from heart disease, cancer, pneumonia, high blood pressure and cirrhosis of the liver. For deaths related to psychological causes, the divorced were worse off than the widowed in eight of ten categories. For example, the suicide rate for widowed women is somewhat more than double that of married women whereas the suicide rate for separated or divorced women is nearly three and a half times greater.

One reason that divorce is so devastating and so hard to adjust to is precisely because the lost spouse is *not* dead. Divorced persons typically feel the same grief, anger, guilt and depression experienced by widowed people, but the divorced spouse remains, often to keep rekindling the anger that led to the divorce. And simply the existence of the ex-mate makes even more difficult the adjustment that is required to accept the reality of a terminated relationship. One study did find that unhappily married couples were more miserable than divorced people. Still, a researcher added, "there's a lot of evidence that divorce is an overwhelming stress for most people, even if they are getting divorced for the right reasons."

"And the Pharisees came to him, and asked him, Is it lawful for a man to put away his wife? tempting him. And he answered and said unto them, What did Moses command you? And they said, Moses suffered to write a bill of divorcement, and to put her away. And Jesus answered and said unto them, For the hardness of your hearts he wrote this precept. But from the beginning of the creation God made them male and female. For this cause shall a man leave his father and mother, and cleave to his wife; and they twain shall be one flesh so then they are no more twain, but one flesh. What therefore God hath joined together, let not man put asunder."

Jesus is talking about the wisdom of God. Man does not set aside God's wisdom without peril. To tear apart the flesh that God has joined together means to inflict deep and perhaps fatal wounds upon oneself as well as others. It means disrupting the wholeness that Jesus knew was necessary for productive or even continued life.

Once again modern science is revealing the profound insight of Jesus, not only in detailing the great psychological damage caused by divorce, but in delineating the reason for the cause — in effect, ratifying Jesus' thesis: "But from the beginning of the creation God made them male and female. For this cause shall a man leave his father and mother, and cleave to his wife." Marriage is so deeply rooted in the human psyche that it cannot be abrogated simply by fiat.

Monogamy, the family, and the father-husband are human inventions that go back at least one million years and probably long before that. In distinction to other mammalian females, women no longer have estrus, a specific time for sexual activity. The opportunity for sexual bonding made possible the nuclear family. The wife-mother's need for support in rearing her offspring and the father-husband's access to unrestricted sex grew into an interdependence that encompassed all phases of life. To be sure, human beings never have renounced the promiscuity that characterizes other primates. But normally most promiscuity is confined to the experimentation of youth. Marriage is so deeply ingrained in humans that even when it fails, with all the trauma involved, most divorced people need to try it again.

The experience of centenarians confirms that marriage is conducive to long life. Only one and a half percent of the American centenarians that I researched were divorced or separated. Two-thirds of the reported marriages lasted from 50 to 80 years. When a spouse died, the centenarian usually remarried, even late in life. Flanders Dunbar, the Director of Psychosomatic Research at Columbia University's College of Physicians and Surgeons during the 1930s and 1940s is one of very few scientists who studied centenarians and nonagenarians. She noted that their marriage rate is very high and their divorce rate very low. "They contrive," Dr. Dunbar said, "to transform marriage from a stress situation to a healthy state of living."

In fourth place on the Holmes/Rahe stress chart is a jail term. Jesus advised his listeners to go to great lengths to avoid jail. "Agree with thine adversary quickly, whiles thou art in the way with him; lest at any time the adversary deliver thee to the judge, and the judge deliver thee to the officer, and thou be cast into prison. Verily I say unto thee, Thou shalt by no means come out thence, till thou hast paid the uttermost farthing."

Similarly, Jesus urged against getting embroiled in legal suits, and to show how strongly he felt on this point he suggested that a most extraordinary concession was preferable. "If any man will sue thee at the law, and take away thy coat, let him have they cloak also." Lawsuits are extremely stressful experiences. Americans seem to have overlooked this hidden cost as they resort to litigation. In terms of health, it may be one of the most costly ways possible of making money. Arnold Hutschnecker, as a practitioner of psychosomatic medicine, was well aware of this. His associations with Presidents Nixon and Ford engendered some political friction. When a controversial report he wrote on violence was made public, political attacks became more strident and at least one newspaper libeled him. I asked Dr. Hutschnecker why he hadn't brought suit against the newspaper to vindicate himself. He said the psychic cost of such a trial wasn't worth it.

The verse about avoiding lawsuits is preceded by: "Ye have heard that it hath been said, An eye for an eye, and a tooth for a tooth: But I say unto you, That ye resist not evil: but whosoever shall smite thee on thy right cheek, turn to him the other also." Jesus tried to break the vendetta mentality that has cursed the Middle East. If we recall that the founder of stress theory said that desire for revenge is about the most destructive emotion that a human being can harbor, Jesus' saying does not seem so outlandish. And if it is taken not as an absolute commandment but as a recommendation for how to behave under most circumstances, the advice becomes reasonable and valuable. It is the same lesson we are just now learning from stress theory: it is bad for your health to engage in an unending series of meaningless and petty fights. It's hard on your nerves, and will take its toll on your well-being. Therefore, try to love your neighbor.

"Ye have heard that it was said by them of old time, Thou shalt not kill; and whosoever shall kill shall be in danger of the judgment: but I say unto you, That whosoever is angry with his brother without cause shall be in danger of the judgment [the court]: and whosoever shall say to his brother, Raca [a term of contempt], shall be in danger of the council [the Sanhedrin]: but whosoever shall say, Thou fool, shall be in danger of hell fire. Therefore if thou bring thy gift to the altar, and there rememberest that thy brother hath ought against thee; leave there thy gift before the altar, and go thy way; first be reconciled to thy brother, and then come and offer thy gift."

The emotion anger is a chameleon. It can produce different effects in different contexts. Jesus conveys as much in the above passage. Anger can lead to violence, anger can be socially disruptive, eroding love and trust in a marriage, alienating friends and neighbors. But anger also can be socially useful in fighting for justice, righting economic wrongs, and delivering political punishment. Anger is a warning to spouses and governments to correct abuses or else action will be taken. Anger, as threat or bluff, can just as well be used as an instrument of state policy. Parental anger, along with parental love, has been a formative emotion of the human species.

In the United States and England, it has been considered improper to display anger in polite and genteel society. This became a traditional attitude in private relationships as well. But in the 1960s and 1970s, a certain number of psychotherapists began to see a psychological danger in the suppression of anger. The new strategy called for a person to bring his anger to the surface, vent it, get rid of it. The expression of anger was healthier than its suppression, at least for the person ventilating his feelings.

In the 1980s, anger came under still further psychological scrutiny, producing different conclusions. For instance, a study of laid-off engineers in San Diego found that men who were invited to express their anger became more hostile toward the company and their supervisors than those ex-employees who were asked to criticize themselves. Leo Madow, a psychoanalyst at the University of Pennsylvania Hospital in Philadelphia, said the "get-the-anger-out, be-honest-with-each-other" approach inspired by the self-awareness movement of the 1970s nearly wrecked some companies that sponsored confessional sessions where employees told how they felt about one another.

Social psychologist Carol Tavris in her book *Anger: The Misunderstood Emotion* found that giving release to anger had an effect opposite to what had been thought. Those people didn't lose their ire, but instead grew angrier. Furthermore, Tavris discovered that suppressing anger does not have harmful effects, a position supported by a number of psychotherapists. Anger becomes dangerous to a person's health when it is *repressed*. Suppression is a conscious act, repression is an unconscious mechanism. The person internalizes the anger without being aware of doing so. There may be psychological reasons why he cannot admit to the anger — at being unloved by a parent, for example.

Internalized anger underlies the famous Type A behavior that has been associated with abnormally high rates of heart attacks. The Type A person is always on the go, likely to be doing two things at once, trying to prove himself, impatient, quick to fly off the handle. Meyer Friedman, who pioneered the Type A concept says it is a behavior-emotion complex adopted by people who are unsure of their competence. Dr. Friedman says that the "chronic and incessant struggle to achieve more and more in less time, together with a free-floating, but covert, and usually well-rationalized, hostility, make up the Type A behavior pattern. The sense of urgency and hostility give rise to irritation, impatience, aggravation and anger: the four components which I believe comprise the pathogenic core of the behavior pattern."

Those are corrosive negative emotions, of course, continually triggering the flight-or-fight stress syndrome and, Friedman believes, the chronic arousal of these mechanisms lays the basis for cardiovascular disease and heart attack. Redford Williams, an internist and psychiatrist at Duke University Medical Center, studied 255 physicians who had taken a standard personality test 25 years earlier. In January 1983, Dr. Williams reported that those subjects who scored in the top half of the hostility scale had suffered five times the number of fatal heart attacks as those in the lower half. In August 1984, Dr. Friedman reported on a federally-financed study of 800 men who had suffered heart attacks. After three years, the men who underwent counseling to curb characteristics of Type A behavior suffered only one half the number of recurrent heart attacks as subjects who did not.

Internalized anger is a modern version of the hell fire that burns until the person is consumed.

Dr. Tavris has advice that parallels Jesus' "first be reconciled to thy brother." In most cases it is better to suppress anger. Count to ten, and if you're still angry, count to 100. Try humor. Dr. Tavris says, "Couples who are not defeated by rage and the conflicts that cause it know two things: when to keep quiet about trivial angers, for the sake of civility, and how to argue about the important ones, for the sake of personal autonomy and change."

There are times when anger is justified, and it can be used constructively: to fight injustice, to change unfair situations, to indict unworthy practices. That is just how Jesus used anger, eliminating a seeming contradiction in his story. He taught the dissolving of unwise and unjustified anger against improper objects — your brother, for instance — but himself raged against the shams and injustices he found in his society.

Dr. Tarvis says the antithesis in exhibiting anger is represented in our popular culture by Superman and the Incredible Hulk. Clark Kent never flies into a rage over some injustice. He coolly dons his flying suit and rights the wrong. "When David Banner gets angry, he becomes, *uncontrollably*, a giant green id, a bilious beast. He is not a man at all, super or otherwise. These incarnations of anger represent dual attitudes:....is it a human blessing, or a bestial sin?"

Incredibly, Jesus answered Dr. Tavris' question. The answer was given earlier as a conundrum from the Gospel of Thomas. "Blessed is the lion which the man eats, and the lion thus becomes man; and cursed is the man whom the lion shall eat, when the lion thus becomes man." When a man conquers his anger, he becomes a lion of a man; when his anger conquers him, he becomes a raging beast.

While Jesus counseled against the negative emotions, his doctrine was a hymn in praise of the positive ones. You can't love too much. "Ye have heard that it hath been said, Thou shall love thy neighbor, and hate thine enemy. But I say unto you, love your enemies, bless them that curse you, do good to them that hate you, and pray for them which despitefully use you and persecute you".

The Christian martyrs, on their way to the fire and the arena, actually behaved that way toward their Roman persecutors and in so doing helped Christianity conquer the Empire. Hans Selye, who maintained that we are not biologically made to love our neighbors as ourselves, nevertheless advocated doing good to others as the best policy: doing good things for others in order to promote one's own self-interest. He called it *altruistic egoism*. The founder of stress theory said the best way to ensure your own safety and further your welfare is to cause in others feelings of gratitude toward yourself. In that way they will want to do good things in return and thus help you. An element of that strategy is in Jesus' advice. "For if ye love them which love you, what reward have ye? do not even the publicans the same? And if ye salute your brethren only, what do ye more than others?"

What has been taken to be Jesus' ethics can be seen to make eminent good sense, to be eminently rational, to be eminently beneficial, to be eminently the best policy when it is considered in terms of the welfare of the individual whom Jesus is addressing — the effect *on that person's mind*.

Jesus is saying, as in his doctrine toward anger: be in control of yourself. If you simply react to every insult and imagined slight that comes your way, you are out of control. Other people are calling the shots. Your mind is the most precious thing you have. You must be its guardian, protector and its conductor — play your own music. Live in the kingdom of God.

The recommendation to love is the most famous part of his doctrine, but his teaching abounds with his advocacy and encouragement of positive attitudes. "Ask, and it shall be given you; seek, and ye shall find; knock, and it shall be opened unto you." Blessed are those who hunger and thirst for righteousness, the pure in heart, the peacemakers, the merciful. "Be ye therefore merciful, as your Father also is merciful."

And one of his most noble exhortations is to act with kindness and compassion: "I was hungered, and ye gave me meat: I was thirsty, and ye gave me drink: I was a stranger, and ye took me in: Naked, and ye clothed me: I was sick, and ye visited me: I was in prison, and ye came unto me." The disciples ask: when did we do these things for you? "Verily I say unto you, insomuch as ye have done it unto one of the least of these my brethren, ye have done it unto me."

Jesus' appeal to the positive aspects of humankind, to realize the best that is in us, included one of his most puzzling qualifications for entry into the kingdom of God.

TWELVE

Become As A Little Child

The disciples ask Jesus who is the greatest in the kingdom of God. "Jesus called a little child unto him, and set him in the midst of them. And said, Verily I say unto you, Except ye be converted, and become as little children, ye shall not enter the kingdom of heaven. Whosoever therefore shall humble himself as this little child, the same is the greatest in the kingdom of heaven."

That was Matthew. Mark says Jesus was "much displeased" when he saw that the disciples tried to keep the children from him. "Suffer the little children to come unto me, and forbid them not: for of such is the kingdom of God. Verily I say unto you, Whosoever shall not receive the kingdom of God as a little child, he shall not enter therein."

In childhood, Jesus saw the immanence of God. Childhood was a precious, wonderful state that must be respected and safeguarded. He was the first outspoken indicter of child abuse as a vicious crime. "Whoso shall offend one of these little ones which believe in me, it were better that a millstone were hanged about his neck, and that he were drowned in the depth of the sea."

The apostle Paul doesn't see childhood as a magical state, but a state of immaturity. "When I was a child, I spake as a child, I understood as a child, I thought as a child: but when I became a man, I put away childish things." Childhood is an episode in the passage to adulthood — an episode that must and should be closed.

Paul's view is closer to the contemporary attitude. We may seem to have a youth-cult fixation in which everyone admires fair complexion, smooth skin and trim figures, but the emphasis is on growing up in a hurry. While youth may enjoy carefree lack of responsibility, young people themselves, as well as their parents, are impatient for them to reach adulthood. Baseball and football are played with professional intensity. Children are dressed like adults. Allusions to sex are ubiquitous. Cigarettes and drugs are accessible to middle schoolers. Adult pressures as well as abuse and suicide are part of the youthful scene. Some observers charge that children are being robbed of childhood.

In any event, childhood is an immature, uncompleted, powerless and vulnerable state. Children lack experience and knowledge and the consequent self-assurance. The fact is that children have low social status with few of the legal prerogatives of adults. Children's welfare and guidance are out of their control, residing with others who exert crucial influences on children's destinies. Certainly, Jesus couldn't have been talking about these characteristics as the kingdom of God.

Except that humility, the one trait that Jesus specifically mentions, is consistent with this childhood status. Humility was a quality admired not only by Jesus, but regarded as a virtue far back in the history of the Middle East. In the "Babylonian Ecclesiastes," cited earlier, the author complains that people abuse the righteous and the humble. Humility was a characteristic prized early in Jewish wisdom literature.

The word humble can be confusing because of its multiple connotations and several meanings. The second definition in *Webster's Collegiate Dictionary* is "reflecting, expressing, or offered in a spirit of deference or submission," such as an apology. The third definition is "ranking low in some hierarchy or scale: insignificant". But it is the first definitiion, we can be sure, that Jesus meant: "not proud or haughty: not arrogant". When the disciples ask him who is the greatest, they mean the word in the same sense as Muhammad Ali's boast. Jesus, with a play on words, substitutes an antonym. The humble are the greatest in the kingdom of God. Jesus said in another place that the humble live in the kingdom of God. *Roget's Thesaurus* equates humble with poor in spirit. The Beatitude tells us that the poor in spirit are blessed "for theirs is the kingdom of heaven."

Humility may be an endangered character trait in a society where everybody wants to be Number One, although this could be more apparent than real because by its nature humility is self-effacing. My research found centenarians in general to be self-effacing people. Every so often a Social Security representative would comment with some astonishment and admiration that the oldtimer was a truly humble person. This kind of remark occurred often enough to recall that Jesus had linked the humble to the kingdom of God.

Jesus must have intended more than humility, however, when he said a person had to become like a little child in order to enter the kingdom of God. "In that hour Jesus rejoiced in spirit, and said, I thank thee, O father, Lord of heaven and earth, that thou hast hid these things from the wise and prudent, and hast revealed them unto babes: even so, Father; for so it seemed good in thy sight." We are never made privy to what this knowledge is.

Could Jesus have intuited a fundamental psychological difference between the states of childhood and adulthood? Research into thanatology, the scientific study of death, reveals that young children do not understand that death is universal and inevitable for all living things, including themselves. We are born into this world believing we are immortal. Because this belief is buried deep in our unconscious, it never leaves us although our rational minds disabuse us of its truth. The experience of each child seems to repeat the experience of the human species in this respect. Like all creatures, our hominid ancestors did not understand that their existence had a natural termination. The human brain had to reach a certain size and power in order to apprehend this awful knowledge. This discovery was not firmly grasped until after the appearance of our species, *Homo sapiens*. There are some indications that the first burial sites appeared possibly as early as 200,000 years ago, but the custom may not have developed until after the arrival of the Neanderthal people 125,000 years ago. The grave, the quintessential human artifact, signified the burgeoning awareness of the mystery of death.

All primitive peoples had myths explaining how death came into the world. Very often, chance played a big role. There was a tree of immortal life and a tree of death. God asked a human being to choose the fruit from one or the other, and the person unfortunately made the wrong choice. The Biblical myth of the Garden of Eden, however, added a far more sophisticated psychological permutation. The tree of eternal life remained (it was because of God's fear that disobedient humans would pluck the fruit from this tree and live forever that they were expelled from Eden), but the other tree no longer was the tree of death. By the implication of this myth, death did not have to be introduced: it already existed. What the fruit from the tree of the knowledge of good and evil did was to open the eyes of human beings to certainty of death for all. The goodness was newly revalued because of the discovery of the evil. The knowledge of good and evil was the goodness of life and the evil of its impermanence. It was this knowledge that banished human beings from the paradise of innocence in which all other creatures, including human children, exist. With untroubled minds, they could live in their God-given natural grace.

During the first two years of life a baby has no conception of death. At the age of about three years, a child begins to grasp some idea of death, equating it with separation. Grandpa has gone to sleep or gone away. The young child cannot tell the difference between a short-term separation and death, which is why the prospect of a parental departure can strike fear into a child. From three to five years of age, the child still does not understand death as final. Grandpa has gone away. When is he coming back? Probably the most persistent of the attitudes is that the child does not accept death as inevitable. He is likely to believe that death happens only by accident or when it is produced by some agent. The man is dead because he was hit by a car or went into a hospital. The youngster decides it is a good idea not to be run over by an automobile and to stay away from hospitals. Associating death only with some obvious cause, children often develop a great fear of murder.

It is perhaps not insignificant that primitive people still hold this immature attitude toward death. Bronislaw Malinowski wrote in a classic anthropological study of Triobriand Islanders in the Southwest Pacific that they could understand and accept death as natural when it happened to a stranger. But when this baleful event threatened a loved one or the person himself, he attributed it to a supernatural agent, some kind of sorcery, the curse of an enemy.

Starting at about the age of five, a child begins to make the long accomodation to the idea that death is final, universal and inevitable. For the first several years in this transition, the child resists accepting death as personal. The youngster is caught between contradictory attitudes of neither denying nor accepting the certainty of his own death. But usually by the age of about ten years, the conflict has been resolved and his own death accepted. "My worst memory," Grandma Moses wrote in her autobiography, "goes back to the time when I first commenced to realize what the world was like [when she was eight years old], and I used to worry."

The discovery of thanatology about the insulation of early childhood from the dread of death offered a clue to the special grace of childhood. I'd had the pleasure of association with three young children of my own. As I looked at their faces and enjoyed the keen minds, I experienced on many occasions an overpowering sensation, which I neither could explain nor articulate, that I was in the presence of God. In these my children I was seeing the face of God. I remember vividly one occasion when my daughter Maggie was two years old. We took a ride on the Staten Island ferry in New York harbor. During the return crossing to Manhattan, she ran along empty benches, up and down, squealing with overbrimming exuberance at the water and harbor scene outside the windows. I referred at the time to this uninhibited outpouring of emotion as transcendant joy. Many times in later years when I went to New York City to work, the sounds from a nearby rooftop playground wafted into my room. Non-stop screaming, shouting, laughing, excitement and joy — the sheer exuberance of living.

These subjective impressions, I believed, related to Jesus' concept of the kingdom of God, but I could not fathom what the clues meant until I learned of a little-known and newly-important scientific discovery.

The story of neoteny begins in 1865, in Paris, in an aquarium, the *Jardin des Plantes*, with an amphibian with the exotic name of *axolotl*. The *axolotl* is an aquatic animal with external gills like the mud puppy. In 1865, some of the *axolotls* in the Paris aquarium spontaneously lost their gills and were transformed into terrestrial salamanders. Until that time *axolotls* were thought to be newts, members not only of a different species and genus, but of an entirely different family of organisms from salamanders. Subsequent research showed that the *axolotl* was the larval, that is, immature, stage in the metamorphosis of a salamander. Immature, but what amazed the researchers is that even in what they now realized was a transitional condition, the *axolotl* was sexually mature: it could reproduce its own young. Generally, if the *axolotl* stays in water, it remains unchanged. In a land environment, it loses its gills and turns into an air-breathing salamander.

In 1884, a Swiss zoologist, Julius Kollman, gave a name to the phenomenon, neoteny. The neo is taken from the Greek word for youth, *neos*. Neoteny means the retention or retardation or stretching out of youthful traits.

Once aware of this fascinating postponement of maturity, scientists began to discover other neotenous occurrences in the animal world. While an interesting phenomenon, the significance of neoteny was unappreciated until scientific attention was drawn to its overwhelming importance in the development of one particular species. Ours. By 1977, one of the most influential scientists in the study of evolution, Stephen Jay Gould, stated: "Neoteny has been a (probably *the*) major determinant of human evolution.

The ascending importance of neoteny coincided with increasing knowledge in molecular genetics. Human beings and chimpanzees are almost identical in their structural genes. This fact presented a nagging puzzle. If humans and chimps are so close genetically, how can we account for the dramatic differences in appearance between the species? "That paradox can be resolved," Gould writes, "by invoking a small genetic difference with profound effects — alterations in the regulatory system that slows down the general rate of development in humans."

Scientific investigators noticed that juvenile skulls of prehistoric hominid species more closely resembled those of modern human beings than they did those of their own adults. As these juveniles grew into adults, they developed heavy brow ridges, projecting jaws, large teeth with pronounced canines. What happened is given the scientific name of gerontomorphism, the development of a form into an old individual. The plasticity of youth grows into the specialization of the mature adult.

Adult chimpanzees, gorillas and other primates are gerontomorphic forms, as were the species preceding the Cro-Magnon people. In both human and chimp infants at birth, the size of the head in proportion to the body is about the same. This also applies to other apes. But after the apes have completed their development, they have proportionately bigger bodies and smaller heads (as well as prognathous jaws). In other words, after full growth the human being anatomically retains, while all other primate species lose, youthful and fetal traits. The skull configurations of newborn humans and chimps are similar. The skulls of adults in the two species are widely disparate. A young chimpanzee is startlingly humanlike in appearance — straight back, erect posture, relatively hairless, distinct neck, relatively large cranium, straight face with unpronounced jaw. When compared in profile to the upper part of an adult chimp, the changes are remarkable. The adult has a relatively small cranium, greatly projecting jaw, receded neck and thick hair over its shoulders, back, arms and chest.

We humans are a prime case of retarded development. Fetal and childlike physical features appearing in the adult human form include large size of brain, large braincase, round-headedness, head situated over the top of the spine, lack of heavy brow ridges, flat face, small face, small jaws, small teeth, relative hairlessness of the body. Neotenous functional traits include low birth weight, fetal rate of body growth during the first year, rapid growth of the brain into the third year, prolonged immaturity, prolonged dependency, prolonged growth period, lack of estrus in females, late development of secondary sexual traits and reproductive maturity.

When it comes to neoteny, some human beings are more equal than others. Females are more neotenous than males. Women have a more delicate skeleton, smaller body size, larger brain in relation to total body size, narrower joints, more delicate skin, less body hair, a more highly-pitched voice. Many feminine traits are attractive to men because they are neotenous. As human beings we are conditioned to respond with a caring, gentle, loving attitude toward what is childlike — diminutive in size, rounded contours, intimations of dependency. The doting terms "baby" and "doll" signify the response that such features elicit. The big eyes, pink cheeks and puckered lips of "baby face" have been favored by many men. Betty Boop cultivated a baby voice. What is evoked is the cuteness, weakness and need to be protected of the dependent infant. "Daddy" speaks with a deep voice and deep pockets.

The long dependency of human young is singular in all of nature and so is the singular human institution, the family. Apes nurse their young longer than humans do, for four years. But after that the young ape must forage for its own living. In adaptation to the neotenous traits of erect posture and the shrinkage of the jaw, the human female developed hemispherical breasts while all human babies are born with the full lips better adapted to suckling at a hemispheric surface. With suckling, which is not the same as sucking, the baby's lips and mouth become a suction pump perfectly designed to withdraw milk from the mother's breast. Psychologically, something magical happens to both mother and child. Within the first hours after birth, the primary bonding takes place. It can only happen when the mother and infant are in contact and occurs optimally when the child is breastfeeding. The communication is two-way. The infant learns this is a good and safe world and at the same time sends messages to the mother that affect her development. Breastfeeding is both a continuity of the shelter and nurture in the womb and the commencement of a loving relationship of two human beings. The act says to the newcomer: welcome to life, welcome to the world, welcome to the human race!

In the Gospel of Thomas: "Jesus saw babies being suckled. He said to his disciples, 'These babies who are being suckled are like those who enter the Kingdom.'" Love, contentment, peace. Is that what Jesus is talking about?

Konrad Lorenz, the founder of ethology, the scientific study of animal behavior, was struck by the wide spectrum of flexibility in human behavior. Flexibility is a youthful trait. In all animals, juvenile plasticity disappears during development into a mature adult. "Human exploratory inquisitive behavior — restricted in animals to a brief developmental phase — is extended to persist until the onset of senility." Why, Lorenz asked, does this youthful trait so fundamental to the essence of humanity persist late into life? His answer was that the same developmental retardation that produces physical and physiological neoteny also is responsible for behavioral neoteny.

Since behavior is a manifestation of thought, we are basically talking about psychological traits. "What," asked anthropologist Ashley Montagu in *Growing Young*, "are those traits of childhood behavior that are so valuable and that tend to disappear gradually as human beings grow older? We have only to watch children to see them clearly displayed: Curiosity is one of the most important; imaginativeneses; playfulness; open-mindedness; willingness to experiment; flexibility; humor; energy; receptiveness to new ideas; honesty; eagerness to learn; and perhaps the most pervasive and the most valuable of all, the need to love." Later, Montagu listed other "neotenous drives of the child": friendship, trust, sensitivity, laughter and tears, creativity, the sense of wonder, optimism, dance, song, and joyfulness.

For how many adults is the journey through life a sloughing off of their youthful legacy in a mistaken notion of what growing older means? For how many is maturing a transition from open-mindedness to narrow-mindedness, from eagerness to learn to close-mindedness, from honesty to hypocrisy, from flexibility to rigidity, from playfulness to solemnity or irritability, from optimism to resignation? How did the lips grow thinner and turn down at the corners? What happened to the bubbles of exuberance? When did the laughter of spontaneous happiness evanesce? Why did the joy of childhood disappear?

"Youth is a wonderful thing; what a crime to waste it on children," said George Bernard Shaw, but now science is saying that it doesn't have to be that way. When the true significance of neoteny is appreciated, Montague writes, "human beings can revolutionize their lives and become for the first time, perhaps, the kinds of creatures their heritage intends them to be — that is, youthful all the days of our lives."

"Verily I say unto you," Jesus said, "Except ye be converted, and become as little children, ye shall not enter the kingdom of heaven." Gould in his scholarly tome *Ontogeny and Phylogeny* says that J.B.S. Haldane, a brilliant British biologist, cited that verse in suggesting that Jesus be viewed as a prophet of human neoteny. Gould says Haldane made the suggestion facetiously. *Facetiously!* It was inconceivable to the scientist that a person two thousand years ago without the entire foundation of scientific knowledge could perceive one of nature's subtlest principles.

Not only did Jesus grasp it, as did Haldane, Jesus knew that it opened the way to the kingdom of God.

C. SOCIAL AND ECOLOGICAL

THIRTEEN

The Golden Rule

Human life functions in three spheres. Jesus' teachings in relation to the psychological and biological spheres have been discussed at length. Every living thing must exist in an environment, the third sphere. For humans, the most important part of this environment is the one they have created for themselves, the social.

In one of his most famous sayings, Jesus distinguished between the social and psychological spheres very explicitly. After he had come to Jerusalem, the Pharisees and Herodians sought to trick him into making a statement that could be used against him as a violation of Roman law and make him vulnerable to a charge of sedition which was punishable by death. Some Jews, especially rebellious Zealots, said it was a violation of Jewish law to pay tribute to Caesar. Tithe money belonged to God.

Therefore the Pharisees and Herodians approached Jesus and said disarmingly that they knew he preached the truth and held loyalty to no man, only to God. "Tell us therefore, What thinkest thou? Is it lawful to give tribute unto Caesar, or not? But Jesus perceived their wickedness, and said, Why tempt ye me, ye hypocrites? Shew me the tribute money. And they brought him a penny. And he saith unto them, Whose is this image and superscription? They said unto him Caesar's. Then saith he unto them, Render therefore unto Caesar the things which are Caesar's; and unto God the things that are God's. When they had heard these words, they marvelled, and left him, and went their way."

Since it was posited that Jesus' ethics, normally taken to be his edicts for social conduct, were primarily intended for a person's own psychological welfare, what was Jesus' social doctrine?

His rules of conduct largely can be summed up in a law which gained such respect for its wisdom that by the middle of the 16th century it was known as the Golden — the most excellent — Rule: "Therefore all things whatsoever ye would that men should do to you do ye even so to them."

Jesus said he was offering nothing new "for this is the law and the prophets." He may have been too modest because even here he was fulfilling the law, enlarging and enlivening it. There is no version of the Golden Rule in the Pentateuch. There is no version of the rule in the Biblical prophets. The law to which Jesus refers is the Talmudic oral law that was later written, enlarged and codified, and served much as United States Supreme Court decisions do in adapting the principles of the Constitution to new developments of contemporary life.

The earlier version of the Golden Rule is a saying by Hillel, a great rabbi whose life overlapped that of Jesus; Hillel died in about ten A.D. Hillel put the rule negatively: "What is hateful to you, do not to your neighbor; this is the whole law, all else is but its exposition." A previous and also negative proscription appeared in the apocryphal book of Tobit, believed to have been written about 250 B.C.: "Do not do to anyone what you yourself would hate."

In the Gospel of Thomas, this negative rule is presented as "do not do what you hate". What is elided is "to others," "to anyone," "to your neighbor." An ethical precept is turned into psychological advice that fits with Jesus' doctrine of "let thine eye be single." How crucial this recommendation is to a person's welfare may be judged by a statement made by Eleanor Robson Belmont. She was an international stage star of the early 20th century who married multimillionaire August Belmont and later helped to save the financially-distressed Metropolitan Opera Company during the Depression by forming the Opera Guild. Her final achievement was living to be 100 years old. When she was asked how she was able to survive for a century, she was ready with her answer. "No diet, no special care, nothing like that," Mrs. Belmont said. "It's doing what you want and doing it happily."

But in Matthew and Luke, Jesus is talking about conduct toward others. He retains the reciprocity expressed in Hillel and Tobit, indeed as contained in the ancient *lex talionis*, the law of retaliation, an eye for an eye. A few verses before the Golden Rule in the Sermon on the Mount, Jesus says, "Judge not, that ye be not judged. For with what judgment ye judge, ye shall be judged." And in Luke: "Condemn not, and ye shall not be condemned: forgive, and ye shall be forgiven: Give, and it shall be given unto you....For the same measure that ye mete withal it shall be measured to you again." In the Lord's Prayer: "Forgive us our debts, as we forgive our debtors." And at Gethsemane: "For all they that take the sword shall perish with the sword."

Jesus reinforces this human justice by also making it divine justice. There were precedents for this in the law and the prophets. In the great law-giving chapter Exodus 20: "For I the Lord thy God am a jealous God, visiting the iniquity of the fathers upon the children unto the third and fourth generation of them that hate me; And shewing mercy unto thousands of them that love me, and keep my commandments." In Isaiah: "I will not keep silence, but will recompense....Your iniquities, and the iniquities of your fathers together, said the Lord, which have burned incense upon the mountains, and blasphemed me upon the hills". In Jeremiah: "Thou shewest lovingkindness unto thousands, and recompensest the iniquity of the fathers into the bosom of their children after them." And the Second Isaiah announced that God's divine justice was made manifest through the instrument of history.

With Jesus, divine justice is dealt individually to each person. The parable of The Wicked Servant contains both human and divine justice. The parable begins with Jesus likening it to the kingdom of God, so that we know he is talking about his own doctrine. In the parable a servant is brought before his lord because of a huge debt owed the master. The servant pleads with his king to forgive the debt, and out of compassion the lord does so. Then the servant turns around and refuses to write off a trifling debt owed him by a fellow servant; instead the servant has the debtor thrown into prison. When the king hears of this, he is outraged. He tells the wicked servant: "I forgave thee all that debt, because thou desiredst me: Shouldest not thou also have had compassion on thy fellowservant, even as I had pity on thee?" The servant was "delivered to the tormenters" until he paid his entire debt. The parable concludes: "So likewise shall my heavenly Father do also unto you, if ye from your hearts forgive not every one his brother their trespasses."

Immediately after the Lord's Prayer, Jesus explains the passage about forgiving debts by saying, "For if ye forgive men their trespasses, your heavenly Father also will forgive you: But if ye forgive not men their trespasses, neither will your heavenly Father forgive your trespasses." And in Mark: "And when ye stand praying, forgive, if ye have ought against any: that your Father also which is in heaven may forgive you your trespasses. But if ye do not forgive, neither will your Father which is in heaven forgive your trespasses."

Scientists have no knowledge of divine justice. Perhaps the closest one can come in science is with some ecological laws of nature that are beyond human control, such as: Refusal to exist in equilibrium with the environment ultimately debases the human habitat, improvident use of resources impoverishes posterity. Protect the ecosystem or pollute yourself, preserve nature's diversity or live with monotony, respect nature's frontiers or exist in a world-wide prison. *The Immortality Factor* pointed to the ecological consequence for achieving biological immortality: a world without children.

But perhaps a motive can be suggested for Jesus' proclaiming divine justice. In psychology, it would be known as a self-fulfilling prophecy. Such is the power of the mind that a prediction is carried out in fact. A voodoo death is a form of self-fulfilling prophecy. Who can tell what effect Joe Namath's categorical declaration that his New York Jets would win an unlikely Superbowl victory had in the confirming outcome — effect both negatively upon the minds of Baltimore Colts players and positively upon his own teammates? We'll never know, but the prediction and victory made Joe Namath a legend in his own time.

Who can calculate the effect that Jesus' pronouncement of divine justice had upon the course of civilization and upon countless human lives? Human beings who believed made their behavior conform to their beliefs. Governors were placed on the minds of kings who ruled by divine right, that is, who were subject to divine law. The unrestrained, monstrous mentality of a Nero or Caligula was reined in by divine justice. How many acts of violence were averted and acts of cruelty mitigated by the fear of divine justice? How many acts of kindness were performed in the hope of divine justice? How much was the world's quotient of human goodness expanded? In effect, belief made divine justice reality in the realm of natural fact.

But Jesus' proclamation of the Golden Rule has had probably an even greater effect upon human affairs. The negative version stated by Hillel promotes detente, peaceful coexistence, avoidance of conflict. It was a great ethical advance over *lex talionis* while using that law's reciprocity as the motivating core of self-interest and justice. That version reflects a law of life already discussed: avoidance of competition wherever possible. Different species of oganisms tend to form their own niches rather than vie as rivals for the same resources.

Jesus' transformation of the rule into a positive ethic goes beyond avoidance of conflict. The Golden Rule encourages active, positive behavior toward one's fellows rather than passive, defensive conduct. Instead of withholding enmity and hate, it promotes offering of kindness and love. It is the ethical counterpart for life's greatest strategy for survival: cooperation.

A new scientific appreciation of the significance of cooperation results from very recent discoveries of fossil evidence of primeval microorganisms, the decoding of DNA, and new knowledge about cells. Microbiologist Lynn Margulis declares in the 1986 book *Microcosmos*: "The view of evolution as chronic bloody competition among individuals and species, a popular distortion of Darwin's notion of 'survival of the fittest,' dissolves before a new view of continual cooperation, strong interaction, and mutual dependence among life forms. Life did not take over the globe by combat, but by networking."

Just recently, Margulis says, life scientists have begun to appreciate that evolution has proceeded by other mechanisms as well as mutation. With mutation, a species might need a million years to adjust to change on a world-wide scale. But bacteria, the most ancient form of cells, can make the adaptation in a few years by the exchange of genetic material. This bacterial "biotechnology" has been going on for billions of years before the first human efforts in the technique. What this means, Margulis writes, is that "all the world's bacteria essentially have access to a single gene pool and hence to the adaptive mechanisms of the entire bacterial kingdom." Cooperation has been built into life since its beginning, and is such a powerful mechanism for survival that bacteria would be able to adapt to a planet devastated by nuclear war.

In such an event, the first would be last. And the last — the most recent species in time and most complex, including *Homo sapiens sapiens* — would be the first to go. There is a correspondence in vulnerability of species to radiation in terms of their complexity. I saw a remarkable demonstration of this phenomenon at Brookhaven National Laboratory on Long Island. Ecologist George Woodwell was conducting a long-term experiment to discover the effects of radiation on an ecosystem, in this case an oak-pine forest. A cesium-17 source turned on intermittantly was surrounded by five concentric zones of graduated life. The center immediately around the radioactive cesium was barren (although I don't know if Dr. Woodwell examined for bacteria). In the innermost concentric zone lichens and some mosses were able to survive. In the next zone farther out were sedges and grasses, then in ring three were shrubs. In the fourth zone were oak trees — only the pines were missing. Beyond that circle the original forest was intact.

The science of ecology has found a number of these first-last/last-first paradoxes. In all kinds of ecosystems there occurs what is called ecological succession. It may take a thousand years, but if the environmental conditions are suitable, a mature forest can develop from bare rock. The process begins with the effects of weathering on boulders. Small crevices are formed, they collect water, the water freezes in winter forcing larger cracks until lichens, the first pioneers of life, are able to gain a foothold. The lichens accelerate the disintegration of rock and start the building of soil until there is enough for a seedbed for mosses and ferns, then weeds. What takes place is that each wave of colonists unwittingly prepares an environment suitable for higher life forms. All kinds of micro-organisms, then nematodes, earthworms, millipedes and small soil arthropods move in. Scores of weed species modify the environment to such an extent that it can sustain the more dominant perennial grasses that eliminate the annual weeds. Shrubs invade, followed by larger woody plants and sumacs, the fast-growing first trees. With each succession of plant communities come different and more animals and birds. Pines outcompete the first tree settlers to be largely replaced themselves by the tree species that dominate the forest in the eastern United States — sugar maple, beech, oak and hemlock. The last to arrive become the first in the sense of the most dominant members of the forest ecosystem.

Various kinds of ecological succession take place in other eco-systems including cities.

Ecologists have found another kind of first-last/last-first phenomenon in what they call dispersal. Dispersal is related to dominance which is practiced among gregarious animals that live in groups. Dominance hierarchy reduces competition and violence within the group, conserves energy that would be wasted in needless fighting and prevents overcrowding. Because socially dominant animals control the habitat, when population density becomes too great, the socially subordinate members are forced to leave. This is a risky move for them because they may be more exposed to predators or they may not find another suitable environment. In some instances, however, the outcasts arrive at even more agreeable environments than they have left so that they prosper and their offspring multiply.

This phenomenon is observed in human affairs with a prime example in the emigration from Europe to the wilderness of North America. The socially dominant Europeans — royalty, nobles, wealthy, the well-connected, sons who stood to inherit — had no incentive to leave what they had. They stayed. The emigrants were the poor, socially less favored, religiously persecuted. They found an environment in which very many people were able to prosper individually while collectively they were able to develop a more powerful nation than they had left.

The socially dominant Jews of Jesus' time did not accept his doctrine, holding to their established traditions. The social inferiors, with little or no stake in the benefits of the society, were responsive. Recognizing the adamant nature of the opposition in the people he wanted to influence, Jesus predicted that the first would be last in the kingdom of God and the last first. He was correct in this prophecy. Those people first told about the kingdom disdained it: Judaism never embraced his teachings. Instead, the gentiles, foreigners from the north, east, south and west of the world — those who learned of him last — became his followers.

The last-first phenomenon explains the parable of the vineyard owner who paid his laborers the same wages even though they worked for different periods of time. It is another parable about the unfairness of life. Very often those who come first have to work harder for their survival than those who come after them. The pioneers who tamed the wilderness in the United States are a case in point. With less effort we enjoy benefits brought about by those who have gone before: those who fought for, sacrificed their lives and won the freedom we sometimes take for granted, those who developed the resources to produce our high standard of living, those who invented comforts that make our lives less onerous and tedious. "The fact never to be forgotten," Rene Dubos wrote in *The Torch of Life,* "is that we are the beneficiaries of the wealth and wisdom that our ancestors acquired through centuries of painful effort. Most of the splendors of our civilization are not of our own making; we are enjoying a heritage rich in material goods, in experience and knowledge."

That's the way it is. The first shall be last in terms of difficulty, the last shall be first in terms of benefits.

In addition to bacterial genetic exchange, there is another prominent form of cooperation in nature: symbiotic alliance. With this process, competition is eliminated by the strategy we know as "if you can't lick 'em, join 'em." This method of combination is very ancient, too, and has yielded one of the most surprising of recent discoveries.

To back up and set the stage just a bit, it was first noticed in 1838 that the bodies of all animals and plants are made of cells. There are free-living one-celled plants and animals as well. The cell is the basic unit of life and all composite creatures are colonies of cells whose cooperation is exquisitely coordinated. In human bodies, trillions upon trillions of cells are simultaneously executing an incredible array of operations without our being aware of anything happening. Cells are so small that even the best light microscopes cannot look into them very well. A century went by before the electron microscope and other sophisticated tools of investigation opened the cell's interior to human understanding. "We have entered the cell, the mansion of our birth," said Albert Claude, the founder of modern cell biology, in his Nobel speech. "If we examine the accomplishments of man in his most advanced endeavors, in theory and in practice, we find that the cell has done all this long before him, and with greater resourcefulness and much greater efficiency."

Within the cell are a number of units that enable it to carry out its essential functions. These clearly demarcated units were named organelles. Two of the most important are the nucleus, which contains the cell's DNA genetic heritage, and the mitochondrion, which has been likened to the cell's powerhouse or source of energy. Without mitochondria, the nucleated cell (that is, all cells except bacteria) cannot utilize oxygen. Without mitochondria there would be no higher forms of life on earth. Now it has been discovered that mitochondria have genetic material that is different from the host cell's DNA in the nucleus. The accepted conclusion is that mitochondria once were free-living forms that traded their independent status for the protected environment inside a larger organism and in return provided an invaluable organic improvement. The same scenario now is accepted for chloroplasts, those photosynthetic parts of plants able to fix the sun's energy and turn it into the chemical carbohydrates that the plant needs to grow and to provide the ultimate food source for the animal kingdom.

Symbiotic relationships between different species are so common that, Dubos says, "they are probably the rule rather than the exception." Bacteria living in the roots of various legumes fix atmospheric nitrogen that is essential to the host plant's existence. Termites could not digest wood without certain protozoa living in their intestines. Pollination of plants is performed by a variety of insect and animal species. In every symbiotic relationship, each partner benefits. The flower gives an offering of nectar and gets a messenger of reproduction.

Lichens once were thought to be mosses until the late 19th century when they were found to consist of two entirely different species —one a fungus, the other an alga — living closely together. The word symbiosis was given to this association of dissimilar organisms after its discovery in the lichen. The alga uses its chlorophyll to make food for itself and the fungus while the fungus has water-absorbent tissue that provides moisture for both organisms. Acids secreted by the fungus leach life-giving nutrients from rock faces and other harsh surroundings. Lichens are able to colonize environments too inhospitable for other plants. The fungi and algae, both of which remain genetically separate, come together as lichens out of need. Together they can survive where neither could make it alone.

It would not be unfair to say that life was able to inherit the planet by living the Golden Rule. Help and you will be helped, give and it will be given to you. The Golden Rule works. It is the epitome of practicality. As life has used it on all levels, so no better ethic has ever been devised for conducting human affairs. If Jesus' more radical prescriptions — love your enemies, do good to them that hate you, turn the other cheek — were intended in the ethical-social sense, why was the Golden Rule included in the Sermons on the Mount and on the Plain? The Golden Rule would not have been needed if the other recommendations were ethical precepts as well — they would have superseded it. Do unto others as you would have them do to you is more moderate than even love thy neighbor.

The writer of Matthew implicitly recognizes the different nature of the two sets of advice by putting them apart by two chapters. In Luke, the Golden Rule and the other recommendations are lumped together as though they were all part of the same thesis. That this joining is an error is suggested by the fact that varieties of the Golden Rule have appeared in many cultures and religions whereas love your enemies is singular with Jesus.   The use of the Golden Rule as the guiding code for social behavior has four advantages:

1. It is totally understandable.

2. It is reasonable — a code of conduct that anyone can carry out.

3. It is valid — the best practicable behavioral law that humans have.

4. It validates Jesus' wisdom, making him at once comprehensible and reasonable.

The Golden Rule takes into account each person's self-interest so that it is biologically sound while encouraging benign behavior in others to contribute to the individual's welfare. Jesus, as we know, advocated all kinds of positive, cooperative actions toward others.

And just because it is proposed that Jesus intended much of his advice in the sense of cultivate your own garden — your mind — and don't let others trample it with their aggressions and meanness, this does not rule out the tremendous social effects produced by loving thy neighbor and turning the other cheek.

Jesus' prescriptions for personal thought in conjunction with the Golden Rule are all that is needed to create a social environment of consideration for others, forgiveness, kindness, gentleness. The kind of environment, in fact, in which the types of people that Jesus liked — the non-aggressive, humble and childlike; the honest and just; the righteous, tolerant and compassionate — could flourish.

In these ecological phenomena described above lies an explanation for the Beatitude "Blessed are the meek: for they shall inherit the earth," which is incomprehensible when regarded as moral exhortation. We powerful human beings act as though we have inherited the earth, and we know we are not a meek species. But it is just now that scientists are beginning to realize that the meek already have inherited the earth and if they hadn't, we never would have appeared on the scene. First came the microorganisms. We still have difficulty comprehending how thoroughly microbes inhabit the planet. For example, close to three tons of bacteria can live in a single acre of soil.

The unicelled organisms had to come first in order to prepare the way for the multicelled ones. Green plants have inherited the earth, and they had to do so in order to provide the nourishment for the animal kingdom. The ecological pyramid of life, determined by the food web, is a measure of levels of meekness. At the bottom and broad base of the pyramid, comprising most of the living biomass, is the vegetation that captures the sun's energy and converts it into food. Above the green plants are the herbivores — the lambs and all other animals that live exclusively on vegetation. Above them are carnivores, the meat-eaters that prey on the more docile plant-eaters. There are a few secondary carnivores — predators of other carnivores — and a few omnivores, like human beings, that can eat just about anything.

At each level of consumption, only about ten percent of the energy stored in the plant or animal can be utilized by the consumer. Because of this 90 percent loss of energy at each transfer, the food supply can support ever fewer individuals at each level and very few at the tops of the food chains, like hawks and leopards. In the scheme of life, the meek must inherit the earth or the aggressive would perish. It was a brilliant perception on the part of Jesus, but not an impossible one. After all, Abraham Lincoln could recognize that the Lord preferred plain, common looking people since he makes so many of them.

D. THE GOOD LIFE
FOURTEEN
The Kingdom Of God

"Again, the kingdom of heaven is like unto a merchant man, seeking goodly pearls: Who, when he had found one pearl of great price, went and sold all that he had and bought it."

Like many other products, pearls have become plentiful in our civilization. They are much more available and much less costly than they were once; also intrinsically less valuable and less beautiful. Cultured pearls, that is, which are made by implanting a shell fragment inside oysters and freshwater mussels. The foreign object in the mollusc is then coated with nacre in the same manner as natural pearls. But genuine pearls, accidents of nature, possess a depth and luster unmatched by cultured pearls. Natural pearls still are rare. Since they are made by nature, genuine pearls vary in size and character. There may be a flaw in symmetry or value may be enhanced by tints of color. Pearls must be evaluated by someone with knowledge of them.

Because of their rarity, because of the uncertainty and difficulty of obtaining goodly pearls, and because they long had been desired for their beauty in human adornment, pearls at the time of Jesus were more prized than precious metals or gems. Pliny the Elder wrote in his *Historia Naturalis* that in the 1st century B.C. pearls were first in value among all precious things. Suetonius reported that the Roman general Vitelius paid for an entire campaign by selling one of his mother's pearl earrings.

There was a story that Cleopatra made a bet with Marc Antony that she could give the most expensive dinner in history. The Egyptian queen removed an earring, crushed it, dissolved it into a goblet of wine, then drank the wine. When she took off the other earring and offered it to her Roman friend, the wager was declared won by her. Pliny estimated that Cleopatra's pearls were worth 60 million sesterces, or 1,875,000 ounces of fine silver.

That is the kind of worth that Jesus placed on the kingdom of God. But the secret of getting to the kingdom is contained in the rest of the parable: the merchant recognized the worth of the pearl and acted upon his assessment. He went and sold all that he had in order to buy the pearl. He changed his life completely because of it. "Not every one that saith unto me, Lord, Lord, shall enter into the kingdom of heaven," Jesus said, "but he that doeth the will of my Father which is in heaven."

The key to the necessity of doing was given by Maxwell Maltz in a popular book in the early 1960s, *Psycho-Cybernetics*. Dr. Maltz was a plastic surgeon who observed that people with some kind of disfigurement, particularly facial, often had a poor self-image, low self-esteem. He discovered the importance of self-image by noticing what happened to people after plastic surgery had improved their looks. Some patients changed immediately. They became new persons. They shucked off their old gloomy, unventuresome outlooks and were ready to begin new lives. Other patients, however, didn't change at all. They remained their same miserable selves unable to believe that the world was now their oyster.

Dr. Maltz came to see that the surgery, the outward change, really was of secondary importance. What mattered was the inner change, in the patient's mind — how he looked to himself.

We already have seen that Jesus appreciated the determining function of the mind in the act of healing and in ordering behavior. That Jesus grasped the importance of the mind in the *Psycho-Cybernetics* sense is indicated by his saying in Mark: "What things soever ye desire, when ye pray, believe that ye receive them, and ye shall have them." In Matthew: "And all things, whatsoever ye shall ask in prayer, believing, ye shall receive."

"This book has been designed not merely to be read, but to be *experienced*," Dr. Maltz wrote in *Psycho-Cybernetics*. "You can acquire information from reading a book. But to 'experience' you must creatively respond to information. Acquiring information itself is passive. Experiencing is active. When you 'experience,' something happens inside your nervous system and your midbrain. New 'engrams' and 'neural' patterns are recorded in the gray matter of your brain."

Maltz recommended to his reader that he practice being the kind of person he wanted to be, that he imagine himself as successful in whatever endeavor he chose, to rehearse acting creatively and positively. Maltz said that so many people have fallen into habits of reacting negatively, by grousing or feeling sorry for themselves, that these reactions were reinforced by repetitions and became ingrained. Such is the power of this kind of imagining that Maltz cited a case where one group, which practiced shooting baskets only in their imagination, improved almost as much as another group where the people actually tossed the ball.

We can see that Jesus understood this principle of experienced learning and at the same time find an explanation for the saying in the Gospel of Thomas: "The Kingdom of the Father is like a man who wanted to kill a powerful man. He drew his sword in his own house; he thrust it into the wall so that he would know if his hand would stick it through. Then he killed the powerful one."

Dennis Garvin, the centenarian who attributed his longevity to the kingdom of God and then added "But you have to live it," intuitively perceived this phenomenon. I believe it also explains the parable of the Hidden Treasure, both versions. In Matthew, "the kingdom of heaven is like unto treasure hid in a field; the which when a man hath found, he hideth, and for joy thereof goeth and selleth all that he hath, and buyeth that field." Just like the pearl merchant, the man recognizes the inherent value of the treasure and gladly gives all his possessions in exchange for it. He appreciates it and he acts. In the Gospel of Thomas, the point is made even more specifically. The treasure exists all along in the field, but the original owner wasn't aware of it nor was his son who inherited the field. The kingdom's treasure became apparent to the field's new owner only after he had plowed it. He had to do the work to earn and appreciate the knowledge that otherwise remains hidden.

This completes the listing of the combinations that, like those which give access to a safe or a computer, open the way to the kingdom of God. This inquiry has postulated that the kingdom is in the mind. These are the keys, assembled during the inquiry, that enable entry into the kingdom:

First of all, there is righteousness. Not a punctilious, letter-of-the-law rectitude, but a genuine righteousness that issues from a person's whole being. Wholeness of the person, of the mind is the essential. Honesty opens access to the kingdom, hypocrisy blocks the approach because hypocrisy fractures the integrity of the self. Good health, physical and mental, are requisites, for both kinds mean wholeness of the mind/body. One must have humility and other childlike qualities in order to get into the kingdom. The arrogant are blind to it. So are the people beguiled by worldly wealth, preoccupied with material concerns, distracted by petty worries about status or exaggerated fears over financial security: all those people who can't distinguish the truly important things in life and thus are unable to set their lives in order with the proper priorities. Preparation is a requisite.

From the Lilies of the Field and the Wise Virgins to The Sower.

The parable of The Sower says the kingdom must be understood. In order to enter it, a person must know what it is. With this knowledge, a person can evaluate the kingdom. The pearl merchant and the man who discovers the hidden treasure were able to make such an evaluation and gave up everything for the kingdom. Their lives were transformed because of it. They saw everything from a new perspective. They experienced it, lived it. One must, spiritually, be born again.

But for people who have done these things, it no longer is "must be:" they *are* born again. They are in the kingdom of God.

Perhaps an ascension that I experienced in World War Two can help serve as a metaphor. I was flying a P-38 out of a base on Attu. The P-38 was a twin-boom, twin-engine fighter plane built by Lockheed and called Lightning. What was most treasured about the P-38 in the Aleutians was the redundancy of engines. The other front-line Army fighter planes, the P-51 and P-47, were single-engine craft. The second engine was insurance against having to ditch the aircraft if one engine failed. I lost an engine once and had no trouble getting back to base.

Attu is the westernmost of a chain of volcanic islands extending from the Alaska mainland 1,500 miles into the North Pacific Ocean. There were two airstrips on Attu, both next to the water with mountains close by. These two strips were the only places on the island where a plane could be brought down safely. In an emergency over the ocean, we knew that the water was so cold that a pilot would freeze to death in minutes.

Soon after being assigned to a squadron on Attu, I took part in a routine flight on an overcast day. One rarely saw the sun. The non-stop, sky-wide cloud blanket was an important element in making the greatest enemy of people sent to the Aleutians their own feeling of depression. In addition to long winter nights and dark days, there were the bitter weather, the treeless and barren islands, and the bleak seascape of a grey and desolate ocean.

Our flight leader decided that instead of just cruising in the vicinity of the island, we should investigate how high the overcast went. I remember that we lifted into the clouds at 2,000 feet. Our flight consisted of four P-38s. There was the flight leader and to his left and slightly in back his wingman. I flew in the second element. My element leader flew to the right and somewhat farther behind the flight leader than the wingman. I was wingman to the element leader, flying to his right and behind.

As soon as we entered the overcast, visibility closed down to a few feet. The fog was so impenetrable that the only plane I could see was that of my element leader, and I had to fly uncomfortably close in order to keep his plane from vanishing. If that happened and I could not recover sight contact almost immediately, I would have to break off because it would have been too dangerous to continue flying close together at high speed without precisely knowing where the other planes were.

The prospect of being on my own was cause for apprehension. While I had the gold bars and silver wings, I still was a relatively inexperienced pilot. I'd logged time in a Link trainer, had flown at night and flown on instruments as a co-pilot in a cargo plane, but I never had been on my own in an actual pea-soup situation. I was unfamiliar with the radio directional pattern of the area and had no confidence that I could get back down on my own to find the airbase without banging into a mountain.

I decided I had better not lose visual contact with my element leader. But this was not so simple either. Presumably the flight leader kept his throttles steady for the climb. Nevertheless, my element leader continually had to make slight adjustments in speed, either to catch up in order to keep the flight leader in sight or to slow down in order not to overrun him. As keenly as my mind was attuned to my element leader's plane, I could not anticipate his adjustments. There inevitably was a time-lag in which he would begin to pull away from me, his plane fading into the mist. Each time this started to happen, I would experience a thrill of fear that prompted an impulse to overcompensate in order to keep the plane in sight. But as I gained or he slowed, I had to chop throttles in order not to slide ahead of him, and then be careful not to drop back too quickly.

The tension of these oscillations went on unabated. At 12,000 feet, we had to put on oxygen masks. Flying in this kind of limbo with no visual orientation except the P-38 receding and looming in the fog and no other sense of motion although I knew we were traveling at close to 300 miles an hour tends to create a feeling of vertigo. The surreality had to be controlled and fought off. 15,000 feet and still climbing. With the tension and fear, the adrenaline was running high, keeping me super alert, but also making this flight almost unbearable and seemingly endless. 18,000 feet. How long could it go on? The P-38 could climb to somewhat above 39,000 feet. What if we still hadn't broken out at the plane's ceiling? What then? I hated to contemplate this ordeal continuing. I wondered how long I could go without making a mistake.

Finally the grey began to brighten. We rose out of the clouds at 20,000 feet. Oh, the feeling of relief! To be still alive and safe! The relaxation at being freed from the tight visual leash and the adrenal sentience combined to produce another sensation: astonishment at then enveloping beauty. The underside of the 20,000-foot cloud cover was a dirty seal over a monochrome world. The motto of that world was "Kill or be killed."

Like some Alice-in-Wonderland, I had been transported from hell through limbo to the empyrean. I glided over a soft, cottony, voluptuous, glistening, immaculate cloudscape. I was immersed in a pristine purity, a sojourner in a serene cleanness. Above was a scrubbed blue sky suffused with sunlight. The sun! Its brilliance glinted off silver wings and glass canopies to refract into rainbow hues. The radiance tinctured the milky terrain with a golden refulgence. I was enthralled.

Any air traveler today can routinely see such a vista if he bothers to look away from his magazine, but he will not be affected in the way that I was that day high above the grim Aleutians. The passenger is detached, uninvolved with the transformation. He would have to experience the day-after-day desolation of life below, the deprivation of sunlight, omnipresence of dangerous options, and the excruciating ordeal endured just before the sunburst of safety. Then, if the passenger had a full hemisphere for observation, he would be able to see what it is like to enter the gleaming interior of a jewel.

The kingdom of God is an altered state of being, a transformed consciousness, a changed perception, a new feeling about one's life and circumstances. This is not necessarily a permanent condition although the possibility for its continuance exists even though the state always remains contingent.

The righteousness — being true to oneself, one's ideals and values — makes it possible for a person to feel good about himself. He can enjoy high self-esteem. Usually this estimate is reinforced by the actions of others who accord the person respect. This does not always happen, however. Sometimes a person marching to his own drummer must defy commonly-accepted standards, in which case he can face public opprobrium. Whistle-blowers are good examples. Their sense of righteousness is such that they risk their livelihoods and even their reputations in order to report a perceived wrongdoing. Going against the herd is one of the most difficult things that any human being can do. Jesus recognized this and made it one of his most important Beatitudes: "Blessed are they who are persecuted for righteousness' sake: for theirs is the kingdom of heaven."

Perhaps the ultimate in neck-sticking-out was performed during the Nazi terror by those Germans and other Europeans who saved Jews from the Holocaust. By some estimates, as many as 200,000 Jews were hidden from the Nazis by non-Jewish rescuers. Some of these brave people who risked their own lives by harboring Jews took in helpless refugees whom they never had seen before, total strangers ("I was a stranger, and ye took me in"). Now a scientific study is finding that these people were able to reach out to others despite personal peril not because they were selfless — quite the contrary! It was because they had a strong sense of self-worth.

Living according to one's beliefs confers another inestimable benefit: peace of mind. Flora Whisenand, who said she was able to live 100 years because she never had done anything she was ashamed of, saw deeply into the secret of her longevity. The point was not that she had been able to survive a century. The real point, and what I believe she was trying to convey to the Social Security man, is that she was able to live for 100 years *with herself.*

Emerson made the connection between righteousness and peace of mind with the concluding words of his great essay, "Self-Reliance." "Nothing can bring you peace but yourself. Nothing can bring you peace but the triumph of principles."

"Come unto me because my yoke is easy and my mastery is gentle," Jesus said in the Gospel of Thomas, "and you will find your repose."

I believe peace of mind explains the riddle that Jesus posed in the 50th verse of Thomas. Jesus told his disciples, "If they ask you, 'What is the sign of your Father who is in you?' say to them, "It is movement and repose."" Animation, or life, and peace.

Joshua Loth Liebman, a famous rabbi, began a book he wrote in 1946 with an account of a list of life's good things that he compiled as a young man. He set down his inventory of what would make him completely happy: health, love, beauty, talent, power, riches, fame and a few lesser attributes.

Liebman proudly showed his list to a wise elder. Any man who could possess all these things, the young Liebman said, would be like a god. The old friend thought it was an excellent selection, but added: "You have forgotten the one ingredient lacking which each possession becomes a hideous torment, and your list as a whole an intolerable burden." With a pencil, the old man crossed out the entire list and wrote in its place three words: peace of mind. "This is the gift that God reserves for his special proteges. Talent and beauty He gives to many. Wealth is commonplace, fame not rare. But peace of mind —that is His final guerdon of approval, the fondest sign of his love. He bestows it charily. Most men are never blessed with it; others wait all their lives — yes, far into advanced age — for this gift to descend on them."

Anyone who must live constantly with any of the negative emotions cited earlier, particularly anxiety and also guilt, grief and despair, knows how they can rob life of its worth. Such feelings, if intense enough for long enough, can make living untenable. Poor health, a threat to life, a severe handicap must be included among the robbers. Unfortunately, some circumstances are beyond our control: peace of mind never can be guaranteed. A past act with unremediable consequences, a loved one with a terminal illness, a son or daughter snared by drugs all cause conditions that are incompatible with peace of mind.

Here lies the explanation for the enigmatic passage in Matthew 11:11-12: "Among them that are born of women there hath not risen a greater than John the Baptist: notwithstanding he that is least in the kingdom of heaven is greater than he. And from the days of John the Baptist until now the kingdom of heaven suffereth violence, and the violent take it by force." The first part is explained, as it was suggested earlier, by the 13th verse: "For all the prophets and the law prophesied until John." John didn't know about the kingdom of God, a new concept born with Jesus. Even followers who understood or accepted only a fraction of Jesus' doctrine were better off than John and his followers.

When one becomes aware of the existence of the kingdom, then one also understands that violence and violent people can destroy a person's peace of mind. This is precisely the weapon of terrorism. Worry, anxiety, fear are allies of injury and pain. With the realization that the kingdom is a precious state comes the appreciation of how terrible is the loss.

Without peace of mind, a person is banished from the kingdom of God. With this inner repose, the final gate to the citadel of he kingdom swings open. It becomes possible for the person at peace with himself to achieve the highest and most pleasurable state of mind. We have many words to describe it: joy, happiness, rapture, euphoria, ecstasy, pleasure, bliss, blessedness, beatitude. It is the very quality which we recognize as characterizing children and differentiating them from adults: unselfconscious joy and exuberance for life. It is a natural high, a high without drugs, a high without chemicals, a high without an enslaving dependency upon any destructive material. The resident in the kingdom of God is high on life.

The life translates into the good life, good in the sense of righteous. That good life translates into the good life as the enjoyable life, a life worth living, peace and plenty.

"The kingdom of heaven is like unto treasure hid in a field: the which when a man hath found, he hideth, and for *joy* thereof goeth and selleth all that he hath, and buyeth that field." The master, returning from a far country, praised the profitable servants and rewarded them: "enter thou into the *joy* of thy lord." Jesus tells his disciples, "These things have I spoken unto you, that my *joy* might remain in you, and that your *joy* might be full."

The progress from peacefulness to an altered state of consciousness has been understood and practiced in the mysticism of many religions, including Christianity. A 14th century treatise of the Western Church, *The Cloud of Unknowing,* tells how to achieve a union with God. The anonymous author says that this goal cannot be gained in the ordinary levels of human consciousness. Necessary lower depths of consciousness are reached by shutting out all distractions and stopping all physical activity. This can be done by choosing a word of one syllable, such as God or love, and repeating the word, concentrating solely on it until all thoughts are banished.

Meditation and mysticism in the Eastern Church used a repetitive prayer. A monk sat alone in silence. He lowered his head, breathed gently, and as he exhaled, said silently, "Lord Jesus Christ have mercy on me." Gradually all other thoughts disappeared.

The principle, with variations, is virtually the same wherever this method is found. Yoga puts great emphasis on breathing. The Jewish Kabalistic tradition included prayer and meditation with a profound contemplation on the divine name of God until the soul was released from its material bonds and the communicant achieved ecstasy. In Sufism, Islamic mysticism, concentration on the name of God was aided by rhythmic breathing, music and dance to induce the trance. Dervishes whirled their way into euphoria. Taoism recommended concentrating on nothingness in order to arrive at absolute tranquility. Transcendental Meditation, practiced today in the United States, employs a mantra word as the beacon for exclusive thought.

Dr. Herbert Benson of Harvard Medical School has secularized the process with the Relaxation Response. In order to elicit this response, a person takes a restful passive position in a quiet environment. The person consciously tries to relax his muscles, becomes aware of his breathing, and with every expiration silently says a neutral single-syllable word like "one." The practice must be continued for at least 20 minutes in order to produce benefits. The Relaxation Response is an antidote for hypertension, quelling the high blood pressure and other effects of frequent triggering of the sympathetic nervous system. The response, practiced regularly, helps people to be more relaxed and to attain greater enjoyment in our tense civilization.

But Jesus was not a mystic in this sense. He did not preach passivity. He was a teacher in the tradition of the Jewish prophets. He did not teach mental isolation from the ills of life nor withdrawal from the world, but rather how to deal with life in ways that were compatible with peace and joy. He did not teach a narrowing of life. *The* life was more life. It meant getting more out of life. "I am come that they might have life, and that they might have it more abundantly." Don't sleepwalk through life. Let the dead bury their dead, he told one man. You come with me and preach the kingdom of God. There is the same point in the parable of The Sower. His way provides more abundance. Live life on all cylinders! Be sentient to what the good life has to offer!

Again, science is beginning to catch up to Jesus and understand how an altered state of consciousness and euphoria can come about through active use of the mind. In the mid-1970s, neurobiologists began to discover brain peptides, hormones of the central nervous system that mediate stress and coping, pain and pleasure — categories crucial to emotional well-being. Several opioid peptides produce various kinds of pain-killing and euphoric effects. The name opioid is an analogue of opium whose chief ingredient is morphine, a powerful pain-killer and sedative producing euphoric effects. A derivative of morphine is heroin, one of the most addictive narcotics known. With the discovery of the opioid peptides, the reason for the almost irresisitible power of these drugs could be understood. The synthetic substances took over niches in the brain already designed for the opioid peptides and evoked more intense euphoric effects.

The result is a kind of perversion of the parables of The Pearl and the Hidden Treasure. In order to enter this kingdom of pleasure, the addict is willing to sell all that he has, go into hock, resort to crime, lay waste to his body and life. Unlike the kingdom of God, this kingdom does not open a person to life, but shuts him off from it. This kingdom does not enhance his fruitfulness and productivity, but imprisons him in a stupor. Ironically, cocaine winds up inducing psychological states inimical to the pleasure promised. This is believed to happen because the drug interferes with the intercellular transfer of neurotransmitters, particularly the neurotransmitter dopamine which has been associated with euphoria. The interference at first produces a glut of dopamine, causing the high, but this is followed by a depletion, causing depression and a desperate craving for another high. A survey by the National Cocaine Helpline found that among 500 users who telephoned, five out of six suffered from depression and anxiety. Two-thirds said they were apathetic and/or had symptoms of paranoia and/or difficulty concentrating. More than half suffered loss of sex drive. One out of two reported attacks of panic, a clinical syndrome characterized by bouts of acute anxiety, hyperventilation and a frighteningly-high heart rate.

From the resort to hard drugs, the abuse of alcohol, the popularity of over-the-counter pain-killers and sedatives, there must be a tremendous amount of misery out there.

But there is another way.

Opioids can be quite powerful in their own right and in their own way. The differences between opioids and narcotics is that the natural substances act to protect and benefit the person. For example, a phenomenon observed in the battlefield but also in auto accidents and other cases of trauma is that although a victim may have suffered a grievous wound he experiences no pain, at least initially. Opioid analgesics can block what should have been unbearable agony. Lewis Thomas in *The Lives of a Cell* related that African explorer David Livingstone was caught by a lion and crushed across the chest by the animal's powerful jaws, but was saved by a lucky shot that killed the lion. Livingstone "was so amazed by the extraordinary sense of peace, calm, and total painlessness associated with being killed," Dr. Thomas writes, "that he constructed a theory that all creatures are provided with a protective psychologic mechanism, switched on at the verge of death, carrying them through in a haze of tranquility."

Almost every death is preceded by reduction of oxygen to the brain, a condition known as hypoxia. Pilots are taught that if they are flying on oxygen and begin to experience a sensation of ecstasy, it means they have lost some or all of their oxygen supply. They must do something immediately — either descend to a safe altitude or correct whatever may be the fault in the oxygen system. Pilots must be warned that this insidious (because so enticing and reassuring) emotional state is a prelude to death. A friend who had suffered a heart attack told me that after he had called authorities he began to slip into this euphoria. Intellectually he knew what was happening, but emotionally he was not alarmed.

A new class of euphoric states now is being explored by a number of investigators. With the national trend to running and jogging, researchers found that the incentives for such an exhausting pastime were not only the ones given — improvement in health, endurance and body trimness. The steady rhythmical physical exercise brought what came to be known as the "runner's high," a pleasurable state that was ascribed to production of endorphins, another of the opioids. Now the runner's high is recognized to be associated with all kinds of situations — playing chess, for instance, or playing a musical instrument, listening to a symphony or a rock concert, performing surgery or building a model airplane.

The common denominator in all of these pleasurable states is concentration, an "active-mind" concentration. Anyone who has ever been involved in a closely-fought chess game or tennis match knows the feeling of virtually being a disembodied mind. When the tennis champion Ivan Lendl was asked how the raucous tennis audiences at the United States Open affected his play, he said that when he was into a match he was not even aware of their presence. Indeed, degree of concentration in a contest between two evenly-matched opponents can make the difference in the outcome. Certain tennis players try to turn this psychological phenomenon to their advantage. When the tide is going against them, they will try to disrupt an opponent's concentration by complaining vociferously over a point, carrying on at length.

The pianist Vladimir Horowitz said he becomes an entirely different person when he is on the stage performing. Psychologist Mihaly Csikszentmihalyi at the University of Chicago has been studying these active-mind altered states. Some of his findings parallel conclusions reached by Hans Selye from his research on stress. For example, Csikszentmihalyi found that the altered states produced by concentration most often took place at work.

Selye said that work is a biological necessity. Most people believe they work for economic security or social status or a successful business career, Selye said, only to find that when they have reached these goals they become bored. All work causes stress, but only work we don't like causes distress. The best way to avoid harmful stress is by working at what one likes and respects. This conclusion was supported by findings in the Duke Longitudinal Study of Aging. The Study lists the three most significant predictors of longevity for men as:

1. Physical functioning
2. Work satisfaction
3. Employment (but a negative factor without number 2).

In my study of 1,200 American centenarians, the abundance of life yielded by work stood out above everything else. Nearly 90 percent of them worked hard and very late into their lives. I could identify only ten centenarians who'd had lives of ease.

Selye believed that a major source of distress among people working in the middle and lower echelons of business, industry, agriculture and public service was dissatisfaction with their lives. They were frustrated by what they were doing, by what they wanted to do and believed they could have done. These people were bored. Selye said that each person must gain enough self-knowledge to know how much challenge to admit into his life in order to avoid boredom without going to the other extreme of too much stress.

Csikszentmihalyi's work has focused on these parameters — boredom on the one hand, anxiety on the other, and the middle way which he calls "flow."

To start with, this psychologist's definition of a self is similar to those already presented by neurobiologist Rose and physicist Harth. To Csikszentmihalyi, a self "is the information an organism has about its own states. The self is structured around intentions, or goals, which provide an axis for ordering information about itself. Information consists of events in consciousness." In order to collect and store information, the self must use what we know as attention, and each of us has only a limited amount of that. Attention cannot be divided very much at any one time so that the interaction between consciousness and its environment is restricted. Each of us is "the unique person defined by the structure of information we have assimilated into our lives." Because attention is the medium through which information becomes experience, it is useful to think of attention as "psychic energy."

Information that conflicts with goals produces disorder in the self-system. The disorder requires that attention be taken away from further acquisition of information and be used to restore order in consciousness. "Thus disorder in the self-system can be viewed as *psychic entropy,* because it decreases the predictability and/or efficiency of consciousness." Csikszentmihalyi says that we experience psychic entropy as self-consciousness, depression, anxiety, loneliness, anger and other disordered states. Ordered processes of consciousness occur when information does not conflict with goals and thus attention can be used efficiently to process further information. These two antipodies are a modern scientific representation of Jesus' concept of wholeness and provide a scientific rationale for the destructiveness of division.

Feelings that characterize ordered states are "unself-consciousness, joy, serenity, involvement, happiness, depending on which aspect of the process is attended to." An observer is struck immediately by the correspondence of this set or series of feelings and those posited for the kingdom of God. Unself-consciousness is a prime characteristic of children. Serenity and joy or happiness are the essence of the kingdom.

Csikszentmihalyi says that for most people most of the time the goals that give structure to the self and dictate where attention is directed are concerned with satisfying biological needs and social status. Under biological needs he lists such things as hunger, thirst and safety. Under "socialization," he puts sex, affiliation, achievement and presented life themes. By presented life themes, he means goals that are inculcated into the individual by his society and culture: doing well at school, going to a good college, getting married, finding a well-paying job, achieving good social status, and happiness based on material possessions.

But there is another category of goals not specified by the genetic blueprint or social coercion. While every person must attend in some degree to these common needs, some individuals create their own goals based on the interaction of the self with its environment. The self uses information from the environment to transform itself. Csikszentmihalyi calls such individually-formulated goals "emergent motives." Long-range emergent motives produce a novel "life theme," one that is not suggested or imposed by society. The pursuit of such a goal for an entire lifetime and its successful realization are rare because the achievement must overcome social inertia. Csikszentmihalyi cites as examples Gandhi and Martin Luther King whose life goals were nothing less than transformation of their societies.   On the intermediate scale, there is individual self-development over the years, personal growth. The self continually builds on new information, combining it with previous experience to keep transforming itself and growing in complexity. The psychologist says that various forms of self-development suggest "that the self has an unstable structure: in order to survive it must grow....becoming a billionaire, a President, the greatest surgeon in the world, is not enough protection. As soon as one's goals are reached, no matter how high they had been set, a new goal must be found. Otherwise the psychic energies of the person, having lost their focus, will begin to be invested at random, causing disorder and confusion." And, finally, disintegration.

On a daily basis, emergent motives are manifested in experiences that the individual has found to be self-rewarding. These "intrinsically motivated experiences," as Csikszentmihalyi calls them technically, are flow, the term used by some people to describe what the experience feels like. When a child plays or a man sits with a fishing pole, the scientist says, "the goal of the activity is usually not something external to be achieved: it is simply to experience the activity." It would be easier and certainly more economical in time for the fisherman to buy his fish at a market, but fishing allows him "to experience a wholesome inner state that is rarely available in daily life where we are constantly being distracted by competing and often contradictory demands." Is there any clearer exposition of Jesus' saying that "whosoever will save his life shall lose it"?

Why are activities intrinsically motivating? Csikszentmihalyi asks. "The answer seems to be that they are rewarding because they provide optimal....states of consciousness that are harmoniously ordered around clear goals." Optimal states of consciousness — flow — are those times when everything goes perfectly. The golf game when you hit every ball just the way you want to. The job interview where you feel so confident that you answer every question with just the right nuance. The play performance when you excel your best efforts and hold the audience in an empathetic grip. The time you played Bach not only without a single mistake but with thrilling vivacity. In other words, peak performance.

Dr. Csikszentmihalyi and colleagues investigated people performing at their peak. Basketball players, composers, dancers, chess masters, rock climbers, surgeons and others were asked to describe what they experienced when they had outdone themselves.

For one thing, their absorption in what they were doing was total. Their attention was sensitized to the shifting demands of the moment.

A rock climber: "I am totally involved in what I am doing. My body feels good....I don't seem to hear anything, the world seems to be cut off from me....I am less aware of myself and my problems."

A composer of music: "My concentration is like breathing....I never think of it. I am really quite oblivious to my surroundings after I really get going. I think that the phone could ring, and the doorbell could ring, or the house burn down or something like that...."

A dancer: "I am so involved in what I am doing....I don't see myself as separate from what I am doing."

The intense concentration bars all distractions. "Past and future cease to exist subjectively," Csikszentmihalyi says. "This continuous focus on the present produces a *distortion of time perspective.* Because the information that ordinarily marks the passage of time is absent from awareness minutes seem to stretch for hours, or hours elapse in minutes: Clock time is replaced by experiential sequences structured according to the demands of the activity."

This intense involvement can only come about when a second condition is satisfied. The challenge and the person's ability to meet it — his skills — must match. The dynamic balance between opportunity and ability means that dissimilar people can achieve flow situations only in different circumstances. A chess master gains no pleasure from defeating a beginner; he is happy only when meeting the challenge of another master. A scientist needs to work on a problem that tests his mettle.

The "Peter Principle" that in organizations a person usually is promoted to the level of his incompetence is a formula for discontent. Where responsibilities exceed abilities, the chance for a flow situation evaporates in a state of anxiety. If a person has more tasks or more difficult ones than he can cope with, he is overwhelmed. The unity (or wholeness) of consciousness is shattered. But the purity of involvement also is diluted by the other kind of mismatch. When a person's skills exceed the challenge and he has less to do than he is capable of doing, he becomes bored. Instead of being painfully tense, existence is unbearably dull. The person is poking along on one cylinder, hardly living — sleepwalking through life. Thoreau could have been talking about either of these conditions when he wrote that the "mass of men lead lives of quiet desperation."

The kingdom of God could be located as lying between the states of anxiety and boredom. But the kingdom of God quite likely connoted something much richer than a secularized flow state. Because our belief systems have changed with greater knowledge, we may no longer be able to reproduce a sense of religious exaltation associated with the almost magically-induced condition.

Two thousand years ago, Jesus said, "If therefore thine eye be single, thy whole body shall be full of light." Today modern science says: "Optimal experience is simply experience that flows according to its own requirements....without regard to ulterior consequences." Two thousand years ago Jesus said: "He also that received the seed among the thorns is he that heareth the word; and the care of this world, and the deceitfulness of riches, choke the word, and he becometh unfruitful." Psychology in the middle of the 1980s says: "Order in consciousness is threatened by conflicting goals, unclear expectations, ambiguous desires." Jesus said: "Do not do what you hate" and "It is easier for a camel to go through the eye of a needle, than for a rich man to enter the kingdom of God." Today's science says: "Most people most of the time feel constrained to alienate their experience —that is, to put up with disorder in consciousness just to survive or in the hope of reaching a rewarding goal in the future."

"The way you think, the way you live," said Tatzumbie Dupea at the amazing age of 110 years, "is heaven now."

Now! The kingdom of God as a state of mind is totally incompatible with the eschatological interpretation as some future external event. The kingdom of heaven as the way one thinks and thus the way one lives is consistent with Jesus saying, "Repent: for the kingdom of heaven is at hand." He proclaims his discovery of the kingdom's existence and tells his listeners it is available to them if they so choose. It explains the answer that Jesus gives in the Gospel of Thomas when his disciples do pose an eschatological question. "His disciples said to Him, 'When will the repose of the dead come about, and when will the new world come?' He said to them, 'What you look forward to has already come, but you do not recognize it.'"

All eschatological references to some kind of future supernatural transformation must be judged as overzealous interpolations to satisfy the commonly-held beliefs and credulity of the times. There is a future element, however, in the kingdom-as-a-state-of-mind. The concept exists now, but it takes time to spread the word about it and then each person must make his own decision about what his future will be. So the kingdom of God can be both a present reality in some people and a future state in others.

The "thy kingdom come" in the Lord's Prayer, clearly implying a future event, has another explanation. Kingdom of God, kingdom of heaven, the life or life are the only code phrases for his concept of the good life. Jesus does not say specifically the kingdom of God in the Lord's Prayer. Similarly, in the confrontation with Pilate when Jesus says his kingdom is not of this world, he is not referring to the kingdom of God.

The confusion of terms does not end here. In Mark and Luke, at the Last Supper Jesus says he will not drink again until he does so in the kingdom of God. That is an eschatological statement and not the kingdom indicated by this study. However, in Matthew, at the Last Supper Jesus says, "in my Father's kingdom," which is not the code phrase. Again, in Mark, Jesus says, "There shall be some of them that stand here, which shall not taste of death, til they have seen the kingdom of God come with power." This verse is often quoted in support of the eschatological interpretation. Luke also uses the term kingdom of God. Again Matthew indicates Jesus is talking about something else. "There be some standing here, which shall not taste of death, till they see the Son of man coming in his kingdom." That is not a state of consciousness.

Jesus said that "the publicans and the harlots go into the kingdom of God before you." How could the disreputable tax collectors and whores enter the mental kingdom ahead of the scribes and Pharisees? The publicans and prostitutes listened to John's preaching about righteousness and believed him. The elite listened to John and rejected him. Whatever the failings of the tax men and hookers, there was no pretense about them. They did not deceive the world about what they were. There was a chance for unity in their minds. This is not possible with hypocrites.

Understanding of what Jesus meant by the kingdom gives a beautiful irony to the parable of The Dishonest Steward. "If therefore ye have not been faithful in the unrighteous mammon, who will commit to your trust the true riches? And if ye have not been faithful in that which is another man's, who shall give you that which is your own?" The manager's habits of deceit and dishonesty have levied the harshest penalty of all — he has robbed himself of the ability to enjoy his own mental well-being.

The kingdom of the mind solves another problem. When the Pharisees asked Jesus when the kingdom of God would come, he answered (in the King James Bible) not to look for its coming because "the kingdom of God is within you." Many scholars, however, prefer to translate the passage as "in the midst of you." The heavenly kingdom that was within Jesus was in the midst of the Pharisees. Either translation is applicable. The kingdom is within you, but it can be within other people as well. That would account for the saying in Thomas that "the kingdom is within you and outside you." This mental, psychological and thus invisible kingdom is, as he also said in Thomas, "spread out on the earth and men do not see it."

Finally, there is the problem of the saying in Luke, "Blessed be ye poor: for yours is the kingdom of God." This looks like a corruption or elision of the Beatitude "Blessed are the poor in spirit: for theirs is the kingdom of heaven," just as Luke's saying "Blessed are ye that hunger" seems to hold the same relationship to the Beatitude "Blessed are they that do hunger and thirst after righteousness." It has been discussed how the poor in spirit or humble relate to the kingdom. Being impoverished usually does not create high self-esteem and peace of mind; usually, just the opposite. However, we in our materialistic society could have developed a quite different view of poverty than Jesus held. Since he saw love of riches, the closed minds of the arrogant and the all-consuming attention devoted to acquisitiveness as barriers to the kingdom, he could have seen the minds of the poor as being unencumbered by those worldly distractions and thus more receptive to inner unity, tranquility and harmony. Poor people usually are humble.

There is reason to believe that the apostle Paul knew what Jesus meant by the kingdom of God in the way that it is has been presented here. The Book of Acts, which immediately follows the four Gospels, says in a number of places that Paul preached, expounded upon and entered into disputes over the kingdom of God. But not once does the book declare what the kingdom is. This is a mysterious omission since the kingdom of God was such an important part of Jesus' teaching. The one hint in Acts of what the kingdom might be about is a red herring. During one of Jesus' post-Resurrection appearances, the apostles ask him if he will restore the kingdom to Israel. "And he said unto them, it is not for you to know the times or the seasons, which the Father hath put in his own power."

Paul in his letters does say what the kingdom is on a number of occasions, but with an inconsistency that obscures the true meaning unless one already has decided upon the answer. The first time Paul mentions the subject, however, in Romans, he is very explicit: "For the kingdom of God is not meat and drink [as Jesus said in the passage on the Lilies); but righteousness, and peace, and joy in the Holy Ghost."

But in the next book, 1 Corinthians, Paul three times uses the verb inherit, implying that the kingdom of God is a future event. In 15:24 it is definitely a future happening: "Then cometh the end, when he shall have delivered up the kingdom to God, even the Father; when he shall have put down all rule and all authority and all power."

But in the next book, Galatians, Paul is back to the concept first presented. He inventories the malefactions that prevent a person from inheriting the kingdom of God. Immediately after mentioning the kingdom, Paul adds: "But the fruit of the Spirit is love, joy, peace, longsuffering, gentleness, goodness, faith, meekness, temperence".

After that, the title becomes more erratic, Jesus' concept disappears, and the emphasis on eschatology grows. In Ephesians, it is "the kingdom of Christ and of God." In Colossians, "the kingdom of his dear Son." In Second Timothy, "I charge thee therefore before God and the Lord Jesus Christ, who shall judge the quick and the dead at his appearing and his kingdom."

In the melange of Paul's references, there is resurrected the divided kingdom that could not be comprehended — the once and future kingdom.

If Paul did know what Jesus meant by the kingdom of God, why would he try to obscure it? Or did he? Were his epistles emended by later transcribers after the Christian Church had taken on a life of its own? Did Jesus explain his kingdom of God in the oral teaching? Was he understood? The scientific knowledge, array of terms and biological mechanisms of today were unknown then. Why did the oral teaching disappear? It could have been suppressed because of the Gnostic threat and eventually forgotten. Even so, why has Jesus' doctrine of the kingdom of God never been grasped during the two millennia of Christianity?

This study's answer to that question is that Jesus' concept of the kingdom of the mind was both far more simple and far more advanced than anyone imagined. His insights were so profound that his kingdom could not be discovered until we gained the requisite knowledge about life.

There is another answer: Jesus' concept of the kingdom of God was not valued. Its significance dwindled and its content atrophied after the event that gave birth to Christianity, inspired unshakeable faith in Christians, and made the triumph of the Christian Church possible: his Resurrection. Jesus' kingdom of God seems meager in comparison to the prospect of living forever. In the Resurrection was the promise of the fate of all human beings. Jesus' kingdom of God hardly could enlist martyrs to lay down their lives in the struggle with Rome. Nor could it be used to control monarchs and other people.

On the other hand, if there is no heaven "up there," if there is no life after death, Jesus' kingdom of God offers everything worth having: good health, peace of mind, feeling good about oneself, enjoyment of the reputation of a good life, enjoyment of life. Even if there is an afterlife, these benefits are precious.

There is a consistency between these goods and what the Jewish people yearned for their Messiah to bring them. Except that they looked for the peace and plenty, hope and happiness, justice and joy to come as a transformation of their society, not through the spiritual change of each individual.

Are there still other aspects to be learned about life from Jesus' teaching? Perhaps the only way we can find out is to wait for our science to catch up.

This study comes to a conclusion which is opposite that reached by Albert Schweitzer. Jesus was not a man of his time. His genius was so far ahead of his time that he is a man for our time.

References & Notes

ONE
The Greatest Story

Page

7   The power and authority of the Sanhedrin is from *Caesar and Christ* by Will Durant, Simon & Schuster, 1944, p 536

8   Biblical quotations are from the original King James Version; Ez 47:11

9   Dan 7:13

The Josephus quotation is from ibid Durant, p 536

The voice in the wilderness: Mt 3:3, Is 40:3

10   O generation of vipers: Mt 3:7

God can choose elect: Mt 3:9

"God is able of these stones...": Mt 3:9, Lu 3:8

John's advice: Lu 3:10-14

"I indeed baptize you with water...": Mt 3:11

The voice from heaven: Mk 1:10-11

John's charge against Herod: Lu 3:19

The Temptation: Mt 4:3-10, Lu 4:1-13

11   "Now after that John was put in prison...": Mk 1:14-15

"From that time Jesus began to preach...": Mt 4:17

Therefore am I sent: Lu 4:43-44

12   "The law and the prophets ...": Lu 16:16

He taught with authority: Mk 1:22

His word was with power: Lu 4:32

"Isn't this Mary's son...": Mk 2:6

Amazed in Capernaum: Mk 1:27

"A prophet is not without honor...": Mk 6:4

Preaching at Sea of Galilee: Lu 5:2-9

"Follow me...": Mt 4:18-22

13   Fame throughout Galilee: Mk 1:28, Lu 5:15

Fame through Syria: Mt 4:24

Sermon on the Mount: Mt 5-7

Beatitudes: Mt 5:3-12

14   "Think not I am come...": Mt 5:17

In the Sermon on the Mount there are 15 references to the law — the first five books of the Old Testament, the Pentateuch or Torah — and seven references to the prophets. In the three Synoptic Gospels Jesus makes 157 references to the law and 195 references to the prophets. References are from annotation in *New American Standard Bible*

Exceed righteousness of scribes: Mt 5:20

On anger: Mt 5:22

Adultery and lust: Mt 5:28

An eye for an eye: Mt 5:38, Ex 21:24, Lev 24:20, Deut 19:21 Penalties under the Hammurabi Code are from *Our Oriental Heritage* by Will Durant, Simon & Schuster, 1935, 1954, p 231

15   Other cheek, extra mile: Mt 5:39-41

Love thy neighbor: Lev 19:18

Love your enemies: Mt 5:43-44

Be ye perfect: Mt 5:48

On alms: Mt 6:1-4

On prayer: Mt 6:5-8

Lord's prayer: Mt 6:9-13

On fasting: Mt 6:16-18

16   "Lay not up for yourselves treasures...": Mt 6:19-21

"No man can serve two masters...": Mt 6:24

"trade curses everything it handles...": *Walden* by Henry Thoreau, Modern Library, Random House, p 63

The lilies passage: Mt 6:25-34

"Judge not...": Mt 7:1-2

"Ask, and it shall be given you...": Mt 7:7-11

17   The Golden Rule: Mt 7:12

On forgiving trespasses: Mt 6:14-15

"Enter ye in at the strait gate...": Mt 7:13-14; the phrase, The Two Ways, comes from *A Synopsis of the Four Gospels* by John Bernard Orchard, Mercer University Press, 1982

"Beware of false prophets...": Mt 7:15

"Ye shall know them by their fruits...": Mt 7:16-17

"Not every one that saith unto me...": Mt 7:21

Sermon on the Plain: Lu 6:20-49

18   Blessed are the poor: Lu 6:20

Blessed are those who hunger: Lu 6:21

Jesus reading from Isaiah in Nazareth: Lu 4:18, Is 61:1

Jesus run out of Nazareth: Lu 4:28-29

Two blind men healed: Mt 9:27-30

The story of Jairus: Mk 5:22-42; also Lu 8:41-56, Mt 9:18-25 (without attribution by name)

19   The importance of faith in healing: Mt 17:14-20

The centurian: Mt 8:5-12

"Many shall come from the east...": Mt 8:11-12

Description of the Pharisees based on, among others, *The Dead Sea Scrolls* by Geza Vermes, Fortress, 1977, pp 119-120

Healing incident and Jesus' rejoinder about ox: Lu 13:11-17

Healing incident and Jesus' question about doing good on sabbath: Lu 6:6-10

20   Picking corn and the sabbath made for man: Mk 2:23-27

Healing the palsied man and forgiving sins: Mk 2:4-12; also Mt 9:2-8, Lu 5:18-26

Re sorcery, see *A History of Religious Ideas,* Vol 2, by Mircea Eliade, University of Chicago Press, 1982, p 333

"Every kingdom divided against itself...": Mt 12:22-28; also Mk 3:22-26, Lu 11:14-20

"But if I with the finger of God...": Lu 11:20

The parable of The Sower: Mt 13:3-23, Mk 4:3-20, Lu 8:5-15

21   Telling the parable: Mt 13:3-9

"Because it is given unto you to know the mysteries...": Mt 13:11-15; Mk 4:11-12, Lu 8:10

The prophecy of Isaiah: Is 6:9

Explaining the parable: Mt 13:19-23

The parable of The Mustard Seed: Mt 13:31-32; also Mk 4:30-32, Lu 13:18-19

The parable of The Leaven: Mt 13:33; also Lu 13:20-21

The parable of the Hidden Treasure: Mt 13:44

22   The parable of The Pearl: Mt 13:45-46

What defiles a man: Mt 15:11-20, Mk 7:15-23

The blind leading the blind: Mt 15:14, Lu 6:39

Instructions to the apostles: Mt 10:5-42, Mk 6:7-11, Lu 9:1-5

"And whosoever shall not receive...": Mt 10:14

"I send you forth as sheep...": Mt 10:16-17

23   "The foxes have their holes...": Mt 8:18-20

"Ye shall not have gone over the cities of Israel...": Mt 10:23

The apostles report: Lu 9:10, Mk 6:30

Private meeting of Jesus and apostles: Lu 9:10, Mk 6:31-32

"But he said, Lord, suffer me first to go and bury my father...":

Lu 9:59-62

24   The Loaves and the Fishes: feeding the five thousand: Mt 14:13-21, Mk 6:32-44, Lu 9:11-17

Walking on water: Mt 14:22-23, Mk 6:45-52

Feeding the four thousand: Mt 15:32-39, Mk 8:1-10

"sighed deeply in his spirit...": Mk 8:12: this "no sign shall be given" answer comes before The Recognition; in Lu 11:29, the clause "but the sign of Jonah the Prophet" is appended: this is after The Recognition; the same clause is added to Jesus' answer in Mt 12:38-39, 16:1-4 before The Recognition

The Recognition: Mt 16:13-20, Mk 8:27-30, Lu 9:18-21

"And upon this rock...": Mt 16:18-19

Jesus tells disciples he must be crucified: Mt 16:21-23, Mk 8:31-33, Lu 9:22

The Transfiguration: Mt 17:1-9, Mk 9:2-9, Lu 9:28-36

25   Malachi's prophecy about Elijah: Mal 4:5

"But I say unto you that Elijah is come already...": Mt 17:10-12

"But whosoever shall deny me...": Mt 10:33-34

26   The sign of Jonah: Mt 12:39, 16:4; Lu 11:29

"This gospel of the kingdom...": Mt 24:14

"And then shall they see the Son of man coming...": Lu 21:27-32

"In the regeneration...": Mt 19:28

Re Suffering Servant, see *The Kingdom of God and Primitive Christianity* by Albert Schweitzer, written 1950-1951, Seabury, 1968, pp 115-124

27   The abridged passage beginning "All we like sheep...": Is 53:6-12

28   "If any man desire to be first...": Mk 9:35

"whosoever will be great among you...": Mk 10:43-45

"Jesus called a little child...": Mt 18:1-4

"The kingdom of God cometh not with observation...": Lu 17:20-21

Pharisees conspire with Herodians: Mk 3:6

29   Caiaphas declaration that it is better for one man to die: Jo 11:50

"O my Father, if it be possible...": Mt 26:39

The Roman soldiers mock him: Mk 15:17-20

"And the scripture was fulfilled...": Mk 15:28, Is 53:12

"My God, my God, why has thou forsaken me?": Mt 27:46, Mk 15:35, Ps 22:1

"Father, into thy hands...": Lu 23:46

"Father, forgive them...": Lu 24:34

"Today shalt thou be with me in paradise...": Lu 23:43

30   "Now is Christ risen from the dead...": 1 Co 15:20-22

"If there be no resurrection of the dead...": 1 Co 15:13-14

31   Re Paul's merger of resurrection with Greek immortality, see ibid
Eliade, pp 350-51

Re Son of man/Son of God, see ibid Eliade, p 343

Re the importance of The Resurrection in preserving Jesus' doctrine,
see ibid Eliade, p 337

32   Mary Magdalene addressed Jesus as *Rabboni* in Jo 20:16

TWO
The Mystery of History

33   "a man of illegitimate birth...": *Jesus Through the Centuries* by
Jaroslav Pelikan, Yale University Press, 1985, p 190

"what is really his from the rubbish...": *Jefferson's Extracts from the
Gospels,* ed. Dickinson W. Adams, Princeton University Press, a
letter to William Short, 1983, p 388

The passage about the evolution of Christ is based on ibid Pelikan

Virgil's prediction is from his fourth Eclogue

"who desires...to be a good man...": Plato's *Republic,* book 2, 2.360-61

34   "My kingdom is not of this world": Jo 18:36

"For unto us a child is born...": Is 9:6

"and yet, on the other hand...": *The Quest of the Historical Jesus* by
Albert Schweitzer, Macmillan, copyright by James M. Robinson,
1968, first German edition 1906, p 238

"surrenders the birth story...": ibid Schweitzer, p 60

36   "in the first He accepted...": ibid Schweitzer, p 61

"*either* purely historical...": ibid Schweitzer, p 238

That the Gospels were written between 60 A.D. and 110 A.D. is from
The Gnostic Gospels by Elaine Pagels, Vintage, Random House,
1981, p xv

37   "*either* Synoptic *or* Johanine": ibid Schweitzer, p 238

"*either* eschatological...": ibid Schweitzer, p 238

38   "make straight in the desert a highway...": Is 40:3

"The general conception of the Kingdom...": ibid Schweitzer, p 239

"He only proclaims its coming...": ibid Schweitzer, p 239

"essential originality and power...": ibid Schweitzer, p 243

"does not give the right clue...": ibid Schweitzer, pp 245-46

"This is the last possible...": ibid Schweitzer, p 249

39   "the teaching of the historical Jesus...": ibid Schweitzer, p 250

Schweitzer's summations: ibid Schweitzer, pp 398-99

"The Jesus of Nazareth who...": ibid Schweitzer, pp 398-99

"a stranger and an enigma": ibid Schweitzer, p 399

The Jesus-is-a-myth exponents are mentioned in *Caesar and Christ* by Will Durant, Simon & Schuster, 1944, p 554

Schweitzer's attitude about eschatology and the Second Coming are from James M. Robinson's Introduction, ibid Schweitzer, p xxi

40-
41   The two paragraphs on Jews and gentiles in Palestine are based on ibid Durant, pp 532-35

41   The reference to Sadducees and Pharisees arguing and to non-sectarian Jews is from *Jesus' Teaching in Its Environment* by John Wyck Bowman, John Knox Press, 1963, p 27

"Behold an Israelite, indeed...": Jo 1:47

The paragraphs on the intellectual changes brought about in the wake of Alexander's conquests in the Hellenistic world are based on *The Gnostic Religion* by Hans Jonas, Beacon Press, 1963, pp 14-31

42   The Mysteries of Cybele and Mithra are from *A History of Religious Ideas,* Vol 2, by Mircea Eliade, University of Chicago Press, 1982, p 280

The keeping of the Eleusinian Mysteries from ibid Eliade, Vol 1, 1978, pp 292-301

Maintaining secrecy in other mystery cults: ibid Eliade, Vol 2, pp 277-80

The importance of secrecy to religious value: ibid Eliade, Vol 1, p 301

43   The description of the Gnostic religion is based on ibid Jonas, pp 32-47; ibid Eliade, Vol 2, p 371; ibid Pagels, p 172

44   The terrifying view of the cosmos is from ibid Jonas, p 322

Jesus' first use of the term "outer darkness" is in Mt 8:12; also in Mt 22:13 and 25:30

The Gnostic meaning of outer darkness is from ibid Jonas, p 116

The reference to Marcion is from ibid Pagels, p 33

The discussion of the Gnostic challenge is from various parts of ibid Pagels

45   The Church's war against esotericism and quotation "Esotericism is documented...": ibid Eliade, Vol 2, pp 368-369

Clement of Alexandria quotation is from ibid Eliade, Vol 2, p 369

46   Origen quotation is from ibid Eliade, Vol 2, p 369

Do not cast your pearls before swine: Mt 7:6

THREE
Riddles

47   Man shall not live by bread alone: Mt 4:4, Lu 4:4

Ye are the salt of the earth: Mt 5:13

Ye are the light: Mt 5:14

A city that is set on a summit: Mt 5:14

Don't let your left hand: Mt 6:3

Where your treasure is: Mt 6:21

No man can serve two masters: Mt 6:24

Consider the lilies: Mt 6:28

Take no thought for the morrow: Mt 6:34

Judge not: Mt 7:1

Ask, and it shall be given unto you: Mt 7:7

Golden Rule: Mt 7:12

Wide is the gate: Mt 7:13-14

By their fruits: Mt 7:20

Fear not them: Mt 10:28

The very hairs of your head: Mt 10:30

What is a man profited: Mt 16:26

What God has joined together: Mt 19:6

Render unto Caesar: Mt 22:21

If a house be divided: Mk 3:25

Which of you with taking thought: Lu 12:25

To whom much is given: Lt 12:48

He that is without sin: Jo 8:7

The truth shall make you free: Jo 8:32

A new commandment I give unto you: Jo 13:34

In my Father's house: Jo 14:2

Greater love has no man: Jo 15:13

"In every work of genius...": "Self-Reliance" by Ralph Waldo Emerson, first paragraph

48   The blind are leading the blind: Mt 15:14

Let the dead bury their dead: Lu 9:60

Not that which goes into the mouth: Mt 15:20, Mk 7:23

They seeing see not: Mt 13:13

He who has ears: Mt 11:15, 13:9, 13:43; Mk 4:9, 4:23, 7:16; Lu 8:8, 14:35

The person who finds his life: Mt 10:39, Mk 8:35, Lu 17:33

Many are called: Mt 20:16, 22:14

The last will be first: Mt 20:16, Mk 10:31, Lu 13:30

"Among them that are born of women...": Mt 11:11

Whoever exalts oneself: Mt 23:12

Whosoever shall humble himself: Mt 18:14

Blessed are the humble: Mt 5:3

Blessed are the meek: Mt 5:5

Blessed are the poor: Lu 6:20

Blessed are those who weep: Lu 6:21

Blessed are those who hunger: Lu 6:21

To him who has: Mt 13:12, 25:29; Mk 4:25; Lu 8:18, 19:26

To become awake to the world of the spirit, see *A History of Religious Ideas,* Vol 2, by Mircea Eliade, University of Chicago Press, 1982, p 382

Sleep as an analogue of ignorance or death: ibid Eliade, Vol 2, p 382

49   "By hearing ye shall hear...": Is 6:9

Jimmy Cagney's quotation "Absorption in things..." is from the *New York Times,* 31 March 1986 at the time of his death

The parable of the Laborers in the Vineyard: Mt 20:1-16

50   "So that last shall be first...": Mt 20:16

"Are there few that be saved?": Lu 13:23

"Strive to enter...": Lu 13:24

"I know you not...": Lu 13:25

"There will be weeping...": Lu 13:28-30

51   The economic conditions of Palestine based on *Caesar and Christ* by Will Durant, Simon & Schuster, 1944, pp 535-36

"And with many such parables...": Mk 4:33-34

"Because of their form...": *A New Quest of the Historical Jesus* by James M. Robinson, Fortress, 1959, 1983, p 198

Changing attitudes toward parables: ibid Robinson, p 199

"So is the kingdom of God...": Mk 4:26-28

C.H. Dodd's realized eschatology: ibid Robinson, p 199

Bultmann's interpretation: ibid Robinson, pp 200-201

52   "irreplaceable loaded language...": ibid Robinson, p 8

The parable of the Mustard Seed: Mt 13:31-32, Mk 4:30-32, Lu 13:18-19

"It is like leaven...": Mt 13:33

The parable of the Hidden Treasure: Mt 13:44

The parable of the Pearl: Mt 13:45-46

The parable of New Cloth, Old Garment: Mt 9:16, Mk 2:21, Lu 5:36

The parable of New Wine, Old Bottles: Mt 9:17, Mk 2:22, Lu 5:37-38

The parable of the Lamp Under a Bushel: Mt 5:14-16, Mk 4:21-25,

Lu 8:16-18, 11:33-36

"Take heed therefore...": Lu 8:18

53   "The light of the body...": Lu 11:34

The parable of the Wheat and the Weeds: Mt 13:24-30; the explanation: Mt 13:36-43

The parable of the Draw Net: Mt 13:47-50

The parable of the Sheep and the Goats: Mt 25:31-46

54   The parable of the Ten Virgins: Mt 25:1-13

The parable of the Household Watching: Mk 13:32-37

The parable of the Watchful Servants: Lu 12:35-40

54-
55   The parable of the Vineyard and Householder: Mt 21:33-44, Mk 12:1-11, Lu 20:9-18

55   The parable of the Two Sons: Mt 21:28-32

When the chief priests and Pharisees "had heard his parables...": Mt 21:45-46

55-
56   The parable of The Wicked Servant: Mt 18:23-35

56   The parable of The Talents: Mt 25:14-30

57   The parable of The Dishonest Steward: Lu 16:1-13

"Woe unto you, scribes and Pharisees...": Mt 23:13

58   "From the days of John the Baptist...": Mt 11:12

"How hardly shall they that have riches...": Mk 10:23-25; also Mt 19:23-26

"If thine eye offend thee...": Mk 9:47-48

"There are some eunuchs...": Mt 19:12

"When the Pharisees had heard...": Mt 22:34-40

"And the scribe said unto him...": Mk 12:32-34

59   "A certain lawyer stood up...": Lu 10:25-28

"There came one running...": Mk 10:17-22

"One came and said unto him...": Mt 19:16-17

"And if thy foot offend thee...": Mk 9:45

59-
60   "And if thine eye offend thee...": Mk 9:47

60   "but go thou and preach the kingdom...": Lu 9:60

"Therefore I say unto you...": Mt 6:25

"Therefore take no thought, saying...": Mt 6:31-33

"Take no thought for your life...": Lu 12:22-23

61   "Thy kingdom come.": Mt 6:10, Lu 11:2

"Ye shall not have gone over the cities...": Mt 10:23

The parable of the Wheat and Weeds: Mt 13:24-30, 36-43

The promise to Peter and other disciples: Mt 19:27-29, Mk 10:28-30

Jesus' prediction that non-Jews would inherit the kingdom: Mt 8:11-12, 21:40-43, Lu 13:27-29

The parable of the Ten Virgins: Mt 25:1-13

The parable of the Household Watching: Mk 13:32-37

The parable of the Watchful Servants: Lu 12:35-40

There be some of them that stand here...": Mk 9:1; also Mt 16:28, Lu 9:27

The parable of the Fig Tree: Lu 21:29-33, Mt 24:32-35, Mk 13:28-31

Repent: for the kingdom of God is at hand: Mt 4:17, 10:7; Mk 1:15

"I will not any more eat thereof...": Lu 22:16-18; also Mt 26:29, Mk 14:25

62   "because he was nigh to Jerusalem...": Lu 19:11

The parable of The Ten Pounds: Lu 19:12-26

"But those mine enemies...": Lu 19:27

"If I cast out devils...": Mt 12:28

"Fear not, little flock...": Lu 12:32

"It is better for thee to enter...": Mk 9:47

"Blessed are the poor in spirit...": Mt 5:3

"And when he was demanded of the Pharisees...": Lu 17:20-21

62-
63   Nicodemus "came to Jesus by night...": Jo 3:2-6

63   "My kingdom is not of this world": Jo 18:36

63-
64   The references to Professor Jaroslav Pelikan are from "Jesus" in 1965 *Encyclopaedia Britannica*; the remainder of the 1965 *Britannica* references are from "Kingdom of God" by Dennis Nineham, Professor of Divinity, University of London

64   The references from the current *Encyclopaedia Britannica* are from "Jesus Christ, Kingdom of God" by M. Jack Suggs

References from *Chambers's Encyclopedia* are from "Jesus Christ" in the 1973 edition by George Walter Tyrrell

References from *Encyclopedia of Religion and Ethics*, Scribners, are from "Kingdom of God" by G.H. Gilbert

64-
65   References from *Baker's Dictionary of Theology*, Baker Book House, 1960, in "Kingdom of God" by George Eldon Ladd

65   References from *The Interpreter's Dictionary of the Bible,* Abington Press, 1962, in "Kingdom of God, Of Heaven" by O.E. Evans

The lecture "The Kingdom of God" was given by Dr. Walter Donald

Kring at All Souls Unitarian Church in New York City, 10 March 1977

66   The Ignatius quotation is from *Jesus Through The Centuries* by Jaroslav Pelikan, Yale University Press, 1985, p 48, attributed to *The Martyrdom of Ignatius*

Eusebius' concept of the kingdom of God is from *Byzantine Christianity* by Harry Margulis, Wayne State University Press, 1970, p 7

Gibbon's quotation is from *The Decline and Fall of the Roman Empire* by Edward Gibbon, Vol 1, Random House, p 442

66-
67   The Tolstoy section is based on *Encyclopaedia Britannica* 1965, *Encyclopedia Americana* 1965, and "The World of Tolstoy" by Peter White in *National Geographic* June 1986

67   Tolstoy-Gandhi is based on ibid Pelikan, pp 213-14

Martin Luther King is based on ibid Pelikan, pp 216-17

67-
68   Schillebeeckx is from *Interim Report on the Books Jesus & Christ* by Edward Schillebeeckx, Crossroad, 1982, pp 129-131

FOUR

New Knowledge

69   The section on the Essenes is based on the following: *The Dead Sea Scrolls: Qumran in Perspective* by Geza Vermes, Fortress, 1977; "New Directions in Dead Sea Scroll Research: The Text Behind The Text of the Hebrew Bible" by Frank Moore Cross in *Bible Review,* Summer 1985; "New Testament Illuminated by Dead Sea Scrolls," a report on Dead Sea Scroll study after 30 years by Joseph Fitzmyer of The Catholic University of America, in *Biblical Archaeology Review,* September/October 1982; "The Kingdom of God" lecture by Dr. Walter Donald Kring at All Souls Unitarian Church in New York City on 10 March 1977; *Caesar and Christ* by Will Durant, Simon & Schuster, 1944, pp 537-38; *Historical Introduction to the New Testament* by Robert M. Grant, Harper & Row, 1963, pp 261-67; "The Essenes" in the Micropaedia, "The Essenes" in "Jesus Christ," "The Essenes" in "Biblical Literature," "Qumran Literature" in "Biblical Literature" in the 1983 *Encyclopaedia Britannica*; "Dead Sea Scrolls" in *Encyclopaedia Britannica,* 1965; "Dead Sea Scrolls," "Essenes" in *Encyclopedia Americana,* 1965

Renan quotation "Christianity is an Essenism..." is from ibid Vermes, p 212

71   The apostle Paul on women: 1 Co 7:1: "It is good for a man not to touch a woman." And 1 Co 7:29: "they that have wives be as though they had none"

Jesus was "a Galilean charismatic..." quotation from ibid Vermes, p 219

Jesus on being a drunkard: Mt 11:19, Lu 7:34

72   "At the heart of Essenism..." quotation from ibid Vermes, p 221

The section on the discovery and derivation of the Nag Hammadi library is based on the Introduction in *The Nag Hammadi Library* by James M. Robinson, the General Editor, Harper & Row, 1977; the Introduction to *The Gnostic Gospels* by Elaine Pagels, Vintage, Random House, 1981; and the followlng articles in *Encyclopaedia Britannica* 1965 and *Encyclopedia Americana* 1965: "Coptic Language," "Coptic Religion," "Egyptian History," "Egyptian Archaeology," "Libraries," "Monasteries," "Pachomius;" maps of "Lands of the Bible Today with Historical Notes" by the National Geographic Society, 1956, 1967

73   Professor Helmut Koester's statement about the Gospel of Thomas is from his Introduction to that Gospel in ibid Robinson, p 117

73-
74   "These are the secret sayings...": from the tranlsation of The Coptic Gospel of Thomas in *Documents for the Study of the Gospels* by David R. Cartlidge and David L. Dungan, William Collins, Fortress, 1980, p 25

74   The parable of the Fig Tree: Mt 24:32-35, Mk 13:28-31, Lu 21:29-33

The parable of the Vineyard and Householder: Mt 21:33-42, Mk 12:1-12, Lu 20:9-18

The parable of the Vineyard and Householder: Th 65

75   The parable of the Wheat and the Weeds: Th 57, Mt 13:24-30, 36-43

The parable of the Draw Net: Th 8, Mt 13:47-50

The parable of the Hidden Treasure: Mt 13:44, Th 109

"I shall give you what no eye...": Th 17, translation in ibid Robinson, p 120

"Do not be anxious...": Th 36, ibid Cartlidge, p 29

"the Life" appears in Th 58 and 114

"The Pharisees and the scribes...": Th 39, ibid Robinson, p 122; it corresponds to Mt 23:13 and Lu 11:52

75-
76   The Recognition: Mt 16:13-20, Mk 8:27-30, Lu 9:18-21, Th 13

76   "Master, my mouth is wholly incapable...": Th 13, ibid Robinson, p 119

"He who drinks from my mouth...": Th 108, ibid Cartlidge, p 35

"Know what is in front of your face...": Th 5, ibid Cartlidge, p 26

"His disciples asked him...": Th 6, ibid Cartlidge, p 26

"Jesus said, "Blessed is the lion...": Th 7, ibid Cartlidge, p 26

"The Kingdom of the Father is like a man...": Th 98, ibid Cartlidge, p34

"If they ask you...": Th 50, ibid Cartlidge, p 30

"His disciples said to him...": Th 51, ibid Robinson, p 123

76-
77 "On what day will the Kingdom come?...": Th 113, ibid Cartlidge, p 35

77 "Jesus said, 'If the ones who lead you...": Th 3, ibid Cartlidge, p 25

"That 'Kingdom,' then symbolizes...": ibid Pagels, p 155

The wisdom section is based on the following: *Israelite Wisdom*, edited by John Gammie, Walter Brueggemann, W. Lee Humphreys and James Ward, Union Theological Seminary, 1978; *A History of Religious Ideas* by Mircea Eliade, University of Chicago Press, Vol 1, 1978, pp 77-80, Vol 2, 1982, pp 257-62; *In Man We Trust* by Walter Brueggemann, John Knox Press, 1972; *Caesar and Christ* by Will Durant, Simon & Schuster, 1944, pp 539-42; "Proverbs" in Micropaedia, "Jewish Philosophy," "Biblical Literature-Proverbs," "Wisdom Literature" and "Mesopotamian Religious Literature and Mythology" in Macropaedia, 1983 *Encyclopaedia Britannica;* "Wisdom" and "Sheba" in 1965 *Encyclopedia Americana;* "Solomon" in *The People's Chronology* by James Trager, Holt, Rinehart and Winston, 1979

Ptahotep based on "The Motif of the Wise Courtier in the Book of Proverbs" by W. Lee Humphreys in ibid *Israelite Wisdom* as well as encyclopedia articles above

77-
78 Babylonian spiritual crisis from ibid Eliade, Vol 1, pp 77-80

78 The Israelite spiritual crisis, formation of Proverbs and much of the part on proverbs is based on the thesis of ibid Brueggemann

81 "I...saw under the sun...": Ec 9:11

"Whatsoever thy hand findeth to do...": Ec 9:10

"Cast thy bread...": Ec 11:1

"Wisdom is better than strength...": Ec 9:16

"Wisdom is better than weapons of war...": Ec 9:8

"Wisdom is a defence...": Ec 7:12

"I perceive that...": Ec 3:22

"it is good and comely...": Ec 5:18

"live joyfully with the wife...": Ec 9:9

The clash of the two traditions and analysis of Jeremiah is based on "The Epistomological Crisis of Israel's Two Histories" by Walter Brueggemann in ibid *Israelite Wisdom*

82 The Deutero-Isaiah analysis is based on "The Servant's Knowledge in Isaiah 40-55" by James Ward in ibid *Israelite Wisdom*

"by his knowledge...": Is 53:11

Personification of Wisdom: ibid Eliade, Vol 2, pp 257-59 and encyclopedias

83   Kings reign by wisdom: Pr 8:15

"Riches and honor are with me...": Pr 8:18-21

The translation "I came forth from the mouth..." is from ibid Eliade, Vol 2, p 261, of Ecclesiasticus 24:3

"Man shall not live by bread alone...": Mt 4:4; based on the Old Testament saying: Deut 8:3

The teacher of wisdom in Ecclesiasticus is based on ibid Eliade, Vol 2, p 261

"Wisdom is a spirit devoted to Man's...": the Wisdom of Solomon 1:6

"Hence no man can utter...": the Wisdom of Solomon 1:8

83-
84   "How can any man...": the Wisdom of Solomon 9:13-18

84   "And the child grew...": Lu 2:40

"And Jesus increased in wisdom...": Lu 2:52

"They were astonished...": Mt 13:54

"Therefore whosoever heareth...": Mt 7:24

"John came neither eating...": Mt 11:18-19

"The queen of the south...": Mt 12:42

86   Rene Dubos, who died in 1982, was a microbiologist, experimental pathologist and researcher in environmental biomedicine who was often taken for an anthropologist and praised by leading anthropologists. Among Dubos' many honorary degrees were three M.D.'s. He was among the first winners of the Tyler award for ecology, recipient of the Arches of Science Award, and many other honors. He deserved the Nobel Prize, which he did not receive, for discovering the first antibiotic and opening up that field to other researchers, some of whom did become Nobel laureates. His book *The Bacterial Cell* was a source of inspiration for the work that earned a Nobel prize for Jacob, Lwoff and Monod in molecular biology. His knowledge was so broad-based that the Director of the National Institutes of Health Dr. Donald Frederickson said: "Among scientists, Professor Dubos is one of the few who truly merit the *ancien titre,* Natural Philosopher." Dr. Dubos published nearly two dozen books and won a Pulitzer prize for *So Human An Animal* which was written in his second language. He was a longtime editor of *Journal of Experimental Medicine,* contributed a column to *The American Scholar,* was a member of both the National Academy of Sciences and the American Philosophical Society, traveled widely, was at home with the classics, and spoke from the pulpit of the Cathedral of St. John the Divine in New York City

"My purpose here...": *Beast or Angel?* by Rene Dubos, Scribners, 1974, p 7 "genetic constitution...": *The Wooing of Earth* by Rene Dubos, Scribners, 1980, p 59

87 "The Cro-Magnon site...": ibid *Beast or Angel?*, p 70

"Since human nature...": ibid *Beast or Angel?*, p 84

"We are still so like our Stone Age...": *A God Within* by Rene Dubos, Angus & Robertson, 1972/73, p 47

88 "In view of the fact...": ibid *Beast or Angel?*, p 43

"Whether or not the words altruism...": ibid *Beast or Angel?*, p 47

You will always have the poor with you: Mt 26:11, Mk 14:7

FIVE
By Their Fruits

91 *The Immortality Factor* by Osborn Segerberg Jr., Dutton, 1974

"With the parable of the sower...": ibid Segerberg, p 52

92 The interviews with centenarians were contained in 13 volumes entitled *America's Centenarians* published by the Social Security Administration from 1963 to 1972

"And the child grew...": Lu 2:40

"And Jesus increased in wisdom...": Lu 2:52

93 "and, behold, a greater than Solomon...": Mt 12:42

"And he turned him unto his disciples...": Lu 10:23-24

Freud's *Eros* and death instinct are from *An Outline of Psychoanalysis* by Sigmund Freud, W.W. Norton, 1940, 1949, pp 20-21

94 *Chance and Necessity* by Jacques Monod, Knopf, 1971

95 Isaiah's vineyard: Is 5:1-7

"in no country in the world...": *The Life of Jesus* by Ernest Renan, Modern Library, Random House, p 114

96 "If thou be the Son of God...": Mt 4:3

The devil's demand to jump from a high place: Mt 4:6

96-
97 "It is easier for heaven...": Lu 16:17; also Mt 5:18

97 Third temptation: Mt 4:8-10

"For what shall it profit a man...": Mk 8:36; also Mt 16:26

"How can any man learn...": the Wisdom of Solomon 9:13-17

"Who ever learnt to know thy purposes...": the Wisdom of Solomon 9:17-18

By their fruits you shall know them: Mt 7:16, 20; 12:33; Lu 6:44

Beware of false prophets: Mt 7:15

"A good man out of the good treasure...": Lu 6:45, Mt 12:35

98 "Not every one that saith...": Mt 7:21

"For every tree is known...": Lu 6:44

Aristotle's comments "An absurd suggestion" and "For these things are natural...": *Physics,* Book II, 99b, 11-19 in *The Complete Works of Aristotle* edited by Jonathan Barnes, Princeton University Press, 1984

"An organism's astonishing gift...": *What Is Life?* by Erwin Schrodinger, Cambridge University Press, 1944, p 82

"The only conclusion I have been..." by Howard Pattee is from *Towards A Theoretical Biology* edited by C.H. Waddington, Aldine, 1968, p 78

99   "Every tree that bringeth not forth...": Mt 7:19

100   "Either make the tree good...": Mt 12:33

"We really do not know why...": *Biology and Man* by George Gaylord Simpson, Harcourt Brace Jovanovich, 1964, p 25

"Know what is in front of your face...": Th 5, ibid Cartlidge

SIX

Like A Mustard Seed

101   "Because of your unbelief...": Mt 17:20; an equivalent passage in Lu 17:6 substitutes a tree for the mountain

The Growth of Seed parable: Mk 4:26-29

102   "When you make the two one...": Th 22, ibid Robinson

103   "And he said, Whereunto shall we...": Mk 4:30-32; the parable of the Mustard Seed also Mt 13:31, Lu 13:18-19

Garrett Hardin quotation "Biological entities..." is from *Diversity and Stability in Ecological Systems,* the report of a symposium held 26-28 May 1969 by the Biology Department, Brookhaven National Laboratory, Upton, N.Y., p 153

"There could hardly be..." by Hardin in ibid Brookhaven, p 153

104   The estimate of 10 quadrillion animal cells in the human body is from *Microcosmos* by Lynn Margulis and Dorion Sagan, Summit, 1986, p 67; in addition, they estimate that the body is composed of 100 quadrillion bacterial cells

The calculations of MacArthur and Connell are from *Where Have All The Flowers Fishes Birds Trees Water & Air Gone? What Ecology Is All About* by Osborn Segerberg Jr., McKay, 1971, p 105

105   The gypsy moth origin from "The Tiny Moth That's Killing the Mighty Oak" by Osborn Segerberg Jr. in the New York *Daily News,* 26 April 1971

The chestnut blight is from *Fundamentals of Ecology* by Eugene Odum, W.B. Saunders, 1959, p 240

106   The human species co-opting nearly 40 percent of all plant

production is from "Human Appropriation of the Products of Photosynthesis" by Peter Vitosek, Paul Ehrlich, Anne Ehrlickh and Pamela Matson in *BioScience*, June 1986

The predicted extinction of more than half of the present species of plants and animals is from *Research Priorities in Tropical Biology,* a report by the National Academy of Sciences, 1980, p 27

"the first and deepest impression...": *The Meaning of Evolution* by George Gaylord Simpson, Bantam, 1949, 1971, p 102

The parable of The Talents: Mt 25:14-30

107   The parable of the Hidden Treasure: Th 109

"somewhat later assumes the aspect...": the essay "Compensation" by Ralph Waldo Emerson, final paragraph

The report of the Joint Economic Committee of Congress was in the Albany *Times-Union,* 26 July 1986

SEVEN

Narrow Is The Way

109   "I love to see that Nature...": *Walden* by Henry Thoreau, Random House, p 283

"Nature has no use for organisms...": *The Lessons of History* by Will and Ariel Durant, Simon & Schuster, 1968, p 21

"The laws of biology...": ibid Durants, pp 18-19

110   "Enter ye in at the strait gate...": Mt 7:13-14

The discussion of human impregnation is based on the *Nova* program "The Miracle of Life" broadcast by WGBH, Boston, 15 February 1983, and *Developmental Physiology and Aging* by P.S. Timiras, Macmillan, 1972, Chapter 2

112   One in five pregnancies aborts spontaneously is from *The Immortality Factor* by Osborn Segerberg Jr., Dutton, 1974, p 131

The curve of mortality is from ibid Segerberg, pp 134-135

"The days of our years...": Ps 90:10

"Strive to enter in at the strait gate...": Lu 13:24-27

113   "The second biological lesson...": ibid Durants, p 10

EIGHT

The Sower

114   "Nature never makes anything...": Aristotle's *On the Parts of Animals*, 691B, 4

Aristotle discusses Empedocles' theory of natural selection in *Physics*, Book II, Chapter 8, even using such terms as fitting, chance and randomness: *The Complete Works of Aristotle* edited by

Jonathan Barnes, Princeton University Press, 1984

114-
115   Darwin's quotations from his Autobiography are taken from *Population, Evolution, and Birth Control: A Collage of Controversial Ideas* assembled by Garrett Hardin, W.H. Freeman & Co., 1964, 1969, pp 146, 147

115   "For he that hath, to him shall be given...": Mk 4:25. The hath-hath not law appears in the following: Mt 13:12, 25:29; Mk 4:25; Lu 8:18, 19:26; Th 41, 70; Th 70 says that what you have will save you

116   "If you express...": Th 70

Re pesticide resistance, "Pests Prevail Despite Pesticides" in *Science*, 14 December 1984, reports the problem of resistance to insecticides is worsening world-wide with many species totally immune to three or more chemicals

Gause's experiment and law is from *Fundamentals of Ecology* by Eugene Odum, W.B. Saunders, 1959, pp 231-34

117   In "The Biological Diversity Crisis," in *Issues in Science and Technology,* a publication of the National Academy of Sciences, Fall 1985, p 21, Edward O. Wilson suggests there may be as many as 30 million species of plants and animals

"I can remember the very spot..." by Charles Darwin in ibid Hardin, p 147

118   "In my Father's house...": Jo 14:2

The parable of the Sower: Mt 13:3-9, Mk 4:3-9, Lu 8:5-8

"some an hundredfold, some sixtyfold...": Mt 13:23

Explanation of the parable of The Sower: Mt 13:18-23, Mk 4:13-20, Lu 8:11-15

119   *Beyond Freedom & Dignity* by B.F. Skinner, Knopf, 1971

The Selfish Gene by Richard Dawkins, Oxford University Press, 1976

Voltaire's quotation about the "holy trinity of destiny" is from a review by Richard Restak of *Promethean Fire* in *The New York Times Book Review*, 24 April 1983

120   "Chance favors only the prepared mind" by Pasteur is from *Louis Pasteur* by Rene Dubos, Scribners, 1950, 1976, p 101; for a detailed discussion of how life copes with chance, see *Evolution and the Theory of Games* by John Maynard Smith, Cambridge University Press, 1982; the fundamental place of chance in biological evolution is discussed by George Gaylord Simpson in *The Meaning of Evolution*, Bantam, 1949, 1971 in Chapter 12 "The Opportunism of Evolution," Chapter 14 "Forces of Evolution and their Integration," and Chapter 16 "Historical Retrospect: the Evolution of Evolution"

121   "some an hundredfold, some sixtyfold...": Mt 13:23

122   *Chance and Necessity* by Jacques Monod, Knopf, 1971

"Determinism and free will are crucial..." was spoken by Dubos during an interview with the author at The Rockefeller University, 18 May 1976

In a letter dated 6 April 1977 to the author, Dubos wrote: "C.H. Waddington in particular has repeatedly emphasized that an animal makes choices as to the particular place where it establishes itself, and these choices in turn influence subsequent evolutionary development."

"Throughout history and prehistory...": *Beast or Angel? Choices That Makes Us Human* by Rene Dubos, Scribners, 1974, p 193

"To be human is...": ibid *Beast*, p 8

122-
123   Dubos has described the polysaccharide experiments in *The Professor, The Institute, and DNA* by Rene Dubos, The Rockefeller University Press, 1976, pp 74-75, and in a memoir tape recording at Columbia University

123   "But he that received seed unto the good ground...": Mt 13:23

124   The discussion of Information Theory and other communication theories is based on the 15th edition of *Encyclopaedia Britannica*, 1974, and the 1965 *Britannica*

"In a purely technical sense..." and "The full information..." are from ibid Wilson in *Issues*

125   Re immunity learning, see *Immunity in Evolution* by John Marchalonis, Harvard University Press, 1977

Re cancer from exotic materials in the environment, Nobel laureate Macfarlane Burnet writes in *Immunological Surveillance*, Pergammon, 1970 on pp 134-35: "The first chemical carcinogens came only with the use of fire for domestic purposes. Since then we have first slowly and in the twentieth century at precipitous speed built a civilization on unbiological materials, i.e., materials that the mammalian body has not been adapted by evolution to deal with...Any reactive chemical molecule which because of the absence of enzymes to deal with it or for any other reason can reach the nucleus of a cell in significant concentration is liable to damage the genetic structure in random fashion."

126   "Only that day dawns..." is Thoreau's final thought in *Walden*

"Therefore I speak to them in parables...": Mt 13:13-15

Isaiah's prophecy: Is 8:9-10

NINE
Out Of The Mouth

128   The exchange between God and Cain: Ge 4:9-10

The exchange between God and Moses: Ex 4:10-12

Jesus' instructions to disciples and "For I will give you a mouth...":

Lu 21:15

129   What comes out of the mouth defiles: Mt 15:10-20, Mk 7:1-23

Isaiah's saying "This people honoreth me...": Is 29:13

The law in Leviticus is Lev 1:2

Jesus on divorce: Mt 19:3-9, Mk 10:2-12

130   The blind leading the blind: Mt 15:14

On embalming of pharaohs is from "X-Raying the Pharaohs" by James Harris and Kent Weeks in *Natural History*, August/September 1972

Hippocrates wrote: "Men ought to know that from the brain, and from the brain only, arise our pleasures, joys, laughter and jests, as well as our sorrows, pains, griefs and tears. Through it, in particular, we think, see, hear, and distinguish the ugly from the beautiful, the bad from the good, the pleasant from the unpleasant...It is the same thing which makes us mad or delirious, inspires us to dread and fear, whether by night or day, brings sleeplessness, inopportune mistakes, aimless anxieties, absent-mindedness, and acts that are contrary to habit."

"O generation of vipers...": Mt 12:34

131   "Thou shall fear the Lord...": Deut 6:13

"Ye shall not tempt...": Deut 6:16

"All the commandments...": Deut 8:1

"And he humbled thee...": Deut 8:3

"A good man out of the good treasure...": Mt 12:35, Lu 6:35

"For as he thinketh in his heart...": Pr 23:7

132   Plato's position on the immortal soul is best expressed in *Phaedo*

For a discussion of how Descartes affected subsequent medicine and biology, see *Man, Medicine, and Environment* by Rene Dubos, New American Library, 1968, pp 76-86

133-
134   Mind-body philosophy and quotation "is no intelligible..." is from 1965 *Encyclopaedia Britannica* in section on "Body and Mind"

134   "To prolong life, therefore..." is from *The Will To Live* by Arnold A. Hutschnecker, Cornerstone Library, 1951, 1975, p 52; body and mind are one is on p 59

"Cartesian dualism..." is from ibid Dubos, p 78

"body and mind are inseparable...": *The Biology of Human Action* by Vernon Reynolds, W.H. Freeman, 1976, p 229

"In the last analysis...": ibid Reynolds, p 17

"As Reynolds shows...": "The Limits of Biology" by Ashley Montagu in *The Sciences*, a publication of the New York Academy of Sciences, May/June 1977, p 22

"Every cell of the human body...": *The Brain* by Jack Fincher, U.S. News Books, 1981, p 7

"The key philosophical theme of modern neural science...": *Principles of Neural Science* edited by Eric R. Kandel and James H. Schwartz, Elsevier/North Holland, 1981, p 3

135   "the manifestation of mind...": ibid Kandel and Schwartz, p 4

"Blessed are the pure in heart": Mt 5:8

When you make the inside like the outside: Th 22

"Another parable spake he...": Mt 13:33; the parable of the Leaven also is told in Lu 13:20-21

136   "Take heed, beware of the leaven of the Pharisees..." is Mk 8:15; the whole episode is told in Mk 8:10-21

"In the mean time, when there were gathered...": Lu 12:1

137   "but the sign of the prophet Jonas.": Mt 12:39, 16:4; Lu 11:29

"How is it that ye do not understand...": Mt 16:11-12; the whole episode is told in Mt 16:1-12

The passage by Pico della Mirandola is from *The Civilization of The Renaissance in Italy* by Jacob Burkhardt, Phaedon, first published in Switzerland in 1860, p 215

138   The discussion of brain and neurobiology is largely based on *The Conscious Brain* by Steven Rose, Knopf, 1975, and *Windows On the Mind* by Erich Harth, Morrow, 1982

139   The usual estimate of brain neurons has been ten billion, but the most recent estimate and the one used — ten billion to 100 billion with 1,000 to 100,000 interconnections — is by Harold Hawkins, a psychologist at the office of Naval Research, quoted in "Investigations of the Brain Finding Clues to the Mind" by Daniel Goleman in *The New York Times,* 22 April 1986; Ted L. Petit, a life sciences professor at the University of Toronto, says flatly there are 100 billion brain neurons in "The Shape of Intelligence" in *The Sciences*, March/April 1987

As more is learned about the neuron, its nucleus, axon, dendrites, synapses, neurotransmitters and their receptors, the greater the complexity as reported, for example, in "Explosion of Data on Brain Cell Reveals Its Great Complexity" by Harold M. Schmeck Jr. in *The New York Times*, 6 March 1984; re intellectual capacity and native intelligence, ibid Petit

140   Re ample potential for continued learning during human lifespan and the need for enriched environments for old people, the most recent research is demolishing previous beliefs of a necessary mental decline with old age, as reported in "New Evidence Points to Growth Of the Brain Even Late in Life," 30 July 1985, and "The Aging Mind Proves Capable of Lifelong Growth," 11 February 1984, both articles by Daniel Goleman in *The New York Times*

Experiments on visual deprivation were conducted by Nobel laureate David Hubel and reported in "New Evidence..." by Daniel Goleman cited above. Quick formation of nerve associations reported in "Very Brief Visual Experience Eliminates Plasticity in the Cat Visual Cortex" by George D. Mower, William G. Christen and Caren J. Caplan in *Science,* 8 July 1983

The benefit of enriched environment for children has been widely reported. Arnold Scheibel, a professor of anatomy and psychiatry at the University of California at Los Angeles, has correlated the explosive growth of neuron connections in a child's speech center from the age of six months to 18 months when the child is exposed to and begins to understand adults talking, also reported by Daniel Goleman in "New Evidence..." cited above

141   Research on the making of a terrorist was reported in "The Roots of Terrorism Are Found in Brutality of Shattered Childhood" by Daniel Goleman in *The New York Times,* 2 September 1986

Churchill's saying "We shape our buildings..." was quoted by Rene Dubos in *So Human an Animal*, Scribners, 1968, p 171

"By the time the scientist..." ibid Rose, p 219

Whitehead on specialists is from *Science and the Modern World* by Alfred North Whitehead, New American Library, 1925, 1948, pp 196-97

Dubos has a long discussion of scientists in *Reason Awake* by Rene Dubos, Columbia University Press, 1970, pp 30-42

142   The two selfhoods in ibid Harth, p 78

"Seek ye first the kingdom of God...": Mt 6:33

TEN
The Finger Of God

143   Curing the palsied man is told in Mt 9:2-8, Mk 2:1-12, Lu 5:18-26

Re Hebrew coupling sin and disease, see *Mirage of Health* by Rene Dubos, Harper, 1959, p 114

"If thou wilt diligently...": Ex 15:26

144   Faith healing at the temples of Asclepius is from *Man, Medicine, and Environment* by Rene Dubos, New American Library, 1968, p 71

The story of Jesus at Nazareth is told in most detail in Lu 4:16-30, then Mk 6:1-6, also Mt 13:54-58

"Ye will surely say unto me...": Lu 4:23

"A prophet is not acceptable...": Th 31 from *Documents for the Study of the Gospels* by David R. Cartlidge and David L. Dungan, William Collins, Fortress, 1980, p 28

144

145   The quotations by Jacob are from *The Possible and the Actual* by

Francois Jacob, Pantheon, 1982, pp 9-11

145   The story of the woman with lupus is from "Thinking Well" by Nicholas R. Hall and Allan L. Goldstein in *The Sciences,* March/April 1986, p 34

The story of tle voodoo death is from "Voodoo Death" by Walter B. Cannon in *American Anthropologist,* April-June 1942

146   "The success of such practices...": *The Mind/Body Effect* by Herbert Benson, Simon & Schuster, 1979, p 23

The story of the man who dropped dead is from ibid Benson, p 26, the anecdote attributed to Dr. Leon J. Saul of Media, Pennsylvania

Dr. Benson on the causes of sudden death: ibid Benson, p 33

146-
147   The reference to George Engel is from ibid Benson, pp 25-26 and *Living With Death* by Osborn Segerberg Jr., Dutton, 1976, p 116. The pioneering work on hopelessness and sudden death was done by Curt P. Richter, a professor of psychology at Johns Hopkins Medical School and published in "The Phenomenon of Unexplained Sudden Death in Animals and Man" in *Physiological Bases of Psychiatry,* edited by W. Horsley Gantt, Charles C. Thomas, 1958. See also *Helplessness* by Martin Seligman, Freeman, 1975

147   Arthur Schmale Jr. reported his findings at the Second Conference on Psychophysiological Aspects of Cancer published in *Annals of the New York Academy of Sciences,* Vol 164, Part 2, pp 307-364; on p 630, Schmale is quoted: "Cancer appears to be one of the diseases that frequently makes its first appearance in a life-setting of experienced hopelessness."

The study on women with breast cancer is reported in ibid Hall and Goldstein

The Simontons' list is from *Mind As Healer, Mind As Slayer* by Kenneth R. Pelletier, Delacorte/Seymour Lawrence, 1977, Chapter 4

The Simontons describe their theories and methods in *Getting Well Again* by O. Carl Simonton, Stephanie Matthews-Simonton and James Creighton, Tarcher, 1978

Pilot Study on effect of imagination on immune responses reported in ibid Hall and Goldstein

148   ibid Pelletier

"It is a remarkable fact...": *Man Adapting* by Rene Dubos, Yale University Press, 1965, pp 266-67

"When Jesus saw their faith...": Mt 9:27-31

Dr. William Osler's credo "The faith that heals..." is from *The Professor, The Institute and DNA* by Rene Dubos, the Rockefeller University Press, 1976, p 13

148-
149   "Certainly the physician's sympathy..." is from *Man, Medicine, and Environment* cited above, p 146

149   "My name is Legion": Mk 5:9 and his story Mk 5:1-19; also told in Lu 8:26-37

"included some 10 pages devoted to...": ibid *The Professor* by Dubos cited above, p 13

150   Mind-nervous system-endocrine system-immune system links are reported in ibid Hall and Goldstein. Also reported in "Psychoendocrine Influences on Immunocompetence and Neoplasia" by Vernon Riley in *Science*, 5 June 1981, giving the link between anxiety, thymus suppression and cancer. Another report: "Coping and Immunosuppression: Inescapable but not Escapable Shock Suppresses Lymphocyte Proliferation" by Mark Laudenslager et al in *Science*, 5 August 1983. Also: "By Training the Brain, Scientists Find Links To Immune Defenses" by Harold M. Schmeck Jr. in *The New York Times*, 1 January 1985

Findings of a link between bereavement and depressed lymphocyte activity were made by Marvin Stein and colleagues at Mount Sinai School of Medicine in New York City and cited in ibid Hall and Goldstein. Arthur Carr and Bernard Schoenberg state in *Loss and Grief* by Bernard Schoenberg, Arthur Carr, David Peretz and Austin Kutscher, Columbia University Press, 1970: "The concept that bereavement is associated with increased mortality is supported by numerous studies." They cite some in their chapter "Object-Loss and Somatic Symptom Formation"

"as a mixture of pseudoscientific..." and "The discovery of pathways that bind the brain..." are from ibid Hall and Goldstein

151   "the manifestation of the mind...", Eric Kandel's definition of behavior, is given in *Principles of Neural Science* edited by Eric Kandel and James Schwartz, Elsevier/North Holland, 1981, p 4

"seems unable to reject..." is from ibid Benson, p 65

The curing of the hemorrhaging woman is told in Mt 9:20-22, Mk 5:25-34, and Lu 8:43-48

Blind Bartimaeus is from Mk 10:46-52

The healed leper: Lu 17:11-19

"They that are whole need not a physician": Mt 9:12, Mk 2:17, Lu 5:31

"If I with the finger of God...": Lu 11:20; the noted historian of religion, Mircea Eliade, says that scholars consider the finger-of-God quotation to be one of four statements by Jesus about the kingdom of God that are certainly authentic: in *A History of Religious Ideas*, Vol 2, University of Chicago Press, 1982, p 338n. The other three are: Mt 11:12, Mk 1:15a, Lu 17:20-21

ELEVEN
If Thine Eye Be Single

152   The first two paragraphs are based on Mt 9:10-13 and Mk 2:15-17; the episode also is given in Lu 5:29-32; Hosea 6:6

153   "Judge not...": Mt 7:1-2

"Why beholdest...": Mt 7:3

"Not everyone that saith...": Mt 7:21

The Dennis Garvin story is from *Living To Be 100* by Osborn Segerberg Jr., Scribners, 1982, p 68

Jesus on righteousness: Mt 5:20

On the Pharisees and scribes blocking the way to the kingdom: Mt 23:13

154   Money is a defense: Ec 7:12

155   Easier for a camel to go through the eye of a needle: Mt 19:24, Mk 10:25, Lu 18:25

The story of the rich young man: Mt 19:16-22; also Mk 10:17-22, Lu 18:18-23

Treasure in heaven: Mt 6:20

The parable of The Dishonest Steward: Lu 16:1-13

"who will commit to your trust...": Lu 16:11

The dilemma for rich children was presented in "Death in Park: Difficult Questions for Parents" by Samuel Freedman in *The New York Times*, 11 September 1986, p 1

156   The John Kenneth Galbraith article "Corporate Man" was in the *New York Times Magazine,* 22 January 1984

157   The parable of The Rich Fool: Lu 12:16-21

"I went to the woods..." is from *Walden* by Henry Thoreau, Modern Library edition, Random House, p 81

158   "A university is essentially...": *The Cox Commission Report: Crisis at Columbia*, Vintage, Random House, 1968, p 196

"...the deceitfulness of riches...": Mt 13:22

158-
159   The comments on J. Paul Getty are based on "Isn't It Funny What Money Can Do?" by Jane O'Reilly in *The New York Times Book Review*, 30 March 1984, a review of *The Great Getty* by Robert Lenzner, Crown, and *The House Of Getty* by Russell Miller, Henry Holt

159   "Seek ye first...": Mt 6:33

The Charles Steurer story is from ibid Segerberg, pp 75-76

"were exceedingly amazed...": Mt 19:25-26

159-
160   The story of Zacchaeus: Lu 19:1-10

160   "Blessed are the meek...": Mt 5:5

Hans Selye comment on loving your neighbor is from ibid Segerberg, p 314, a report on *The Stress of My Life* by Hans Selye, Van Nostrand Reinhold, 1979

Research on sexual fantasy reported in Jane Brody's "Personal Health" column in *The New York Times*, 27 August 1986

"Be ye therefore perfect...": Mt 5:48

The attitude that Jesus' ethics only could be followed by hermits and monks was presented in lecture "The Ethical Principles" by Dr. Walter Donald Kring at All Souls Unitarian Church in New York City, 24 March 1977

Johannes Weiss' comment "That is why His ethic..." is from *The Quest of the Historical Jesus* by Albert Schweitzer, Macmillan, 1961, p 240

161   Schweitzer's view on ethics from ibid Kring

Comments of Dr. Frederick Grant are from "Jesus Christ" in *Encyclopedia Americana* 1965

"the ethical teaching of Jesus..." is from *From Jesus To Paul* by Joseph Klausner, Menorah Publishing Company, New York City, 1943, p 587

"Judaism will never allow...": ibid Klausner, p 609

"Whosoever therefore shall break...": Mt 5:19

161-
162   "The light of the body...": Mt 6:22-23

162   "where your treasure is...": Mt 6:21

On two autonomic nervous systems getting out of sync: "Voodoo Death: New Thoughts on an Old Explanation" by Barbara Lex in *American Anthropologist*, 76, 1974

164   Louis Harris poll reported in "73% of Americans Suffer Headaches" by Harold Schmeck Jr. in *The New York Times*, 22 October 1985

Hans Selye's views on stress were discussed in ibid Segerberg, Appendices 11 and 17 summarizing Selye's books *The Stress of Life*, McGraw-Hill, 1956; *The Stress of My Life* cited above; *Stress Without Distress*, J.B. Lippencott, 1974

165   The story of Flora Whisenand in ibid Segerberg, pp 73-74

166   The famous lilies passage is Mt 6:25-34

The John Tuggle story is from a column by Bill Verigan in the New York *Daily News*, 17 October 1984. Tuggle died 30 August 1986 at the age of 25

Reports on the Holmes/Rahe scale in *The Immortality Factor* by Osborn Segerberg Jr., Dutton, 1974, pp 95-96, and *Living With*

Death by Osborn Segerberg Jr., Dutton, 1976, pp 88-89

167   Recent research on divorce is reported in "Divorce's Stress Exacts Long-Term Health Toll" by Jane Brody in *The New York Times*, 13 December 1983

"And the Pharisees came to him...": Mk 10:2-9

168   The changes in human man-woman relationship based on "Family Matters" by Jane Lancaster and Phillip Whitten in *The Sciences*, January 1980, pp 10-15; "Theory on Man's Origins Challenged" by Erik Eckholm in *The New York Times*, 4 September 1984; "Of Human Bonding" by Helen Fisher in *The Sciences*, February 1982; see also the *Sex Contract: The Evolution of Human Behavior* by Helen Fisher, Morrow, 1982

"They contrive to transform marriage..." by Flanders Dunbar is from *Living To Be 100* cited above, p 285

"Agree wiyh thine adversary...": Mt 5:25

169   "If any man will sue thee...": Mt 5:40

The Arnold Hutschnecker story is based on an interview with the author in New York City, 19 October 1976

"ye have heard that it hath been said...": Mt 5:38-39

"Ye have heard that it was said by them of old time...": Mt 5:21-24

170   The discussion of anger is based on "Venting Anger May Do More Harm Than Good" by Jane Brody in *The New York Times*, 8 March 1983, and Jane Brody's "Personal Health" column in *The Times,* 9 March l983

Anger: The Misunderstood Emotion by Carol Tavris, Simon & Schuster, 1982

170-
171   The discussion of Type A behavior is based on "Type A Behavior: A Progress Report" by Meyer Friedman in *The Sciences*, February 1980

171   The Redford William research was reported in "Heart Attack Rate 5 Times Higher in Angry Men" by Al Rossiter Jr., United Press International, 12 January 1983

Meyer Friedman's report on reduced recurrence of heart attacks after counseling against Type A behavior was in "Modifying 'Type A' Behavior Reduces Heart Attacks" by Jane Brody in *The New York Times*, 7 August 1984

"Couples who are not defeated by rage..." by Carol Tavris was reported in Jane Brody's "Personal Health" column cited above

172   Tavris' contrast of Superman and the Incredible Hulk is from Tavris, p 27

"Blessed is the lion...": Th 7 is from *Documents for the Study of the Gospels* by David R. Cartlidge and David Dungan, William Collins, Fortress, 1980, p 26

"Ye have heard that it hath been said, Thou shalt love thy neighbor...": Mt 5:43-48

Selye on altruistic egoism from *Living To Be 100* cited above, p 314

"For if ye love them...": Mt 5:46-47

173   "Ask, and it shall be given...": Mt 7:7

The Beatitudes cited are Mt 5:6, 8, 9, 7

"Be ye therefore merciful...": Lu 6:36

"I was hungered...": Mt 25:35-40

TWELVE
Become As A Little Child

174   "Jesus called a little child...": Mt 18:2-4

"Suffer the little children...": Mk 10:14-16

"Whoso shall offend...": Mt 18:16

"When I was a child...": 1 Co 13:11

The Erosion of Childhood by Valerie Polakow Suransky, University of Chicago Press, 1982

175   "In that hour, Jesus rejoiced...": Lu 10:21

177   *Magic, Science and Religion* by Bronislaw Malinowski, Doubleday, Anchor, 1925, 1955

"My worst memory goes back to the time..." is from *My Life's History* by Anna Mary Robertson "Grandma" Moses, Harper & Row, 1948

178   "Neoteny has been a (probably *the*)...": *Ontogeny and Phylogeny* by Stephen Jay Gould, Belknap/Harvard University Press, 1977, p 9

179   "That paradox can be resolved...": ibid Gould, p 9

The discussion of neoteny is based on ibid Gould and *Growing Young* by Ashley Montagu, McGraw-Hill, 1981

180   "Jesus saw babies being suckled...": Th 22 is from *Documents for the Study of the Gospels* by David R. Cartlidge and David Dungan, William Collins, Fortress, 1980, p 28

181   "Human exploratory behavior..." by Konrad Lorenz is from ibid Gould, p 402

"What are those traits of childhood behavior...": ibid Montagu, p 2

Montagu's "neotenous drives of the child": ibid Montagu, p 131

Youth is a wonderful thing..." by George Bernard Shaw is quoted in *The International Dictionary of Thoughts*, J.G. Ferguson Publishing Company, 1969

"human beings can revolutionize...": ibid Montagu, p 2

181-
182   "Verily I say unto you...": Mt 18:3

182   The reference to J.B.S. Haldane in ibid Gould, pp 401-02

THIRTEEN
The Golden Rule

183   Re three spheres of human functioning: the Duke University
Longitudinal Study of Aging conducted in Durham, North Carolina
from 1955 to 1979 on 268 subjects for 788 qualities in the physical,
psychological and social categories: see *Living To Be 100* by Osborn
Segerberg Jr., Scribners, 1982. The National Institute of Mental
Health Longitudinal Study examined 47 men 65 years and older for
more than 600 characteristics in categories denoted as medical and
physiological, psychological and psychiatric, and social-psycho-
logical: see ibid Segerberg; also "The Need for a New Medical Model:
A Challenge for Biomedicine" by George L. Engel in *Science*, 8 April
1977

"Tell us therefore, What thinkest...": Mt 22:17-22; there are similar
passages in Mk 12:13-17, Lu 20:19-26

"Therefore all things...": Mt 7:12

"for this is the law...": Mt 7:12

184   Hillel's negative Golden Rule is taken from *From Jesus To Paul* by
Joseph Klausner, Menorah Publishing Company, 1943, and from
"Hillel" in the 1965 *Encyclopaedia Britannica*

"Do not do to anyone...": Tobit 4:15

"do not do what you hate": Th 6 is from *The Nag Hammadi Library*
by James M. Robinson, the General Editor, Harper & Row, 1977, p
118

"No diet, no special care..." by Eleanor Robson Belmont in ibid
Segerberg, p 221

"Judge not...": Mt 7:1-2

"Condemn not...": Lu 6:37-38

"Forgive us our debts...": Mt 6:12

"for all they that take the sword...": Mt 26:52

184-
185   "For I the Lord thy God am a jealous God...": Ex 20:5-6

185   "I will not keep silence...": Is 65:6-7

"Thou shewest lovingkindness unto thousands...": Jer 32:18

The parable of the Wicked Servant: Mt 18:23-35

"For if ye forgive men their trespasses...": Mt 6:14-15

"And when ye stand praying...": Mk 11:25-26

186   Ecological consequences of biological immortality: *The Immortality*

Factor by Osborn Segerberg Jr., Dutton, 1974, pp 249-263

"The view of evolution as chronic bloody competition...": *Microcosmos* by Lynn Margulis and Dorion Sagan, Summit, 1986, pp 14-15

"all the world's bacteria...": ibid Margulis, p 16

189   The parable of the Laborers in the Vineyard: Mt 20:1-16

"The fact never to be forgotten...": *The Torch of Life* by Rene Dubos, Simon & Schuster, 1962, p 120

190   "We have entered the cell...": "The Coming of Age of the Cell" by Albert Claude in *Science* 8 August 1976, the Nobel lecture delivered in Stockholm, 12 December 1974

"they are probably the rule rather than the exception": "Biological Memory, Creative Associations, and the Living Earth" by Rene Dubos in *The Nature of Life*, University Park Press, 1978, the printed record of the 13th Nobel Conference at Gustavus Adolphus College in October 1977

192   "Blessed are the meek...": Mt 5:5

193   The Lincoln quotation is cited in several reference works and in John Hay's Letters and Diary 23 December 1863

FOURTEEN
The Kingdom Of God

194   "Again, the kingdom of heaven...": Mt 13:45-46

The section on pearls is based largely on "The Pearl" by Fred Ward in *National Geographic* magazine, August 1985

194-
195   "Not everyone that saith unto me...": Mt 7:21

195   *Psycho-Cybernetics* by Maxwell Maltz, Pocket Books, 1960, 1969

"What things soever...": Mk 11:24

"And all things...": Mt 21:22

"This book has been designed...": ibid Maltz, pp xii-xiii

196   "The Kingdom of the Father...": Th 98 from *Documents for the Study of the Gospels* by David R. Cartlidge and David L. Dungan, William Collins, Fortress, 1980, p 34

"the kingdom of heaven is like unto treasure...": Mt 13:44

The parable of the Hidden Treasure: Th 109

200   "Blessed are they...": Mt 5:10

"I was a stranger..": Mt 25:35

The study of people who helped Jews during World War Two is

described in "Great Altruists: Science Ponders Soul of Goodness" by Daniel Goleman in *The New York Times,* 5 March 1985; the study with many researchers is directed by sociologist Samuel Oliver at Humboldt State University, Arcata, California

"Self-Reliance" by Ralph Waldo Emerson

"Come to me because my yoke is easy...": Th 90, ibid Cartlidge, p 33

"If they ask you, 'What is the sign...'": Th 50, ibid Cartlidge, p 30

Peace of Mind by Joshua Loth Liebman, Simon & Schuster, 1946

"You have forgotten the one ingredient...": ibid Liebman, p 3

201   "This is the gift...": ibid Liebman, p 4

"Among them that are born of women...": Mt 11:11-12

"For all the prophets and the law...": Mt 11:13

202   "The kingdom of heaven is like unto treasure...": Mt 13:44

"enter into the joy of thy lord...": Mt 25:21

"These things have I spoken unto you...": Jo 15:11

The discussion of altered states of consciousness in various religions is based on "Your innate asset for combating stress" by Herbert Benson in the *Harvard Business Review* July-August 1974

203   The discussion of the Relaxation Response is from ibid Benson

"I am come that they might have life...": Jo 10:10

The discussion of opioid peptides and drugs is based on the following: "Synthesizing the Opioid Peptides" by Jean L. Marx in *Science,* 22 April 1983; "Brain Peptides: What, Where, and Why" by Dorothy T. Kreiger in *Science,* 2 December 1983; Frontiers of Research in Neurobiology" by David A. Hamburg in *Science,* 2 December 1983; "Cocaine's Vicious Spiral: Highs, Lows, Desperation" by Erik Eckholm in *The New York Times,* 20 May 1986; "Cocaine Survey Points to Widespread Anguish" by Richard D. Lyons in *The New York Times,* 3 January 1984; "Cocaine and anxiety" in *The New York Times*; "Drug Abuse in America: Widening Array Brings New Perils" by Harold M. Schmeck Jr. in *The New York Times,* 22 March 1983; "The Addict's Brain: Chemistry Holds Hope for Answers" by Harold M. Schmeck Jr. in *The New York Times,* 25 January 1983; "Brain Peptides Controlling Behavior and Metabolism" by Clifton A. Baile, Mary Anne Della-Fera, and Deena Krestal-Rickert in *BioScience* February 1985; "Methadone Conformation and Opioid Activity" by William L. Duax et al in *Science,* 22 April 1983; "Opiate Receptor Distribution in the Cerebral Cortex of the Rhesus Monkey" in *Science,* 22 October 1982; "The Reward System of the Brain" by Aryeh Routtenberg in *Scientific American,* November 1978; "Endorphins: Studies of these morphine-like substances are shedding light on acupuncture, addiction and pain-control" by Avram Goldstein in *The Sciences* March

1978; "Opiate-like Substances in Brain May Hold Clue to Pain and Mood" by Harold M. Schmeck Jr. in *The New York Times*, 2 October 1977

204   The anecdote about David Livingstone is on p 50 in *The Lives of a Cell* by Lewis Thomas, Viking, 1973

205   Daniel Goleman identifies five groups of investigators into altered and euphoric states of mind in "Concentration Is Likened To Euphoric States of Mind" in *The New York Times*, 4 March 1986

Ivan Lendl made his statement at the time of the U.S. Tennis Open in September 1986

Vladimir Horowitz made his statement in a report by Ned Potter on the CBS Evening News, 8 September 1986

205-
206   Selye's findings on work, stress and distress reported in Appendix 19, *Living To Be 100* by Osborn Segerberg Jr., Scribners, 1982

206   The Duke Longitudinal Study of Aging reported in Appendix 3, ibid Segerberg; see *Normal Aging* and *Normal Aging II*, edited by Erdman Palmore, Duke University Press, 1970, 1974

Work habits of American centenarians reported in ibid Segerberg

The discussion of Mihaly Csikszentmihalyi's work is based on "Emergent Motivation And the Evolution Of The Self" by Csikszentmihalyi in *Motivation and Adulthood*, edited by J.L. Maehr and D. Kleiber, J.A.I. Press, Greenwhich, Connecticut, 1986

209   "mass of men lead lives of...": *Walden* by Henry Thoreau, Random House, p 7

210   "If therefore thine eye be single...": Mt 6:22

"He also that received the seed...": Mt 13:22

"Do not do what you hate": Th 6, ibid Cartlidge, p 26

"It is easier for a camel...": Mt 19:24

"The way you think...": Tatzumbie Dupea in *America's Centenarians* by the Social Security Administration, 1963-72

"Repent: for the kingdom of heaven is at hand": Mt 4:17

"His disciples said to him...": Th 51 from *The Nag Hammadi Library* by James M. Robinson, the General Editor, Harper & Row, 1977, p 123

210-
211   "Thy kingdom come": Mt 6:10

211   "My kingdom is not of this world...": Jo 18:36

Jesus' remark at Last Supper about when he will drink wine again: Mk 14:25, Lu 22:18, Mt 26:29

"There shall be some of them...": Mk 9:1; in Luke, it is 9:27

"There be some standing here...": Mt 16:28

"the publicans and the harlots": Mt 21:31

"If therefore ye have not been faithful...": Lu 16:11-12

"the kingdom of God is within you": Lu 17:21

212   "the kingdom is within you and outside you": Th 3, ibid Cartlidge, p 25

"spread out on the earth...": Th 113, ibid Cartlidge, p 35

"Blessed be ye poor...": Lu 6:20

"Blessed are the poor in spirit...": Mt 5:3

"Blessed are ye that hunger": Lu 6:21

"Blessed are they that do hunger and thirst after righteousness...": Mt 5:6

References to the kingdom of God in Acts: 1:3, 8:12, 14:22, 19:8, 20:25, 28:23, 28:31

The question about restoring the kingdom to Israel: Acts 1:6-7

212-
213   "For the kingdom of God is not meat and drink...": Ro 14:17

213   References to those who shall or cannot "inherit the kingdom of God": 1 Co 6:9, 10; 15:50

"Then cometh the end": 1 Co 15:24

"But the fruit of the spirit is love...": Gal 5:22-23

"the kingdom of Christ and of God": Eph 5:5

"the kingdom of his dear son": Col 1:13

"I charge thee therefore before God...": 2 Tim 4:1

Biblical Verses
GOSPELS

Apocrypha

New Testament

Index

ABOUT THE AUTHOR

Osborn Segerberg Jr. is an author, science writer, investigative researcher and journalist. He has written extensively about the life sciences in four published books, guide books for the New York State Education Department, magazine articles, and four television documentaries broadcast on PBS. He has written about religion in two of his books, *The Immortality Factor* and *Living With Death.* In his journalistic career, Mr. Segerberg has reported and written about many of the major events in the post World War Two period. He has written for the CBS Evening News, NBC News' Today, ABC News' 20/20, United Press, United Press Movietone, television and radio stations in New York City. His articles have appeared in the New York *Daily News, Esquire, New York, Philadelphia* and *Sea Frontiers.*

The Riddles of Jesus and Answers of Science stems from ten years of research, thought, study and rethinking a life-long experience with Christianity.